Praise for WHAT YOU DID NOT

"A well-told story of flight from poʟɪᴛɪ.. ⟩
new surroundings, and an eloquent meditation on nᴏ·ᴠ. ɪʀ
history with us over many generations."
—Lorien Kite, *Financial Times*, Top 10 Books of the Year

"This is intensely felt history, with personalities reconstructed from fragments of their written style. Mark Mazower found a kind of Jewish/
East European *War and Peace* waiting to be pieced together from
archives that began in the family attic…a marvelous declaration of his-
toriographical intent." —*Times Literary Supplement*

"An inquiry into the importance of roots and the psychic contentment
that comes with belonging…*What You Did Not Tell* is a marvelous
book from the pen of a fine historian, written in a foreign country and
steeped in nostalgia." —*Jewish Chronicle*

"'How is it that the places we live in come to feel that they are ours?' a
noted historian asks in this exacting memoir…Mazower, plowing
through letters, diaries, and archives, finds that his grandfather's story
encompasses many of the horrors of twentieth-century Europe."
—*The New Yorker*

"A deeply personal book, but one that will resonate with many readers,
particularly those grappling with a fraught heritage."
—*Minneapolis Star Tribune*

"After discovering his grandfather's work as an agent for the Jewish
socialist Bund, [Mazower] explored the efforts people later took to hide
their involvement in the revolution. Through the story of his grandfather, Mazower reconstructs the history of this largely forgotten Jewish socialist group that, he writes, was instrumental to the revolution's
success." —*Publishers Weekly*

"This is historical storytelling at its very best." —*Standpoint Magazine*

"[This book] sheds light on the acute political, social, and intellectual dilemmas that confronted European Jews (and others too, but most particularly Jews) in the early twentieth century. Beyond that, it is an affecting human portrait, drawn from life. Mark Mazower writes with sensitivity, imagination, and a literary flair worthy of his other better-known forebear." —*Jewish Review of Books*

"Mazower tells a story that is both a family saga and something larger... His book places his family history firmly within the dark history of twentieth-century Europe of which he has written so compellingly. Yet he ends *What You Did Not Tell* not with a gloss on history but with a tribute to the reticent English father who did his best to turn away from the dark." —*The Nation*

"A powerful study of resettlement, persecution, and survival...[in which] we find a dazzling constellation of figures, including senior Bolsheviks, dedicated political activists, émigré historians, philosophers, writers, and engineers, thrown into turmoil by war, ethnic cleansing, and their dangerous habit of dissent." —Jeremy Harding, author of *Border Vigils: Keeping Migrants Out of the Rich World*

"*What You Did Not Tell* is a memoir that only one of our finest historians could have written. To call it a 'memoir' even is to represent only a small part of Mazower's investigation into his family's past. This is a saga of cities—Vilna, Moscow, Paris, London, and New York—and a profound meditation on what it takes to call a place home. It spans more than a century and sheds sparkling light on the Bundists, the first mass Marxist party in Russian history. It is history made intimate, history made personal—a story of idealism, exile, revolution, and defeat. One of the great thrills of *What You Did Not Tell* is to behold Mazower's deep knowledge of Europe meld with his own ancestral past."
—Michael Greenberg, author of *Hurry Down Sunshine*

What You Did Not Tell

A FATHER'S PAST

and

THE JOURNEY HOME

❧

Mark Mazower

Other Press ⊞ *New York*

First softcover edition 2018
ISBN 978-1-59051-986-8

Copyright © Mark Mazower, 2017

Production editor: Yvonne E. Cárdenas
Text designer: Julie Fry
This book was set in Dante.

1 3 5 7 9 10 8 6 4 2

Library of Congress Cataloging-in-Publication Data
Names: Mazower, Mark, author.
Title: What you did not tell : a father's past
and the journey home / Mark Mazower.
Description: New York : Other Press, [2018]
Indentifiers: LCCN 2018014435 | ISBN 9781590519868 (pbk.)
Subjects: LCSH: Mazower, Mark—Family. |
Historians—England—Biography.
Classification: LCC DA3.M68 A3 2018 | DDC 940.5—dc23
LC record available at https://lccn.loc.gov/2018014435

For Selma and Jed

and for their cousins

Nina and Clara

Rachel, Cleo and Nicholas

Max, Seth and Elliot

Contents

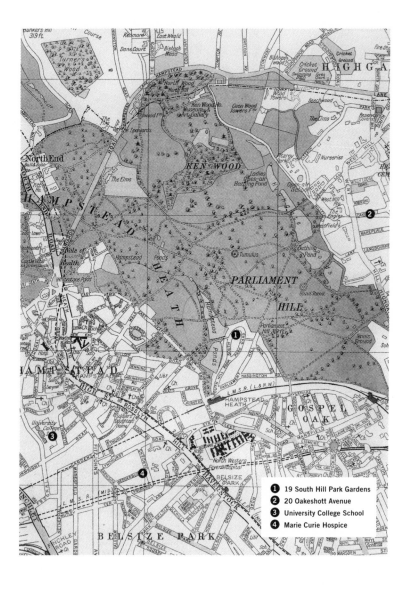

1 19 South Hill Park Gardens
2 20 Oakeshott Avenue
3 University College School
4 Marie Curie Hospice

On West Hill

I thought I knew Dad well, but the day he died I began to realize how much of his life was unknown to me. We had come back home from the hospice and somebody asked what kind of funeral his parents had had. As none of us was sure, I did what my historian's training and instinct suggested: I went to the archive. Upstairs in the wardrobe were his boxes of family papers, and on one of them he had written: Diaries, 1941–1996. I climbed on a chair and fetched it down and sat with it on my parents' bed. I am pretty sure it was the first time I had opened it.

I had always felt close to Dad, and when my brothers and I were growing up, he had been the most comforting of presences. Once, I remember, we were driving through the Cotswolds, just he and I. It was a spring day, and I must have been twelve or thirteen. We were looking at houses because he and Mum were thinking about buying a weekend cottage. The map was spread out on my lap, and I recall feeling proud that he was relying on me for directions. He drove and I gazed out of the window as the fields flashed past, comfortable in our easy silence and mutual trust.

A comfortable silence is not an impenetrable one. Dad had not been a talkative man, and he shied away from the personal like a nervous horse. Difficult questions could elicit a faint smile before he responded. But we could ask him anything, and he would tell us stories about his childhood and his parents. Some years before his death, he and I decided to get these stories down—he was a grandfather by then and time was passing—so we went to his room at the top of the house and I switched on the tape recorder. Our conversations ran over several afternoons, and I don't remember that there was anything he refused to talk about. The limits were really inside me: I felt inhibited about raising some things with him, and there were many others it never occurred to me to ask.

Inside the box there were a couple of old address books and half a century's worth of his Letts pocket diaries, neatly arranged in chronological order. He had used them mostly to jot down appointments and I soon found the information we needed. There were no intimate confessions or emotional out-pourings—no surprise there—and you could have counted on the fingers of one hand the points at which Dad had recorded a mood or feeling. Yet those resolutely unintrospective pages spoke after their fashion, and as I read on, I slowly began to piece together the pattern of daily movements and social contacts that had characterized his life.

He had grown up in the North London neighborhood of Highgate and the diaries testified to his enduring attachment to it. At the start of January 1942, when he noted in his Schoolboy Diary that he "saw Daddy off in Waterlow Park," he was just sixteen. He was about to return to the school he was attending in Somerset as an evacuee; his rapidly aging father was making his way through the bombed-out city to his wartime job in postal censorship. A decade later, Oxford and military service were behind him, and the year his father died was also the year his cousins visited from Paris and he "took the children for a walk on the Heath." "Children" did not mean my brothers and me because we had not come along yet. But sure enough the Upright Diary for 1954 notes a "walk on the Heath with Miriam" on April 11; barely a month had gone by since he and Mum had met. And before long we were there too and they were playing with us in the meadows above the ponds or walking amid the rhododendrons behind Kenwood House.

When they became parents, Mum and Dad started filming us, and as we grew older a favorite treat on wintry weekend afternoons was to get out the projector, draw the curtains, and watch ourselves as toddlers: Dave's first steps, tottering towards the camera across the sands in Devon; Ben in the pram in our back garden; Jony on the climbing frame. One of their earliest efforts dates from the summer of 1958. It is a sunny day and Mum must have been holding the camera—they had borrowed it from a friend. They are on Hampstead Heath for a picnic and as usual they have laid the tartan rug on the ground because the grass is often a little damp even in July and August. Dad is on his back, holding me above his head: He is full of life and looks strong and happy, much as I remember him throughout

my childhood. Yet when I freeze the frame, I notice something
else now, lurking in the distance: There behind him, across the
ponds and above the tree line, is the spire of St. Michael's at the
top of Highgate West Hill. It marks with a strange precision
the very spot where I would wait each day to catch a cab to
visit him in hospital half a century later, in the last few months
of his life.

It was the summer of 2009 and a sabbatical had brought me
back to London. Shortly after I arrived, his health had taken a
turn for the worse. Not having a car, I used to walk up Highgate Hill and wait there for a taxi. The autumn was unusually
mild—as I remember, there were hardly any rainy days—and
the stroll allowed my mind to float away from the image of Dad
lying in his ward towards the things he liked to talk about: the
war, his childhood, history, Russia.

About fifty yards from where I would be standing there was
a sign that marked a fork in the road: It had one arrow pointing to "Highgate Village," the other to "The North." As the
cars sped past, in and out of town, there was something about
that sign—perhaps it was the stark choice it offered, or maybe
it was the midcentury font—that got me thinking about the
places Dad had called home. I realized that his eighty-plus years
could be plotted—stints in the army and college and business
trips aside—as a series of points around Hampstead Heath, the
great rolling expanse of which unfolded below me. Unlike his
parents, who had been uprooted from Russia and parted from
their families and had suffered great hardship by the time they
settled in London, his experience of home over the course of
his life was pretty much contained within the circle of a day's

walk from where I was standing. Now it was ending only a couple of hundred yards from where it had begun, and I wondered whether the contentment I associated with him—an acceptance of life, a kind of happiness, really, if it is not presumptuous to call it that—was linked in some way to his enduring bond with the area, whatever it was that had drawn his parents not just to England but to this part of London in particular, and led them to make it their home and his.

Since moving to New York a few years earlier, I had started to feel acutely nostalgic for my native city. When I was growing up, things were in many ways not very different from how they had been in Dad's time: The Lyons teahouses had gone, and the first Sainsbury's supermarkets had arrived. But the Victorian classrooms in the school down the road, the grim toilets across the playground, the warm public libraries, the whole class-driven ethos of England had stayed more or less intact. By the start of the twenty-first century, all this was disappearing fast. Transformed by massive inflows of capital, London was changing before my eyes. As Dad lay ill, I thought about nostalgia and what precedes it. How is it that the places we live in come to feel that they are ours? What had it meant for Dad's taciturn father, Max, never to see his birthplace again? How had

Dad's affectionate, intuitive mother, Frouma, come to terms with being separated from her family in Moscow for thirty years? What invisible psychic struggles, what efforts of renunciation, had gone into making a home in Highgate for their son to grow up in? These questions acquired new meaning for me once I returned to Manhattan. The more I thought about them, the more this double loss—Dad's death and the vanishing of the London I had known as a boy—came to seem inextricably intertwined.

Behind them lay a third, more distant loss as well. I had never really known Dad's parents because Max had died before I was born and Frouma when I was six. But it was clear enough from everything we had been told that Dad's silence had nothing on his father's. How else could one account for the fact that although Max and Frouma had been close, he had never apparently told her the name of his own mother? Unlike Dad's, Max's silence had hidden real secrets. Before he met Frouma, he had been a revolutionary socialist in Tsarist Russia, something he never spoke about later, once he had left his underground existence behind. Many of his closest comrades ended up in violent deaths, shot either by the Bolsheviks or by the Nazis. His decision to come to England, to marry and start a family with Frouma, had been a precondition for our existence. In her, he had found someone for whom the nurturing of family ties was a way to withstand the pain of history. But for Max, settling down had depended upon his renunciation of activism: The building of a home and political disillusionment could not be separated.

Perhaps this explains why my image of him was suffused with the melancholy aura of dashed hopes. In the courage and commitment of his youth, I saw something exemplary for our more jaundiced age with its demagogues and its obscene wealth and its ever more intense introspectivity. Today many people seem to be too chastened and paralyzed by their suspicion of social utopias, even the most practical ones, to want to fight for anything much at all beyond the perfection of their own souls. Max had fought hard for others—driven by a very old-fashioned passion for justice that had been animated by a firsthand knowledge of poverty and exploitation. He'd had a visceral opposition to tribalism of any kind, ethnic and religious above all, an opposition that came from the gut as much as the brain. The movement for which he had fought more than a century ago had lost out and languished in oblivion, but that hardly seemed to matter. History's losers have more to teach us than its winners. No victories last forever—it is what you do with defeat that counts.

Back in Highgate, I found myself thinking about Fisher and Sperr, an antiquarian bookshop on the high street next door to the Hilltop Beauty Salon. Why it had come into my mind I am not sure—maybe because nothing preserves defeated ideas better than an old bookshop, which keeps intact the possibility of their discovery and reincarnation. And perhaps for that reason I remembered how dismayed I was only a few months after Dad's death when a dusty green curtain appeared across the familiar bow window to mark John Sperr's passing. The shop had been there so long I had somehow assumed it would go on forever; Mr. Fisher had disappeared years ago, but John Sperr had manned the desk to the end. He had become forbiddingly deaf and barked at visitors, but once you had his confidence, the key came out, the cavernous back room with its treasures was grudgingly unlocked, and the light was turned on. Inside it was always freezing and the books were crammed high, gathering dust and rarely touched. One afternoon, I found a small

leather-bound edition of the *Anthologia Lyrica Graeca*, its title
page bearing in a precise but minuscule schoolboy hand the sig-
nature "V. E. Rieu" and the date "Nov. 10th 1902." I bought it
because I had heard of Rieu, who would later become the first
translator of Homer in paperback and the founder of Penguin
Classics, the great disseminator of the world's learning. He had
lived and died nearby, leaving his library to be dispersed and
then reassembled in a bookdealer's afterlife.

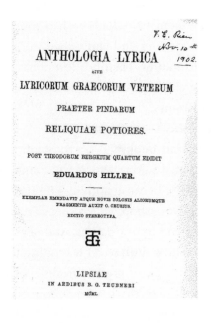

Rieu was not the only local resident to have valued ideas
and books: Like an urban mountaintop, Highgate's elevation
seems almost designed to inspire thought. "Once up the hill
and the trouble of ascending it is at an end, it is felt that a haven
has been reached," noted Ernest Aves, an acute observer of the
streets of Victorian London, after he had walked up into the village one mild December day in 1898. "Philosophers or Friends

ought to be living here."[1] So they have, along with poets and novelists, conservative romantics, anarchists and revolutionaries; the most famous communist in history lies in its cemetery. Many, like Karl Marx, were émigrés. Others, like Rieu, were the children of foreigners. It is as if the city views from London's northern heights drew in the contemplative and the idealists, and gave its charms a special significance for those who had braved political turmoil and sought sanctuary without ever wanting to give up on the world.

"Mostly it was footsteps, rustling leaves," in John Betjeman's words—the bard of Victoriana had passed his infancy on Highgate West Hill. When Dad was growing up there, horses still pulled the milk float along Langbourne Avenue and sheep were herded down North Road. The pace of the neighborhood suited his parents, and once they had settled down on the Holly Lodge Estate, an interwar development of half-timber houses and wide avenues on the flank of West Hill, they refused to uproot themselves again. When family circumstances drove them to sell their first house and move to a smaller place, the van picked up their furniture and deposited it at their new home five minutes later: It was just around the corner. And later still, when Dad's father died, his mother moved into a block of flats less than a quarter of a mile away. There is a privilege in being able to stay put, in choosing when to move, and the upheavals, fears, and deprivations of their early lives had equipped Dad's parents to appreciate it.

This was the terrain Dad grew up in, and he knew it intimately. It gave him confidence, I think, the kind that perhaps comes only by knowing where you are from and having been

happy there and having kept it close. In hospital, some time in
his last weeks, I brought him the memoir of a man who had
grown up in the poor backstreets of Highgate New Town
below the cemetery, and when I queried the name of a road the
author had mentioned, Dad identified it immediately because
he had canvassed there for the Labour Party before its historic
victory in the magical election summer of 1945. As his health
grew worse, while he was lying in a noisy ward that overlooked
the streets sloping down to the West Heath ponds, there were
few things that worried him as much as momentarily forgetting
how to get from home to the hospital. A local map restored his
natural sense of direction.

This ability to orient himself, to know where he was, had
always been important to him. Among the first photographs
he took when he was a boy, in the early 1930s, were shots of
the Heath, tokens of the lure of the place, its grip on his imagination. The trees are mostly bare, and to judge from what the

blurred figures above the ponds are wearing it is probably a spring day. It is not the people that have caught his child's eye but the slopes, the skylines, and the hedgerows. Already one can see an attachment forming, and the way he passed that on was only one of his gifts to us.

His, and his parents' too. For them, it had come at a price — the price all refugees have to pay — because making their home in England had meant forsaking other, older places, with memories of their own. One or two of these we knew a little about because during our childhood we would from time to time overhear Dad speaking in fluent Russian on the phone to relatives in Moscow and Leningrad. Other places were never anything more than names — Smolensk, Vilna, Grodno, Riga — that cropped up occasionally in anecdotes. I was not sure where they were exactly, or who had lived in them. It had all seemed so far away.

CHAPTER ONE

The Bundist

At the time Dad was born, his father was doing well. Max was a company director several times over, and he ran the Engineering and Mercantile Company Ltd, which exported Sheffield-made machine tools to Eastern Europe. In the photograph, the three-piece suit, the tightly buttoned jacket, the cuffs, and the lightly held cigarette convey respectability, the poise of someone comfortable dealing with balance sheets, trading positions, and capital.

But his air of latent watchfulness hints at a man on his guard, and the wary glance off to the side suggests that his careful appearance concealed as much as it revealed. A leading anarchist named Rudolf Rocker once wrote in his recollections of the political exiles he had known in turn-of-the-century London that they were taciturn men, disinclined to talk much, and Max was of that kind: His wife, Frouma, called him *zhivotik*—"little stomach"—because words stayed down there and rarely made their way up into his mouth. He had no difficulty with languages—he spoke four fluently and his English was impeccable, with no trace of an accent. But Max had learned to say no more than was necessary in any of them.

He belonged to the same generation as Vladimir Lenin, the Menshevik leader Julius Martov, and the future Soviet foreign minister Maxim Litvinov, and his path had almost certainly

intersected with theirs because when he had entered business
in the years before the First World War, working for a Rus-
sian shipping firm in the city of Vilna, he had simultaneously
been involved in running an underground socialist movement.
Its full name was Der Algemeyner Yidisher Arbeter Bund in
Lite, Poyln un Rusland (the General Jewish Workers' Union in
Lithuania, Poland and Russia), but it was known simply as the
Bund. Today it has been almost entirely forgotten: Its language,
Yiddish, barely survives, and the people who supported it — the
Jewish working classes of the Russian Pale of Settlement — were
mostly wiped out in the war. Yet in its time the Bund played an
absolutely critical role in the birth of left-wing party politics in
the Tsarist empire. Leading a double life as a merchant's book-
keeper and revolutionary agitator, Max had learned early on
the value of those habits of caution, silence, and mistrust that
were necessary for survival. He never forgot them — or the loy-
alties he grew up with. To the end of his life Max was not just a
man of the Left: He was a Bundist.

To be a Bundist. It all started, perhaps, with a feeling — a feeling
of outrage at the enduring divide between rich and poor:

> *Beneath the salt sea of humanity's weeping*
> *A terrible chasm abides*
> *It couldn't be darker, it couldn't be deeper —*
> *It is stained with a bloody red tide…*[1]

On the one side, the suffering worker, the pauper, the slave;
on the other, the emperors, the barons, the exploiting classes.
The Bund's anthem, a kind of proletarian "Marseillaise" for a
future revolution, was a call to rise up in anger, to choose the

side of justice, to fight under the red flag of socialism. *Brider un shvester*, it opened—"Brothers and sisters in toil and struggle": A desire to combat the millennial injustice of the world was matched by a deep sense of comradely solidarity. From the start, the Bund generated a remarkable warmth of affection among its militants, an almost unrivaled fealty to one another and to the Bund as a whole, as though the thing itself was more than a mere party or an organization, something living and beloved. In Yiddish, the word was *mishpokhedikayt*, the sense of family. Perhaps this feeling that it seemed to engender was responsible for allowing it to prosper as long as it did in a world of far more ruthless enemies, and to linger in people's hearts long after.

But of course the Bund was not just a matter of sentiment—it would never have appealed to a realist like Max if it had been—it was also a serious vehicle for ideas about political transformation. Late nineteenth-century revolutionary socialism was an argumentative milieu preoccupied with doctrinal differences, a world in which parties split and amalgamated, and factions formed and reformed in an endless debate about the lessons the past held for the future of mankind. Inside the broad tent of Russian social democracy, Mensheviks quarreled with Bolsheviks and both of them argued with the Bund. They all met under the stern gaze of Karl Marx, whose writings inspired them. But while the Bolsheviks adulated Lenin with his conception of the tightly controlled and centralized party, the Bund had no Lenin and wanted no single leader. Mensheviks and Bolsheviks both claimed to speak on behalf of all the inhabitants of the Russian Empire; the Bundists regarded themselves as the voice of Russian Jews in particular. For them, national, cultural, and linguistic differences needed to be acknowledged, not ignored.

But the Bundists were not nationalists, and far from being solely concerned with a Jewish future, they thought that the Zionist idea of establishing a national home for the Jews in the Middle East was a fantasy, and a dangerous one at that. Being a Bundist meant focusing on the here and now, participating with others in the socialist movement's common struggle for a better future, and working to overthrow the autocracy in Russia as a part of that struggle. At least that was the dream as the twentieth century began, when Max had been active and when the Bund was the largest and most effective revolutionary force in the Tsarist empire. By the 1920s, the Bund was a shadow of its former self; its heartlands had been torn apart, Bolshevism had triumphed in Russia, and the dream lay in the past.

Max was more than fifty when Dad was born, so the hidden book of his former life was a thick one, and the few anecdotes he imparted to his young son raised as many questions as they answered. He was, Dad said much later, an enigma, a man who kept to himself. To one of Dad's childhood friends, he seemed to be a figure of mystery, reading quietly upstairs, descending for his evening drink. It was easy to imagine stories of espionage, the plotting of exiles, secret contacts with government ministers. Silence invites speculation, and Max's silences were manifold.

Frouma did not know a lot more because she had only met her husband at the start of the 1920s, after he had put his activist years behind him, and even though they had a loving relationship, he spoke little about his past. When Max died in 1952, Frouma received a letter in Yiddish from a New York publishing house, the Ferlag Unzer Tsayt, an outpost of Eastern European Jewish political life that had implanted itself on the Upper East Side. After the Second World War it was one of the main outlets for what remained of the once powerful Bund, and it was run by an erstwhile comrade of Max's who wanted to write his obituary. In response to his queries, Frouma confessed that she knew almost nothing about what Max had been doing in the period before she met him: "As an old member of the Bund, which during the period in which he was active was an illegal organization, my husband even in his later life never liked to speak about his share in it." It was not only about his activism that Max kept his lips sealed. Frouma went on to say that both of his parents had died by the time she married him and she did not even know the name of his mother. She had never met any of his relatives and so far as she knew, his closest friends were dead. His precise date of birth, she said, Max had not even been sure of himself. The best she could do was to send them a photograph of him that appeared with the caption: "Mordecai Mazower. A leading Party worker in Wilno, Łódź and other cities during Tsarist days."

During Tsarist days. At the dawn of the twentieth century, Vilna was one of the largest cities in the Russian Empire, positioned at the intersection of the railway lines to Europe and the Baltic and a key hub for the imperial communications system. It was there that on April 12, 1901, customs officials caught sight of a young man staggering out of the train station under the weight of a suspicious-looking sack. As he began to load it into a horse-drawn cab, they asked him to open it. It turned out to contain bundles of illegal Yiddish newspapers and leaflets. A search also revealed a note with instructions scrawled in Russian: "Corner of Ignatievskaya Lane and Blagoveshchenskaya Street facing the Polish church where there's the office of the dentist Katz, on the third floor ask for Mazower, and then for Max—if he's not at home, then go to the Nadezhda Co. office on Bolshaya St. and ask for him there."

Bahnhof in Wilna

The Vilna police quickly established the seditious nature of the material. The newspaper, *The Worker's Voice*, was, in their words, "openly antigovernment in its content." It argued for the need to replace the existing capitalist system with a socialist one favoring the workers' struggle against the Russian government which it described as "the most savage in the civilized world." It was published by the Bund. There were also pamphlets for the Russian Social Democratic Workers' Party, calling for demonstrations on May 1 — a date of special anxiety for the police, only a few weeks away — and highlighting the slogan "Down with the savage Asiatic autocracy, the enemy of democracy and socialism."

When the young man was charged with belonging to "a secret society that calls itself the General Jewish Labor Bund of Russia and Poland," he claimed never to have heard of the organization; he had merely been carrying the parcels as a favor to someone he met in the street. The Ignatievskaya apartment belonged to a widow, Sara Mazower, who lived there with her three sons, one of whom was called Mordkhel (Max). Nothing incriminating was found there, or at the offices of Nadezhda, a shipping company where he worked. Max himself—described in the police file as an accountant—pled not guilty to belonging to the Bund and to disseminating illegal revolutionary publications. He said he had no idea who had written down his address or why, and his boss testified to his good character. Unimpressed, the Vilna prosecutor named him as one of four men who were members of a "secret criminal organization" participating in the labor movement and distributing antigovernment materials. The police detained him, aware that his name and that of the trading company he worked for had been cropping up in other investigations. They knew that suspicious characters had previously been seen entering his mother's apartment. But they could find nothing more, and eventually released him on bail, leaving him under surveillance but free to resume his double life.[2]

"Forgetting some things is a difficult matter," says the hero of *The Gadfly*, a novel by Ethel Voynich that was dear to Max's heart. I can't help wondering what things he had wanted to forget, what in particular lay buried deep in his very earliest memories, before the double life of his early manhood began. Readers of *The Emigrants*, W. G. Sebald's strange set of dreamlike meditations, will recollect the mysterious character of the book's opening—Dr. Henry Selwyn, an elderly English doctor tending his secluded and melancholy walled garden in a village outside Norwich, who turns out to have been born Hersch Seweryn into

a Russian Jewish family from somewhere in the vicinity of the
town of Grodno, a day or two's ride from Vilna, at the end of
the nineteenth century. Max never lived in decaying splendor
in the English countryside, but in his own way he journeyed as
far as Sebald's fictional hero, and like him, he found in England a
sanctuary for his own guarded version of bourgeois civility. But
perhaps the real reason he reminds me of Selwyn lies elsewhere,
in the odd coincidence of the fact that his starting point—a place
and a milieu he never talked about at all—had also been Grodno.

Grodno at the time of Max's birth was a town of some thirty-five thousand people in the Pale of Settlement — that vast swathe of western Russia to which the Jewish population had been almost entirely confined by imperial order. By the late nineteenth century, the Pale contained ninety-five percent of the empire's Jews, which is to say, nearly half of all Jews in the world at that time. Grodno's Jewish community dated back to the fourteenth century and Mazowers had lived there for several generations at least. Indeed Max was originally named Mordkhel after his grandfather, who had been born in 1792 and would have been one year old when Grodno hosted the very last meeting of the parliament of the old Polish republic.

After Poland was partitioned, the town had been transferred to Russian rule where it languished, an outpost on the empire's northwestern borderlands, until the economic upswing of the late nineteenth century. By then, the Pale had turned into a demographic time bomb because between 1820 and 1880 the empire's Jewish population had risen from 1.6 million to 4 million people who were constrained to live in increasingly crowded and impoverished circumstances. It was in the urban areas that their plight was most starkly visible. Most of Grodno's inhabitants were Jews, roughly twenty-seven thousand by the mid-1880s, many of whom lived in squalor in the disease-ridden shantytown behind the Neman River where filthy unlit hovels, sunk into the earth, their walls crumbling and patched with paper to cover the holes, were each inhabited by anywhere up to fifteen people. In summer, amid the stench of the puddle-filled alleys, children played half naked and barefoot. Conditions were no better in the villages where insanitary shacks might be shared by two or three destitute families, living off a daily diet of a few onions, a herring, and some bread.[3]

There was a small wealthier class, mostly connected with the tobacco factory that provided much of the town's employment. Max never spoke about his upbringing, but one of his cousins was doing well enough as an accountant in the factory to be able to afford an apartment outside the Jewish quarter, a private tutor for his children to make sure they spoke Russian properly, and a small wooden dacha four or five miles outside of town, where they spent summers collecting wild strawberries and mushrooms. This cousin later helped out Max with shelter and money, when he was on the run, and later still, in London in the 1920s, Max would return the favor by supporting one of his cousin's sons.

Max's parents were probably neither prosperous nor starving. Dad thought Max's father, Iosif (Yosl/Osip), had owned a small mill. Semyon, one of Max's brothers, once wrote that their father had been a "clerk on a small salary." What is clear is that he was already old and on his second marriage when Max was born. There cannot have been much to go round because there were several children to support from his first wife before he had another three boys in quick succession. Max was the first. According to Frouma, all Max knew for sure was that his birth took place on the "fifth day of Chanukah," in the year 1874, or so she thought. But even that is uncertain because in 1909, in the absence of a formal birth certificate, Max obtained a notarized declaration by two elderly Grodno inhabitants in which they testified that "as is well known to us and as we well remember, there actually was born unto the lawfully married commoner of the town of Grodno, Yosl Mordkhelovitch Masower and his wife Merka-Sara Jankelevna, in the month of October of the year 1873 a son who was named 'Mordkhel.'"

Although Max was known much later on to his in-laws in Paris as Dr. Mazower, or more simply *le docteur*, that was really a tribute to his careful dress, his diction, and his reserve rather than to any diplomas or degrees. He never passed through the science faculty of the Université de Liège or the commercial school at the Riga Polytechnikum like some of his émigré friends in London; in fact he never had much of a formal education at all. But he was a fast learner and could easily see how limited the prospects in Grodno were because people were already emigrating in large numbers from the province in the 1880s. Then came a catastrophic blow, or perhaps a blessing in disguise: When Max was about fourteen years old, his father died. Loss of a breadwinner could send a household plummeting into poverty and the family finances faced disaster. Max and his two brothers left Grodno with their mother almost immediately; there was evidently little to keep them.

Some of their relatives were heading across the Atlantic but the four of them moved only as far as Vilna, a city many times the size of Grodno, where they rented a small apartment. Max became the main money-earner and the family's situation stabilized once he found a job in the office of a prosperous Jewish shipping merchant called Lazar Rapoport. His brother Zachar joined him there, while Semyon, the youngest, was apprenticed to a typesetter in a printing shop. All of them joined the Bund and ran into trouble with the police as a result. Zachar, who later trained as a dentist, would manage in this way to reach the lower fringes of the professional classes. Semyon never escaped the world of manual labor, and he suffered from poor health all his life, and by the age of fifty could no longer work because of failing eyesight. Max seems to have been the most enterprising and rose the furthest. Starting out as a clerk he quickly became his employer's confidant and the manager of his personal affairs, and by the time of his arrest, he was running the office whenever Rapoport was away. He was a capable, discreet, and energetic young man, with a developed sense of responsibility and a wry sense of humor. In 1902, Rapoport wrote him a reference: Over the ten years he had known Max, he wrote, he had come to appreciate him as "a highly honest, cultured, and diligent person, and as an impeccable employee." A model of bourgeois virtue.

And by then, thanks to Vilna, an increasingly formidable revolutionary as well. In a family saga of cities—London, Paris, Moscow—Vilna was the first and perhaps the most important. Grodno was in essence a Jewish town of mostly wooden, low buildings with one large factory, but Vilna was a microcosm of the Russian Empire. Today the capital of Lithuania, it was then a flourishing polyglot emporium that was becoming a cauldron of political rivalries as the competing struggles of Polish nationalism, the Yiddish cultural revival, and Russian socialism intensified. The Tsarist authorities felt the presence of enemies all around them; according to the police, the city was teeming with revolutionaries. In their judgment, the "most serious and zealous" belonged to the Bund, and Vilna was its birthplace.

The authorities could more or less keep an eye on the elegant new boulevards and squares in the city center, but their hold was much more precarious over the back alleys where prostitution and begging were rife and sewage trickled along the open streets. No less than forty percent of Vilna's population was Jewish, among them a large proportion of the workers in the city's textile mills and sweatshops, packers, porters, peddlers, and bristle-makers, and it was in the encounter between these laboring men and women and the young more educated Jewish students of the city that the Bund originated. In the early 1890s, just a few years after Max's arrival, youthful Jewish socialists formed discussion circles to educate themselves in political theory. Soon they moved on to the more practical business of mobilizing the city's Yiddish-speaking workers into unions. Then, in October 1897, representatives of several Jewish labor organizations from the main towns and cities of the region met in the attic of a modest house on the outskirts of Vilna and founded the Bund, the first mass Marxist party in Russian history. These activists wanted to build a grassroots workers' organization and had the connections, the patience, and the skills to do so. Over the next ten years they expanded the Bund into the largest and most powerful labor movement in the Russian Empire.

Vilna was an entry point to European languages and culture, a place where you could have your photograph taken at the Maison Schmidt on the rue Grande and still be in the Russian Empire. Thanks to the railway, the city was a center of migrant agents, making money by helping peasants to emigrate. The trains brought books, pamphlets, and newspapers from west and central Europe, and they brought students returning from Berlin and Zurich. It was an environment in which modern ideas were valued and circulated. Mordkhel from Grodno changed his name to make it sound more Russian and more European. He appears first to have gone by Markus—"Markus Osipovich Mazower" is how Rapoport styles him in his letters of reference—and then by Max, which is how he would be known for most of his life. Vilna's cafés, factories, bookstores, and Viennese-style apartment blocks acculturated him into the

manners and dress of the imperial bourgeoisie. From this time
onwards his manner of dress was proper, with a tie and waist-
coat, and his coat generally buttoned up high. With his neatly
trimmed goatee and mustache, he has an almost dandified air in
early pictures, wearing the uniform of middle-class civilization
that was a kind of passport across the Continent. It is surely no
coincidence that it was only once he got to Vilna that the first
photos of him were taken, photography itself enabling a kind
of ratification of good social standing. Yet the city also turned
him into what Russians call an *intelligent*, a member of the intelligentsia. And into a conspiratorial revolutionary as well. For
it was not only in Marxist theory that revolution presupposed
the emergence of bourgeois values; this was true in life as well.
Leading Bundists aimed for outward respectability; many of
the members of its central committee sported derbies, a symbol in those days of the bourgeois style. Work in a merchant's
company gave Max the skills, the language, and not least the
shipping network for his revolutionary activities. Knowledge of
Russian, something less than than five percent of Jews in the
Pale acquired, gave him access to the classics of Marxist theory
and a worldview.

That Max was aware of the irony of this situation we know
thanks to the story told later by one of his comrades, a man
called Sholem Levine. He was a young Bundist who came to
Vilna in the winter of 1899 to set up an illegal printing press.
When he ran short of the money to rent an apartment, his girlfriend had an idea: They should tell her family they were getting
married and use the dowry her well-off brother had promised
her. In his memoirs Levine goes on to describe how as a member of the Vilna central committee, Max was asked to approve
the scheme. He did so, commenting wryly: "It is a blessing

[*mitzvah*] to take money from a bourgeois in order to set up an illegal printing shop." It's the only sound of his voice we have from these first years, practical, joking, and authoritative at the same time. At the age of twenty-five, he was already, only two years after the Bund's founding, a member of the directorate running the organization in its most important town.[4]

Because his employer, the Nadezhda Trading Company, was based in St. Petersburg and involved in shipping goods across the empire, it offered the perfect cover. The Vilna Bundists were respected in the party for their tight security procedures, and thanks to their caution and discipline, penetration by police agents was limited. As a result, the authorities were usually one step behind them, something which was not true in other cities. By the time of his arrest in 1901, Max had in fact been responsible for at least five years for printing and distributing illegal literature in Yiddish across the region from Warsaw to Białystok and Vitebsk; he was also supervising the publication of an illegal journal, *Der Klassen Kampf* (Class Struggle), an organ of the Vilna committee. And there were other tasks: forging passports on forms stolen from municipal offices; buying guns; purchasing printing equipment abroad and getting German technicians in to help them operate it. Vilna was the revolutionary hub for northwestern Russia and Max was at its center. Known to the agents of the Okhrana, the Tsarist secret police, who shadowed him, as "the Handsome One," to distinguish him from his brother Zachar, Max was the consummate organizer, a figure of the shadows, someone who seems never to have sought the podium but knew what to do when a new press was needed, an activist smuggled in or out of danger, or workers brought out on strike.[5]

Along with smart clothes and the outlook of a member of the intelligentsia, Max acquired a cover name, an integral part of revolutionary culture in all the underground parties in those days. In the Bund alone we find all kinds of pseudonyms deployed: References to hair color— "Red," "Black," "Max the White" — were common. A glutton was known as "Gravy"; "the Philosopher," "the Madman," and "the Fighter" were self-explanatory. Often people went simply by some version of their first name, suggesting that it was not security that motivated them so much as the desire to join in the intimate circle of those on first-name terms.[6] In Max's case, security was clearly a consideration, and it is not at all easy to figure out the name he had used: Indeed even Frouma, his wife, got it wrong after his death. The main problem is that Bund correspondents, whether in letters or party documents or newspaper articles, avoided mentioning one another by their real names, so it is often hard to figure out which nickname refers to whom. In a much later work, however, Jacob Hertz, a chronicler of the movement, identifies Max as the author of several articles under the pseudonym "Daniel," and a file found recently in the Moscow archives confirms this. In 1904, an agent for the Okhrana was tracking letters sent from a Bundist official in Vilna called "Wolf" to a certain "Daniel," in Warsaw. Wolf was part of a network in Vilna that included Max's brother Zachar, and Daniel was obviously an experienced Bundist operative because his security procedures were tight. He made sure that the letters were not sent to him directly but to a drop-off point, a haberdashery in Warsaw. Even then they were not picked up by him but by a third party, a young nurse who was a relative of the shopkeeper; she then presumably passed them on. The letters themselves had mostly been intercepted and appeared to concern deliveries of clandestine pamphlets to the Polish capital, although it was hard to tell because they were in a code the police could not break. But they had, the agent reported to his superiors in Moscow, been able to figure out who Daniel was: the eldest of the Mazower brothers, Max.[7]

He had not chosen the name by chance: It was a nod to his roots back in Grodno, and perhaps also to his hopes. The original reference was to the Old Testament prophet who is promised a revelation of what the future holds when the kings of the age have been defeated. But it had been adopted as a pseudonym by a figure from the previous generation, Aaron Lieberman, whom some called the father of Russian socialism. Like Max, Lieberman came from the Grodno region and he too had received his education in study circles in Vilna some years earlier. Like Max, his primary concern was to spread socialism among the Jewish laboring classes and he too rejected

nationalism, believing that "Jews are an integral part of humanity and cannot be liberated except through the liberation of
humanity." In 1876 Lieberman had fled Tsarist persecution. He
had founded the first association of Jewish socialists in the East
End of London before emigrating to the United States, where
he died in 1880, a still-young intellectual and an activist whose
memory was revered not only by Max but by many others.

Lieberman's generation had little time for Yiddish, the
earthy fusion of medieval German, Hebrew, and Slavic that was
the language spoken by most Jews in the Pale. Russian was the
language of education, as they saw it, and of the socialist culture to which they aspired. Lieberman himself often wrote in
a rather complex Hebrew. Unlike others, however, Lieberman
had encouraged the use of Yiddish, and this may have been the
most important thing of all for Max and his milieu, for whom
reviving "the jargon" was at the heart of their politics. The reason was eminently practical: Successful agitation required going
to the masses, and as more than ninety-five percent of Jewish
workers in the Pale could not understand Russian—knowing how to speak it, as Max could, was already a mark of
distinction—this meant reaching out to them in a language
they could comprehend. Yet Yiddish was at that time a spoken
language not a written one, so the early Bundists became trans-
lators, poets, and playwrights.

In Vilna they formed a "Yiddish committee" that met
secretly in respectable apartments belonging to sympathetic
pharmacists and doctors. This group looked for materials that
would promote "socialist feelings" and awaken the spirit of
protest; its members sometimes wrote stories of their own,
or they chose short stories from Russian and other languages,
novels as well as classics of Marxist political economy. Many

of these works would not have passed the censors so they had to be handled carefully. Max was a member of the committee, chiefly responsible for printing and distribution. Although he had almost certainly been speaking Yiddish in Grodno before he learned Russian, I am not at all sure that he ever spoke the language of his childhood once his work with the Bund was over—as an educated man, his preferred language was always Russian. But at this time, alongside his help with the administrative arrangements, he translated short stories and reviewed Yiddish plays, and he numbered several writers among his friends. On one book in particular he must have spent a good deal of time because he translated it in its entirety: a radical fin de siècle English novel called *The Gadfly*.[8]

The Gadfly was the work of the Anglo Irish writer Ethel Voynich, who was involved with the anti-Tsarist London newspaper *Free Russia* and was active in radical circles. A Russian speaker, she was the daughter of the logician George Boole and had married a Polish exile who became one of the great antiquarian bookdealers (scholars today remember him as the man who discovered the mysterious and still-undeciphered Voynich manuscript). But Voynich was just as remarkable as either of these men and her novels made her, for a time, a household name. Set in Risorgimento Italy, *The Gadfly* featured a fugitive freedom-loving hero who writes incendiary tracts and satires. Loosely based on the figure of Giuseppe Mazzini, the famous Italian republican of the mid-nineteenth century, the novel offered an obvious allegory of the struggle for liberty in Russia. It was a success in England—enough to annoy Joseph Conrad, who was already thinking about the themes that would later result in *The Secret Agent*, his remarkable study of terrorism—and it appealed enormously to the Left elsewhere too.

Not only did it circulate widely among socialists in a Russian translation but its popularity continued to soar after 1917, and during the twentieth century it became a communist publishing sensation, reckoned to have sold more than four million copies in the USSR alone.

It had an equally dramatic if more indirect success in the capitalist West. Sidney Reilly, the famous British "Ace of Spies," is supposed to have modeled himself on Voynich's hero, although separating fact from fantasy in the case of Reilly is difficult. He claimed to have had an affair with the author, though like most of his claims, this one was probably false. All we know for sure about Reilly is that his real name was Rosenblum, that he was Jewish and born in Russia around the same time as Max, that he worked for the British Secret Intelligence Service trying to overthrow the Bolsheviks after 1917, and that he was shot by the OGPU in 1925.[9] Many years later, Ian Fleming, who was fascinated by Reilly, used him as the model for James Bond, making *The Gadfly* an unlikely source of inspiration for the most famous spy of the Cold War.

Max and Reilly evidently shared a fascination with the book. But for all the air of mystery that surrounded him in later life, Max was a very different kind of character from the colorful Reilly. The latter was an adventurer and a womanizer, a man who seems not to have shied away from murder, lied with abandon, liked the good life, and had few evident political principles. What I think appealed to Max in Voynich's work was something that would have been secondary for Reilly: its idealization of the selflessness and suffering of the revolutionary life. Serious about educating himself and others, Max wrote a long historical introduction to his Yiddish translation. It is a dry piece of work, the style in keeping with what we know of some of his other writings, but Voynich's novel was anything but. Did he choose that particular book because it articulated, in a way he could not himself, the passion and pathos of the lonely path he had chosen?

By the time his translation of *The Gadfly* appeared—published in Vilna in 1907—Max had already been tested more than once by arrest, imprisonment, and flight. His name had been on the radar screen of the Okhrana since the mid-1890s and there had been that incident in 1901. With the Bund growing in power, it was only a matter of time before he was arrested. In February 1902 he was again detained and this time was sentenced to three years' exile under police supervision in the remote village of Uyarskoe near the town of Kansk, a destination that lay more than three thousand miles to Vilna's east along the Trans-Siberian Railroad.

Something of the rigors of that experience, which Max never spoke about, can be gleaned from the memoirs of Marie Sukloff, another Jewish socialist from the Pale who ended up not far away. In them, she describes an exhausting, unpredictable journey lasting many days in crowded, freezing convict cars, broken only by stops in the filthy, typhus-infested forwarding prisons that lined the route, prisons that generally required marches under guard from the train down roads covered with ice and snow. In Kansk, political prisoners were held in unheated barracks even through the winter months, and then sent on by foot through the snowbound Siberian woods to the isolated peasant communities that were their ultimate destination. Books were scarce, alcohol was the chief distraction, and the illiterate villagers tended to be both suspicious and respectful of the "noble" strangers in their midst. Confined amid the forests of the Yenisey River, Max bore it for only a few months. On July 13, 1902, he escaped and the police issued an alert for "Mazover, Mordkhel Ioselev, a commoner from the town of Grodno." Officers were told to look out for a man with "dark blond hair" and brown eyes, five foot five inches tall. It was too late. The Voynich's periodical *Free Russia* mentions in its November 1902 issue that among the five Bundists reported recently to have fled Siberia for "freer countries" was a certain "M. Mazover."[10] His destination was Germany, where he joined a circle of Bundist students at the university in Berlin. Trotsky's sister was there, as were many future luminaries—and opponents—of the Bolshevik state.

Penetration of the Bund by Tsarist spies was always a threat; indeed a wave of arrests had nearly killed off the movement in the first months of its operations, and although it recovered quickly, the reverberations lingered. The organization in Vilna took steps to guard against infiltration and did not shy away from punishing informers when it unmasked them. After a Bundist tried to assassinate the governor of Vilna in 1902, there was a massive clampdown. But the Russian authorities were not the only enemy. Devout members of the Jewish community regarded the Bundists as godless materialists and terrorists, and they particularly did not like the fact that there were young women activists in their midst. For its part, the Bund spoke the language of proletarian revolution and regularly castigated the cowardice of the wealthier Jews who thought their money could buy them security. Bund cadres were known to burst into synagogues to make socialist speeches, and as a result rabbis denounced the organization in their sermons. The movement also combatted Jewish gangs from the criminal underworld, which were linked to the prostitution and gambling rackets that flourished in the towns of the Pale because they had strong ties to the police and employers, who used them as strikebreakers.

But the most significant enmity for the future came from the Left. Although Lenin had initially been impressed by the Bund's achievements, in the early years of the new century he came to see it as a threat and started to oppose the idea that Russian Jewish workers needed their own movement. A serious rift between Lenin and the Bund developed as a result, one that would never heal. The Bund's insistence that it spoke for the empire's Yiddish-speaking Jewish proletariat was anathema to Lenin's vision of a tightly centralized single Social Democratic Workers' Party reliant on the Russian language and controlled by him. Behind this was the larger question of how the numerous nationalities within the Tsarist empire should be brought into the revolutionary fold, especially when many of them did not speak Russian. Confronted with the power of the Bund, Lenin immersed himself in its arguments, read its publications, and began—respectfully at first, then with increasing impatience—to hammer out his objections.

It was a theoretical argument but it was also a personal one, conducted at close quarters, for in these years both Lenin and several of the leading Bundists in exile were living in the small Swiss town of Bern, so the Bundists had ample opportunity to see their opponent and get to know him. "Outwardly he failed to make a good impression," recalled the Bundist theoretician Vladimir Medem. "From what I had heard, I envisaged a towering revolutionist...one of the 'big guns.' But what I saw before me was a little animated individual...with a small flaxen beard, bald head and tiny brown eyes. A clever face but not an intelligent one. He reminded me then, and the comparison came instantly to mind, of a crafty Russian grain dealer." Lenin was not a forceful or imposing speaker, but Medem could not help being struck by two things: his iron will, and his distrust of people.[11]

Max was caught up in the growing antagonism at first hand because shortly after his escape he was invited to participate in one of the Bund's most critical meetings—a closed session of top party leaders that was held in Geneva in the spring of 1903. Lenin had just published another direct attack on the Bund in an article entitled "Does the Jewish Proletariat Need an Independent Political Party?" and his answer to his own question was predictably negative. The meeting was called to formulate a response. Only about ten people were present, including several Bund founders, so Max's presence is an indication of his respected position inside the organization. There was the chain-smoking Arkadi Kremer, the "father of the Bund," a theoretician of revolutionary agitation whose pamphlet on the subject had a huge influence on Lenin; John Mill, whose English-sounding name disguised one of the Bund's most important figures, was the founder of its powerful foreign committee; and Evgenia Gurvitz, one of several women in prominent positions. Max represented the Vilna committee, alongside another comrade, Julius Lenski, who had escaped from Siberia with him. (Later on, Lenski would join the Bolsheviks and then, according to one inside source, become a senior figure in the Cheka, the precursor of the KGB.)

The Geneva participants reaffirmed that Jewish workers did indeed need their own political movement and vowed to resist efforts to dissolve the Bund within the larger Russian Social Democratic Workers' Party. Thus matters came to a head. At its congress later that year, the party famously bifurcated into

Menshevik and Bolshevik factions. Less commonly remembered is that at the same time the Bundists accused Lenin and his followers of dictatorial tendencies and withdrew entirely. They insisted on being accepted as the sole representatives of Russian Jewish workers in the party, and they also demanded that the party sign on to the idea of cultural autonomy for different national groups within the empire. A few years later, the party agreed to the second condition and the Bund agreed tacitly to drop the first and was readmitted. Over time it became aligned increasingly with the party's Menshevik wing, which is why many former Mensheviks turn out to have started in the Bund, and why Max preserved close friendships over the years with Menshevik comrades and their families. There can be no doubt that his knowledge of Bolshevism—and his mistrust of its authoritarian leader—went back to this time, long before the revolution, when Lenin had regarded the Bund as one of the greatest threats to party unity.

Although the Bund's leaders worried about how workers in the Pale would respond to the rupture with their comrades, the workers seem to have scarcely noticed and the Bund's membership went from strength to strength. Growing confidence that Yiddish-speaking proletariat in the Pale would naturally gravitate towards them was the main reason why its leaders dropped their demand for formal recognition of their role in Jewish life; it was happening anyway. The Bund was by some considerable margin the largest and best-organized socialist movement in the empire, dwarfing Lenin's quarrelsome band of followers. Unlike the Bolsheviks, the Bund successfully combined revolutionary agitation with organizing workers to improve wages and working conditions. In the summer of 1904, a year after the London congress, it had some twenty-three thousand members, a number that grew to about thirty-four thousand at its zenith during the 1905 revolutions. By comparison, the entire membership of the Russian Social Democratic Workers' Party at the start of 1905 numbered fewer than ten thousand, and of these the Bolsheviks were in a minority.

A more urgent worry than arguments with comrades on the Left was escalating right-wing violence inside the Russian Empire. Backed by the Tsarist authorities, anti-Semitism was becoming increasingly murderous and 1903, the year of the Geneva meeting, was the worst for pogroms since the 1880s. That Easter a crowd in the town of Kishinev made international headlines when it went on a rampage with the cry "Kill the Jews," leaving many dead and a trail of destruction. Some months later, in the small town of Gomel, five hundred kilometers southeast of Vilna, mobs of railway workers and peasants were joined by local detachments of infantry after their officers had harangued them on the need to defend the "Father-Emperor" against his internal enemies: Hundreds of shops were wrecked and more than a dozen people were killed.

But among them, unusually, were some of the pogromists themselves: The attacked had fought back. The Bund rejected the terrorist tradition of Russian revolutionary activism, but it was certainly neither pacifist nor prepared to allow the terror unleashed by the authorities to go unchecked. Gomel had a large Jewish population and the Bund armed units ahead of time to protect Jewish neighborhoods—there were roughly two hundred men in the core groups, both Jews and Christians. After the pogrom was over, the details of what had happened were publicized in the widely circulated pamphlet *The Truth*

About the Gomel Pogrom, which came out in the name of the central committee of the Bund. It was in fact written by Max and it is, I think, the first document we have in which we can fully hear his voice.

The pro-government press had blamed the violence in Gomel on "the audacious attitude of the local Jews towards the Christians." But Max picks apart the official version in forensic detail. It is likely that he had gone to Gomel immediately after the pogrom and talked to people there. (Someone from the Bund certainly had, as had several journalists.) He describes the detailed preparations that the local authorities had been making for months to arm and provoke Christians against Jews, hoping to use anti-Semitism to drum up loyalty to the tsar. He names the officials involved—the town's captain of police, who had incited peasants from neighboring villages; the commander of the infantry regiment; the merchant Petroshenko; the notary Plakhov; the prison chief; and even some highschool students. The superintendent at the railway workshops had supplied the hammers, bars, and rods that were used to smash shops and beat people. Max also describes the extensive preparations Bund activists had undertaken for self-defense. When the pogrom broke out, everyone had been waiting. The row at the fish market that had ostensibly started things off had merely been the trigger. And it had only been when the troops fired on the rioters, instead of abetting them, that the looting and killing ended.

What strikes me now, in light of what we know about Max later in his life, is his extraordinarily factual tone. But he certainly does not shy away from judgment. He identified the main culprits as the local authorities: "The edifice of the autocracy is built only on murder and lies. Every provincial satrap considers himself an autocrat in his own right and considers every insult to his own person to be a revolt against His Majesty the King." But Max had little respect for the local Jewish community leaders who had taken it upon themselves to speak in the name of their co-religionists and been "overwhelmed by an attack of their usual cowardice and fearfulness." Instead of helping arm Jewish fighters, they had sent a deputation to assure the local governor of their loyalty: The "Jewish bourgeoisie" had thus revealed its "enslaved, servile spirit." All they had gotten in any case was a harangue for allowing the Bund to organize within their midst and a reminder that the Jews had been better off in the old days when they kept out of politics completely.

The lesson Max drew from all this was clear: Only under the leadership of the "Jewish socialist-minded proletariat," fighting under the "Social-Democratic flag" alongside the "proletarians of all nations" could a sufficiently powerful counterweight to the Tsarist regime be built. "Only the proletarian struggle will lead to a victory over Tsarist despotism and over the entire capitalistic world, with all the suffering that is bound up with it." Whatever differences the Bund might have had with its comrades in the Social Democratic Workers' Party, it was and remained a Marxist party, committed to solidarity among the workers of all nations and to the toppling of capitalism. The pamphlet was suffused with confidence; ethics and history were marching in step. The days of tyranny were numbered.

Gomel was a propaganda victory because, thanks largely to the Bund, the Jews had for once not taken things lying down. "What had occurred was a fight...rather than a pogrom," was how one Yiddish newspaper put it. "A newborn unprecedented type appeared on the scene," wrote a participant later, "a man who defends his dignity." Yiddish authors referred to Gomel as a time of renewed hope. "The youngsters intervened," says a character in a story by S. An-sky, "the new type who, people say, are not Jews at all, who keep none of the commandments… and they saved the entire Jewish community."[12] The social democrats in Kharkov said that the events in Gomel had "taught the Russian workman, as dozens of good books would never have taught him, to respect his Jewish comrade as a fighter." For their part, the Russian authorities were worried: They feared the spread of insurrection, and they were right to do so. Armed self-defense units, so-called *kamf-grupe* (fighting groups), were formed by the Bund in other towns as well, organized into core members and reservists. Soon there were probably between five hundred and a thousand core members in the Pale overall, and thousands more in reserve. Mostly they were Jewish, young men in workers' blue shirts and caps, but they were joined by Russians, Lithuanians, Ukrainians, and Poles. With funds pouring in from London and the United States, the organization was able to smuggle in revolvers and upgrade its printing presses. It was more powerful than ever.

CHAPTER TWO

1905

The revolution arrived sooner than anyone had anticipated. When Russia went to war with the Japanese in 1904, the campaign turned into a humiliating disaster, and the world watched in disbelief as a major European power was humbled for the first time by an Asian foe. At the start of the following year, as the struggle in the Pacific went from bad to worse for the Tsarist regime, demonstrators marching on the Winter Palace in St. Petersburg were brutally dispersed by bullets and cavalry charges, leaving hundreds dead. The events of Bloody Sunday and its aftermath triggered rallies and uprisings across Russia as protesters took to the streets and occupied factories. The parties of the Left were taken by surprise at first but they mobilized quickly. Max, who seems to have been working undercover in Warsaw, was now given the biggest assignment of his career: to help coordinate the Bund's activities in Łódź. He never spoke a word about this afterwards in all his years in London, not to his son and probably not to anyone else either. Nevertheless, the weeks he spent there formed the climax of his life as an agitator—an epic struggle that nothing, not even 1917, ever eclipsed.

An industrial city twice the size of Vilna, Łódź—with its numerous textile mills and large working class—had several nicknames: "the Polish Manchester" for one, "the city of chimneys" being another. One of the most densely populated and polluted urban spaces in Europe, it had been growing astonishingly fast—there had been a nearly fivefold increase in its population in just twenty-five years. It was close to the German border, on the western edge of the Russian Empire, and as a result, it was ethnically very different from the towns of the Pale. There was a large Polish population alongside the Jewish community and a sizable German minority as well. But the wave of strikes that broke out in 1905 crossed the lines of religion and involved some of the most extraordinary scenes of insurrection seen anywhere in Russia before the 1917 revolutions. What started as spontaneous protests soon turned into rolling factory sit-ins involving more than half the city's workforce, bringing the economy to a halt and alarming local industrialists. The Bund mobilized thousands of Jewish workers and began coordinating with Polish socialists as well as with the Lithuanian Polish socialist party led by Feliks Dzerzhinsky. The Yiddish-speaking Dzerzhinsky had been a student in Vilna and had many Bundist friends. (Later he joined the Bolsheviks and created their secret police, the feared Cheka.)

It is to this period of extraordinary tension, a time when it seemed that the entire Tsarist edifice might be toppled, that we can date the second major document we know Max authored, a single-sided proclamation in Yiddish that was pasted up on the walls of the city at the end of May.[1] The events that precipitated it unfolded against the backdrop of news that the Japanese navy had annihilated the imperial Russian fleet at the Battle of Tsushima, a victory that would force the tsar's government to sue for peace. In Łódź, Cossacks fired on a group of children and killed one of them on Wschodnia Street, a Bundist gathering place. Funerals were often revolutionary dramas in those days—it was for that reason Russian soldiers often buried fallen protesters secretly at night—and the bodies of the dead came to possess intense power over the crowds. Perhaps to forestall any attempt by the authorities to intervene, people gathered in front of the hospital where the boy had died and Bund activists went through the town encouraging workers to turn out. The cortege set off, at its head two hundred and fifty children, some in rags and barefoot, holding hands. An estimated ten thousand people marched behind them—Jews and Poles, men and women, workers and seminary students—and the sidewalks and balconies were thick with onlookers. A squad of Cossacks in civilian clothes looked on at the cemetery as the children raised a red flag and a black banner commemorating the dead, and there were speeches in Yiddish and Polish. It was a demonstration of unity against the regime. Afterwards, thousands of copies of Max's description of these events were printed and circulated.

"Proletariat of the world, unite!" it opens, for the Bund was completely committed to Marxian socialism:

Great are the defeats which the autocracy suffered during the entire bloody [Russo-Japanese] war in the Far East. And do you really think it is weak? If that is what you think, it is not quite true, as anyone who was present on Wschodnia Street on Saturday, May 27, would readily attest. There the Tsarist regime fought the "internal enemy" and came out with a "thorough victory." The Asiatic autocracy [i.e., the Tsarist regime] was able this time simply to destroy its enemy, and in fact quite easily. It's true that the enemy was completely unarmed, had little acquaintance with the great arts of war, and what's more, was small in number and posed no threat to the Tsarist throne of all Russia. The enemy consisted of a horde of little children who were outside in the carefree

Sabbath daylight, making mischief, playing a little and imitating what the grown-ups do. The children lifted a red cloth as a flag and imitated and demonstrated, singing joyous revolutionary songs and shouting "Down with autocracy!" It is unbelievable but these are the facts. Young children were shot for no reason other than because they are living in a time of revolution.

The children, writes Max, can't understand why anyone would be afraid of them. But "that frantic and poisoned creature, autocracy" is restless and jumping at shadows. Recently, he goes on, the police also shot a "Christian member of the brotherhood of workers. Blood mixes with blood and flows from every corner of Russia to the murmuring ocean." Then came the call to arms:

> But who among us can stand by, detached from this historical process, in which a population of 130 million people liberates itself from the capricious rule of Tsarist despotism? Only one who has lost all human feeling, one who is already entirely enslaved…
>
> Let anyone who possesses a spark of human dignity, anyone who does not wish to be adrift and who strives for a free life, join in the working-class struggle as soon as possible and stand under the red banner for the liberation of the proletariat, which means the liberation of the entire world.
>
> The new bloodshed that took place before our eyes is terrible. Our society is slavishly silent, as if nothing were happening at all. But we, the workers of Łódź, have not been able to keep silent and have poured out our protest in mighty demonstrations at the funeral of the late comrade Grabczynski and the small child, the terrible victims of absolutism.

Sunday and Monday, May 28th and 29th, grieving Jewish and Christian workers, brothers together, protested mightily and openly before the entire world against such wild capriciousness and such a murderous political order.

"Down with autocracy!" "Long live socialism!" — this has been our only answer.

To step forth in the heroic struggle for our complete liberation continues to be our hard and fast decision.

Honor the memory of the fallen comrades!

Down with autocracy!

Long live the revolution! Long live socialism![2]

In the days that followed, the authorities almost totally lost control of the city. After factory bosses appealed for reinforcements, several more regiments were sent in. But when a police volley killed a young Jewish girl haranguing the crowd from a box in the market, the last and most serious phase of fighting took place. Behind makeshift barricades, formed from market carts, boxes, and paving stones, Polish and Jewish worker militias armed with rocks, bottles, bombs, and pistols fought together under the red flag. Pitted against them were army and Cossack units, the gendarmerie, and local anti-Semitic groups. Schools shut down and shops were shuttered. By June 24, wrote a reporter,

[Łódź] resembles Paris in the days of the commune...The streets are filled with the debris of demolished barricades. Blackened ruins of shops pillaged and burned by the rioters stand out in the darkness like sentinels of anarchy...Only the flickering fires of the soldiers' camps in the squares light the streets. Desultory revolver shots, answered by quick volleys, are heard at frequent intervals in the city. Houses are barricaded, their doors and windows boarded up or filled with mattresses to ward off the bullets from Cossack carbines. For two days the streets of Łódź have been the scenes of battle. On the tsar's side, ten regiments of Cossacks, dragoons, and infantry; on the people's side, one hundred thousand striking workmen arrayed under the red flag. The fighting spirit of the people is fully aroused. They have tasted blood and want more. Today at Bałuty, a suburb of Łódź, four Cossacks were killed and sixteen others wounded by a bomb that was thrown into their barracks. Twenty-three of their horses were killed...The shooting was renewed late tonight. Cossacks are robbing the dead of jewels and money.[3]

It took days of heavy fighting and the proclamation of a state of siege before the uprising was finally crushed. By the end of June, more than one hundred and fifty civilians lay dead—that was the official total; a more realistic figure is probably between one and two thousand—and hundreds had been wounded.

In later years, Max's aging comrades would regret that he had not written more, and one can understand why—his blend of irony and moral outrage must have made his proclamation powerfully effective. The movement's socialist credentials are on vivid display in his words but the target is carefully chosen: neither capitalism in general nor the bosses, but the imperial regime and the indiscriminate violence of those defending it. Socialism here means the emancipation of society in general, and the freedom for young children to have their innocence back and to be able to play in the streets without alarm. The tsar's fear is what lies behind the violence, the fear—entirely justified in Max's eyes—that history is against him. It is not a sectarian message, and it emphasizes in particular the necessity for cooperation between Jewish and Christian organizations that was such a striking feature of the Łódź events.

The politics of it is not the only thing that strikes me now; there is some intensity of feeling behind it too. This was a call to arms triggered by outrage at the killing of children, at the cruelty of adults. Max had lost his own father and grown up fast. Perhaps as a result, when he became a father much later on, he was reserved, as if feeling his way into the role, and when Dad was a boy, Max was more or less incapable of demonstrating physical affection with him. Yet Dad never questioned that his father loved him, and felt both protective and proud of him as Max aged. Dad unquestionably sensed the real warmth of emotion that subsisted at some deeper level in a heart that had been enfeebled and acutely disappointed by history, that had taught itself to subordinate the personal to the political, and that later on could no longer easily show itself. To my knowledge, Dad never read his father's writings for the Bund. But I do not think their passion and emotional energy would have completely surprised him.

In Vilna, the Bund hung on for longer. The city had become, for the Bundists, "our Vilna" in which revolutionary meetings were held openly and orators kept crowds spellbound. Max returned from Łódź to a new assignment, and so, after nearly fifteen years, he finally left Lazar Rapoport's employment to run the first more or less legal Bundist newspaper, *Folks-Tsaytung* (People's Journal). Rapoport had been Max's staunch defender, one of those indispensable protectors to whom Russian revolutionary organizations owed so much: The St. Petersburg shipping company he ran had given the Bund enormous assistance. In abandoning his double life in favor of full-time political work, Max likely felt it was now or never, that the Tsarist autocracy was on the way out. If so, he had it wrong and must have soon realized his mistake. The tide was in fact slowly turning the other way, against revolution, as the authorities in Moscow and St. Petersburg regained their nerve and the arrests began again in greater numbers than ever.

In the summer of 1906 Max sent in his last report. It was from the town of Bila Tserkva, near Kiev, a region into which the Bund was trying to expand. His article is dry, matter-of-fact, analytic, downplaying his own role—he had probably gone primarily not as a journalist but as an agitator among the workers. A strike had started there, he tells readers, with "thirty old Jews," rope-makers, who acted spontaneously and then came to the Bund for help in formulating their demands. Other trades and industries followed—hairdressers, carpenters, bakers, workers in a paper mill: All demanded a pay increase, and in each case, Max reports, they prevailed. The "organization," as he calls the Bund, took the opportunity to encourage the workers to form unions, and the result was that more than one hundred of them joined the Bund. He comes across as the accountant of revolutionary potential, totting up successes, helping patiently to make the movement grow. This was the Bund's way, expanding through its practical support for underpaid laborers. For Lenin and the Bolsheviks, they were just "organizing weakness," mistakenly focusing their efforts on a section of the population that by itself would never bring about revolution. The Bolsheviks thought this was "economism"—as if fighting for higher wages alone could bring the end of capitalism. They preferred to change political consciousness through a nucleus of committed party cadres. The Bund saw things differently: For them the whole purpose of what they were doing was to make ordinary workers conscious of their strength by helping them to organize. It was a strategy that had paid off in the preceding decade. But it was to pose an impossible problem once the Tsarist regime, shocked by the events of 1905 and 1906, clamped down on any form of unrest with unprecedented severity.

Max had been an organizer par excellence — this was where his revolutionary talents lay. Writing was secondary; he was neither a rhetorician nor a lover of the limelight, and it is not a coincidence that he published nothing at all under his own name. His systematic mind and bent for facts and figures had been devoted to problems of distribution, supply, communication. The scope for him to work in this way now vanished. Early in 1907, as the roundups intensified, the police caught up with him once more, and after being arrested, he was sent back to Siberia, this time to live with a peasant family outside the city of Tomsk. It was one of the very few episodes from his life in Russia that Max spoke about later, perhaps because it had marked his exit from active politics. Dad always remembered the story of his father's escape, how Max had been supposed to register at the police station every day, and how he got the local policeman to trust him by playing chess with him — the policeman, stuck in that remote backwater, had nothing much to do. Gradually Max was allowed to come in every two days and then every week, until one day he calmly came in, played his usual game of chess, and boarded the train to Tomsk. He passed swiftly through Moscow and Vilna, narrowly escaping another police trawl there, before realizing the city was no longer safe and making his way abroad. His Vilna years were over. Henceforward, he would put his resourcefulness, his administrative expertise, and his deep-rooted caution towards building a new life and looking for a new home.

CHAPTER THREE

The Yost Typewriter Company

The initial months Max spent in exile following his escape from Russia are a blank, but it must have been sometime later when he was lodging with a revolutionary comrade in Dresden that his eye was caught by a job advertisement in the newspaper: The London office of a well-known American typewriter firm was looking for a marketing manager with a knowledge of Russian. He answered it and was invited to interview, and in November 1909 he crossed the Channel and arrived at the Holborn headquarters of the Yost Typewriter Company. It was almost certainly his first time on English soil.

At thirty-five, Max had reached a turning point. From the perspective of younger Bundist activists, he was already an old man, a *zokn*. For more than a decade, he had been living a semi-clandestine existence, under constant police surveillance. Since 1901 he had been sent twice to Siberia, escaping both times; he had lived an exile's life in Switzerland and Germany; and he had directed Bund operations in Vilna, Warsaw, and Łódź. He had been on the run, arrested, and questioned many times over, and he had sacrificed the prospect of domesticity for the cause of socialism. In Russia the Tsarist repression was in full swing: The second Duma was dissolved in the summer of 1907 and the prime minister, Pyotr Stolypin, was presiding over mass arrests and courts-martial, sending tens of thousands

of his opponents to Siberia. The kind of union organizing that
had been the source of the Bund's strength was in these circumstances impossible. Having fled the country, Max seems to have
felt, like other Bundists of his generation, that the revolution
was over for good. Many members felt the same and the party
itself shrank fast; by 1910 its numbers had dropped dramatically,
to about two thousand or so. Some of the other mass parties
suffered similarly: the Social Democracy of the Kingdom of
Poland and Lithuania, a major force in Russian Poland, collapsed from some forty thousand members in 1907 to around a
thousand by 1910.

Berlin, Geneva, Paris, New York, and Munich were the
most important centers of Russian political activism in these
years and the obvious destinations for those fleeing Tsarist persecution. England was less popular, a way station to the United
States for some of the million or so Eastern European Jews who
emigrated after 1880 from Russia and the Hapsburg empire. In
London's East End, amid the roughly ninety thousand poor
Jewish immigrants crowded into its slums and tenement buildings, there was a small Bundist presence. They had been sending funds to Vilna, which Max would have known about and
perhaps handled, and he would have read articles in the Yiddish
press about the workers' movement there. He may also have
had some London contacts of his own: Ethel Voynich's *Free
Russia* had reported his earlier escape in its pages and several
Vilna-born socialists whom he kept up with in later life were
already living there. In other words, the British capital was
probably not an entirely unknown quantity to him. Yet Max
knew so little English when he answered the Yost Company's
advertisement that his first correspondence with them was in
German, and he had so little money that he'd had to ask a rela-

tive back in Grodno to send him enough for a new suit for the interview. The firm was run by cosmopolitan men, however, and he must have impressed them. The managing director was Milton Bartholomew, a dynamic and ebullient Englishman who was keen to expand Yost's business into the Tsarist lands. The office manager, Samuel Wechsler, was a Jewish immigrant born in Bessarabia who had achieved Edwardian respectability and a house and family of his own in Cricklewood within a decade of arriving in London. Bartholomew and Wechsler liked Max; they gave him a position as Traveler and the job of opening up the Russian market at a modest salary of £100 a month, which would be supplemented by commissions if he did well. He would be going back to Russia not as a revolutionary but as a kind of glorified salesman. Most likely he was at this point able to return legally—either through an amnesty or because a sufficient period had elapsed since his original sentence—but possibly he was simply confident of being able to reenter the country illicitly. A series of rented rooms in North London became his base while he spent most of the year abroad.

A picture of Max's guarded, sensitive face stares down at me from the wall in my office each day, and it still strikes me as hard to imagine him ever selling typewriters. Yet he worked for Yost for a decade—a tumultuous one that spanned the First World War and the Russian Revolution—and in that time he turned out to be much better at his job than anyone could have imagined. Dad once came across an old-model Yost in a Cotswold museum and it was like a fish out of water: "What it was doing there, God alone knows." But the more I looked into it, the more sense the typewriter made. For there had been a time when this epitome of yesterday's technology had once conveyed all the excitement of the future and Max, coming out of a world where typewriters were still scarce and print was revolutionary, had understood how to seize the opportunity it presented.

> In the typewriter competition held at Pavia, Italy, during May, the Yost won first prize in the Hors Concours — or extraordinary typewriter competition. Mr. Warren, the operator on the Yost, did 1,881 strokes in three minutes, or about 170 short words per minute. Warren also carried off the second prize in the precision competition, which meant an hour's work for making up a balance sheet. In all, the Yost carried off about seven medals from the competition.
> — "Yost Happenings," *Typewriter Topics* (1907), 176

George Washington Newton Yost was an American inventor, a big figure in the rise of the typewriter. The introduction of this machine, along with the telegraph, the telephone, the moving picture and the motorcar, marked a moment in the emergence of modern life nearly as important as the earlier invention of print itself in the decisive move away from a society based on the handwritten word. Starting out as a designer of farm equipment and then a salesman for the Remington arms company, which pioneered the first popular models of the Type-Writer, Yost had gone on to found the firm that bore his name, and its fame grew so fast that the deceased spiritualist Helena Petrovna Blavatsky is said to have specified the use of a *"new* Yost machine" when she dictated her memoirs from the spirit world in 1896. A decade after Yost's death, the company was expanding all over the world. In their London showroom near the Holborn Viaduct, smartly dressed young women sat at rows of machines, a vision of independent, wage-earning, white-collar femininity that captivated more than one Edwardian novelist and plenty of young girls of the time as well.

It was boom time in the typewriter business. The U.S. government had begun ordering thousands of typewriters a year in the 1890s, but it took Europe a decade to catch up. Public typewriter contests took place as ways of advertising the machine's virtues, and more than five thousand spectators watched a so-called "endurance contest" in Paris between teams of rival typists. The Yosts were technically innovative, elegant, and efficient, although they faced competition from more established makes. Max's task of establishing a network of sales offices and buyers in Russia meant he had to be abroad about nine months of the year. In his first year he sold more than £12,000 worth of goods as he traveled across the Russian Empire, returning to London where, along with the company's other "Continental managers," he posed for a group picture, standing characteristically to one side. He cuts an elegant figure, smart, quietly dapper, but his hands are by his sides, a man prepared. The following years he ranged across Russia as far as Kirghizia. And then came the war, a new kind of test. Somehow he managed to go on working for Yost throughout. His sales figures for the imperial market shot up astronomically as the needs of the war prompted the Russians to buy more machines. Never again would he be as successful as he was at that time. In 1916 alone he earned enough in commissions to double his income, which is how the once poor revolutionary saved up the capital to buy a house and make possible the family life he later established in London.

Doing business in the middle of a world war that was followed by a revolution and civil war demanded a willingness to gamble and confidence in one's own judgment. Many of the usual business methods were suspended and prewar trading routes by land were blocked, which made St. Petersburg (or Petrograd, as it was called in the years after) more important than ever, since all imports into Russia from Europe had to go through there. At first Max stayed with his youngest brother, Semyon, behind the Moskovsky railway station. Semyon, who printed clandestine pamphlets for the Bund and other Russian social democrats, had moved from Vilna to St. Petersburg at about the same time Max had gone to London. As his business at Yost boomed, Max opened an office on the Nevsky Prospect, which became his base for the war years. When his stock of typewriters ran low, he dealt in thermos flasks, paper, pens, and other office supplies, and several times, faced with the difficulty of remitting foreign exchange, he simply used the company's profits to buy other goods that he exported to London for sale there, leaving his bewildered bosses to dispose of pigs' bristles, eggs, and other unexpected items. Max had turned out to be exactly the kind of resourceful yet utterly dependable entrepreneur the managers of the Yost Typewriter Company relied on, and at the start of 1918, having been in Russia for several years without a break, he received a letter from his head office congratulating him on his work: "The Directors of this Company...feel that you have really done remarkably well under what are probably trying circumstances—hitherto unexampled!" This was something of an understatement: The regime of Tsar Nicholas II had collapsed, as had the Provisional Government, and the Bolsheviks had just seized power. The Romanov dynasty was defunct, Russia was in turmoil, and the imperial German army was poised to invade from the west.

With its heavy restrictions on trade and heightened suspicions of foreign capitalists, counterrevolutionaries, and spies, the October Revolution left Max doubly vulnerable. Not only was he working for a British company but there was also his Bundist past, which obviously counted against him with the Bolsheviks. The bitterness that dated back to 1903 had not healed. Indeed the events of 1917 made it worse because although the Bund's members hailed the first revolution that spring, and many were elected to the new workers' councils, they were of two minds about Lenin. Quite a few Bundists went over to the Bolsheviks, but the vast majority (including Max and his brothers) did not, believing they were dictatorial and dangerous. The Bolsheviks reciprocated their suspicion. In August 1918, a ham-fisted British attempt to mount a pro-Tsarist coup frightened the wits out of the country's revolutionary rulers, although the Cheka dealt with it easily enough in the end. But then came two serious acts of terrorism. In the first, an assassin shot dead the Cheka's Petrograd head, Moisei Uritsky, and because Uritsky was a former Bundist, the investigators of his murder erroneously assumed at first that he was targed by Bundists or some other Jewish activists as punishment for leaving them. On the same day, there was nearly a second, much more consequential assassination, when the half-blind Jewish revolutionary Fanny Kaplan shot at Lenin in Moscow and came close to killing him. The All-Russian Extraordinary Commission for Combating Counter-Revolution and Speculation—to give Dzerzhinsky's Cheka its full name—now went into overdrive. For several months, it mounted a kind of Red Terror, and among those it arrested were many Jewish activists. On October 20, 1918, Max's offices were raided and the goods impounded. Suspicion and uncertainty were at their height, and the Cheka was the most feared agency in revolutionary Russia, operating virtually without restraint and executing thousands of people without trials. If the numbers of those killed were small compared with what was to come under Stalin, they dwarfed the numbers of the victims of the Tsarist secret police and presaged repression on a new scale. Max was arrested but fortunately he was not detained for more than a few months at the most, because by February he was free and able to pay off his office staff. He began operating again from other premises, before the Cheka found that too.

He clearly had sangfroid, but I wonder also about those contacts of his from prewar days who may have helped keep him alive. As he explained later to his employers back in London, the revolution had elevated the fortunes of many of his former comrades. There was the Bundist Mark Liber, for instance, a man Max had known for at least fifteen years, who had a personal connection to the Cheka's head. (Feliks Dzerzhinsky had once been engaged to Liber's sister until her untimely death left him devastated.) One of Dzerzhinsky's aides had been a Bundist from Vilna, and he too was a man whom Max knew well. Max may even have known Dzerzhinsky, if not from

Vilna in the 1890s then from Łódź in 1905. And that was just the leadership of the Cheka; there were Bundists and Mensheviks in other government agencies as well. In fact, the influx was so great that many Bolsheviks were worried, and a few years later a functionary in Minsk complained that "one has the impression that the Bund, and not our party, is in power."[1]

Released from the clutches of the Cheka, Max took precautions. He joined the All-Russian Union of Cooperative Societies, an organization which was not yet under Bolshevik control and which was to play a central role in Soviet trade and diplomacy in the coming years. He sensed that the Bolsheviks were too powerful to be toppled. At the same time, he could tell that despite its hatred of capitalism and the ongoing civil war, the revolutionary government needed to organize exports in order to acquire the foreign currency it badly needed. As a Russian speaker familiar with British business practices Max had the kinds of skills they depended upon to begin trading again, so his interests as a merchant and the union's interest in exporting Russian goods dovetailed. An additional advantage for him was that working for the union gave him a cover that would stand him in good stead if he needed to leave the country suddenly. That moment came soon enough. When the Bolsheviks began registering the names of the managers of all foreign firms in the country, he decided it was no longer safe to stay. Tipped off that he was about to be arrested for espionage, he obtained permission to travel to Polotsk in western Russia on co-op business. He closed down his office in Petrograd, handed the company accounts over to his brother, and in early December 1919, after undergoing what he tersely described to his employers as "more severe experiences and much risk," he left. He was headed for the border.

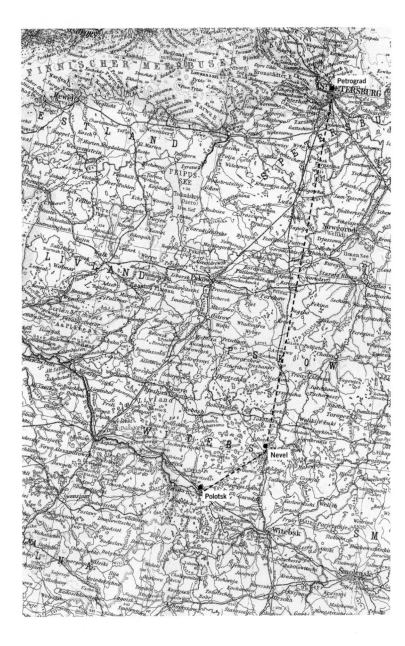

CHAPTER FOUR

Border Crossing, 1919

Refugees are rarely in a position to choose their traveling companions, and when Max fled Petrograd, it was in the company of a group of smugglers and black marketeers. There was also a wealthy banker and his wife, and a leading Menshevik opponent of the regime, Eva Broido. She was the only one of them he knew. She had a bad cough—a mark of her years in Siberia—and had brought her twelve-year-old daughter to make the crossing with her.

Heavy fighting had been under way for months between the Bolsheviks and the Polish army, so they were heading for a war zone: Max and his companions hoped to cross the front during the winter lull. From Petrograd a train took them south through the forests to the small railway town of Nevel. There they changed into a cattle car pulled by a smaller locomotive, which stopped now and then for troops to clamber on, men arriving for the coming spring offensive. When the train eventually halted, as it seemed in the middle of nowhere, the black marketeers and the soldiers got out and trudged off and the others were told to wait. They could hear distant gunfire but there were no dwellings to be seen. Snow stretched across the fields to the horizon. I wonder what went through their minds as the train reversed away and it grew dark. Eventually a guide did appear, with a sledge and a horse to load up their belongings, and they trudged through the drifts until they reached their destination, the old town of Polotsk.

The front had come to rest along the frozen Dvina River that bisected the town, and most of the inhabitants on the Russian side had fled. For several weeks, Max and the rest of the little group made themselves as comfortable as they could in the cellar of a burned-out house. They lit a fire and a local man brought them food while they waited for word that they could cross. The Broido girl spent the days reading popular French novels that she found in the house. Many years later, she could not forget the strange contrast between the abandoned streets outside and the book-lined rooms of the empty house in which they were holed up. The adventures of Rocambole that she devoured, classic nineteenth-century yarns, featured a fearless hero always beset by disaster, yet somehow finding a way to embark upon the next set of daring deeds. Her mother told her about her own experiences of reading in prison, of being so gripped by a Dumas novel that she was reluctant to leave it when the day came for her to be released. Her daughter felt the same way when the guns across the river finally fell silent and she was obliged to leave her beloved Rocambole behind unfinished.

Once the crossing was arranged, they were told to leave any letters, printed documents, and photographs, and to carry only small sums of money. Max was traveling light; he had left most of his belongings in Petrograd. At dawn, clutching their bundles, they trudged through the snow down to the first checkpoint by the bank. Max waited in line, but when his turn came the Red Army guards were bored and scarcely looked at his papers. Across the ice, and through the Polish lines, he and the others found lodgings for the night with an elderly Jewish man who led them off up the other bank.

It is hard to estimate now what risks they faced. Certainly large sums of money had changed hands to smooth their passage and Max appears to have been briefly arrested at some point, paying out another 15,000 rubles to be released—a sum that dwarfed the 300 rubles he had spent on his train ticket out of Petrograd. Then there was the pretty Lithuanian nurse who had joined their party in Polotsk and crossed with them, hoping to meet up with her mother on the other side. They were shocked when the Polish officer who was arranging their transport out of the town insisted she stay behind. Her companions protested—it was obvious what he wanted—but the next day, when they left, she was nowhere to be seen. The passage across the border had been dangerous for them all, but women on their own were always the most vulnerable. Max's companionship had probably given Eva Broido and her daughter some protection. But none of them had been able to help the nurse. Broido's daughter, not far off her in age, never forgot the scene.

In Vilna, Max said good-bye to the Broidos and made his way to his brother Zachar's apartment. The streets were patrolled by Polish soldiers and paramilitaries. The city he had grown up in, the city of his Bundist past, his former home, had suffered badly. As German rule disintegrated, there was one short-lived administration after another—seven or eight of them in two years. The Red Army had tried to set up a Soviet republic. Then the Poles pushed the Russian forces out, and in April 1919, as the Poles took over, they targeted the town's Jews and killed dozens of them in the belief they had supported the Reds. One of them had been a close comrade of Max's before the war, a brilliant Yiddish writer and publisher named Vayter who had been with him in Łódź. Max did not linger. Once he had obtained the papers he needed and contacted his employer in London, he traveled on to Warsaw and then took the train across Europe to Paris. By the end of April 1920, after a six-year absence, he was back in his lodgings in North London.

CHAPTER FIVE

Brits and Bolsheviks

"At the request of Mr. Cassatt, I am writing you the following lines regarding the present situation in Russia." Thus, in impeccable English, begins the analysis that Max wrote at his employers' request shortly after his return. Even today it is unnerving to see with what lucidity he understood the complex political dynamics of a country in the throes of civil war. He anticipated that the regime would stay in power despite the ongoing war with the Poles, and he outlined to his employers the mechanisms through which the government was taking over private concerns. The key thing, he advised them, was to work through the Russian trade delegation that was en route to London: "There is no other way to do business with Soviet-Russia."

Max had fled Russia at the end of 1919 because he feared a return visit from the Cheka. The charge of espionage was bandied around by the Soviet authorities, then and later, and generally of course it was unfounded, the product of paranoia not evidence. Nevertheless, the British secret intelligence service, then in its infancy, was active in Russia and was certainly using businessmen to help gather intelligence on the Bolsheviks. The question of whether Max might have been spying for the British is not a stupid one.

Those years were, in a way, the start of the Cold War and there were larger-than-life characters on both sides: Dad had always been fascinated by them. We used to talk about Sidney Reilly, certainly the most colorful of MI6's early agents in Soviet Russia, and one of the bookshelves in Dad's office at the top of our house was dominated by the fast-paced accounts of figures like Paul Dukes, another MI6 man, whose fluent Russian had been learned at the Saint Petersburg Conservatory. I wondered if the thought about Max being a spy had crossed Dad's mind. But because MI6 keeps its archives firmly shut, checking in its files was not straightforward. The best I could do was to explain what I was after to a fellow historian, a colleague who was used to roaming the no-man's-land between academia and the intelligence world, and as she had some sort of security clearance or access, she was kind enough to check. Nothing there, was the answer. So that had to be that.

Yet once one's mind starts running down such channels, it takes on a momentum of its own and I was reluctant to end the sleuthing, not least because espionage seemed to provide such a dramatically satisfying explanation for Max's determined silence. So I turned to the countervailing possibility: Had Max perhaps become a spy for the communists? It seemed unlikely, given the long animosity between them and the Bund. On the other hand, Bundists did move into the Bolshevik camp after 1917, some more willingly than others, and one can retrospectively invent all kinds of reasons why it might have happened to him.

I have already mentioned that through his work in the Bund Max might have easily come to know Feliks Dzerzhinsky and others whom the revolutions of 1917 brought to power in Russia. But there was the London phase of his life too. A few Bolsheviks had also been living there before the First World War and some of them might have known Max from then, especially as they frequented the same neighborhoods around Hampstead Heath. Perhaps the most important of these was Lenin's former arms procurer and smuggler in chief, Maxim Litvinov. After 1917, Litvinov quickly rose to the highest echelons of power, and by the time he was forced from office by Stalin on the eve of the Second World War, he was Europe's longest-serving foreign minister. He intrigued me because his background was so similar to Max's and there were many points when their paths might have intersected.

They had been born only two years apart in nearby towns in the Pale and both had gravitated to the Russian Social Democratic Workers' Party and then been imprisoned. They had escaped—Max from Siberia, Litvinov from the main prison in Kiev—within a few months of each other and both had ended up living in North London before the First World War. Litvinov married an Englishwoman, Ivy Low, and settled down with her and their baby in Golders Green, becoming the informal leader of the small group of Lenin's followers in the capital.

Finding out who exactly had known whom among the Russian exiles in London in those days is not at all easy. Revolutionaries were not good at writing down gossip and tended to subordinate the personal to the political. An evocative memoir of those prewar years by one member of the Russian community, Ivan Maisky, made one thing clear: Ideological differences had not stopped Mensheviks and Bolsheviks and others in the Russian socialist movement from mixing. Maisky himself, who would later become the Soviet ambassador to London, was a Menshevik before 1914, yet he had seen plenty of Litvinov and other followers of Lenin. He is a wonderful guide to some of the extraordinary personalities he encountered—the aging anarchist Prince Kropotkin; a picnic on Parliament Hill with the revolutionary feminist Alexandra Kollontai. But there is nothing in his book about Max.

Britain's domestic security service, MI5, is more accommodating than MI6, so I did manage to see some of their files on Bolsheviks in London. Litvinov's has recently been declassified and fascinating it is, with hilarious accounts of polite interrogations with Colonel Kell at Scotland Yard one minute and dinner parties with Bloomsbury worthies like Bertrand Russell the next. But there is no mention of Max. Nor does he appear in the equally voluminous mass of papers the snoops collected on a fellow comrade of Litvinov's, Fyodor Rothstein, a "red-hot socialist" (according to the file) who had been born in the Pale just two years before Max. Rothstein had lived in Highgate, across from Waterlow Park, and most of the Russian socialists visiting London seemed to have passed through his house at one time or another. By the war he was firmly in Lenin's camp and later became the Soviet ambassador to Persia. But he had moved in Bund circles in the East End earlier, and he had a brother named Samuel, and there was a Samuel Rothstein who was an early business partner of Max's in these years. Still, this was very little to go on.

There was only one other person besides Maisky who I knew had written about the social circles of London's Bolsheviks, and that was Litvinov's wife, Ivy; somewhere there was an unfinished autobiography that talked about their early years together. Her papers are scattered across several continents, but a number of boxes are held at St. Antony's College, Oxford, and I made an appointment to visit the archive. It was a place I knew well. Years earlier I had done my doctorate there and my supervisor, a wise, deeply humane anthropologist named John Campbell, had died only weeks before Dad. His grave under the trees at Great Tew in the Cotswolds was a spot I visited regularly. I felt abiding affection for his memory and this extended to the college too. I wondered what I might find there. I had always been dimly aware of its purportedly close connections to British intelligence during the Cold War—devotees of John le Carré will remember the odd obscure reference to St. Antony's in his books—but it had never occurred to me that I would be looking in that direction for the sake of my own family's history.

An old Victorian convent had formed the original college building, and part of it has now been converted into a comfortable reading room for students of the vanished Soviet empire. On the table the college archivist had placed a single enormous cardboard box: inside was a mass of amateurishly typed drafts and counter-drafts in no particular order. Ivy Low had moved on the margins of London literary life before she met Litvinov, and she had evidently been a prolific writer. I had to wade through reams of irrelevant material before I came closer to what I was looking for. It was just a couple of pages, an incomplete draft in which she tried to reconstruct what had happened when news of the revolution in Russia had first reached her and Litvinov in North London in the spring of 1917. She had just given birth to their first child. It had been a momentous time:

> The nurse who brought me the baby to feed in the morning said there was nothing special in the paper. "Just another Zeppelin raid over the West End." As Golder's Green was in the west end (or at least the northwest end) this was of course nothing special. Maxim called me to the telephone. "Haven't you heard? The revolution has broken out in Russia." I was quick to see where it affected us. "Darling, we're not refugees

any more!" I spent the rest of the morning talking to Aunt
Edith and Catherine over the telephone.[…]

Maxim came round to the nursing home later that same
day more excited than I had ever seen him, continually mop-
ping at his forehead, though it was March. He and Mitrov had
been to the House to call out Ramsay MacDonald…and ask
him what he was going to do about the Revolution? It seemed
Ramsay MacDonald was not quite sure at the moment,
he hadn't had time to think it over yet. Next they called at
Chesham House (the old Russian embassy) and asked them
why they hadn't taken down the portraits of the Royal Family
in the hall. They weren't sure at the Embassy, either, though
Maxim noted the glances of interest and he thought sympathy from certain youthful members of the embassy staff.

The London Russians immediately applied to the British
Govt for a convoy to Stockholm, on their way to Moscow.
But the Govt hedged, first sending over two old stagers, Ple-
khanov and ~~Chaikovsky~~ (*Kropotkin*) (Were they SRs?) who
had been lying very low in London throughout the war so
that hardly anybody realised they were there. (Perhaps this
isn't true?) The Govt knew they could depend on these
old stagers to support continuation of the war at all costs.
Whereas the SD group contained subversive foundation
members of the Bolshevik faction (?) like Litvinoff (who else?
Mitrov was a Menshevik. Rothstein? Maisky? It would be nice
to have a few names here.)[1]

As the question marks and strike-throughs suggest, when Ivy
started writing this, in the years after her husband's death, she
was elderly and there was a lot she was not sure about or could
not remember. Even so, one name leapt out at me because I had

come across it already in some of our family letters—Mitrov, the man who had gone with Litvinov to the House of Commons in March 1917. He was a former Duma deputy, a Menshevik, who had ended up in Hampstead and was making a living as an expert on the Baku petroleum industry in Azerbaijan. He also happened to be a friend or acquaintance of Max. Into the 1930s, after Mitrov had returned to live in the USSR, Max and Frouma followed his news and tried to help out when his son came to England to study. To date he remains the only link I have been able to trace between Max and Litvinov, the man whom I have come to see as leading a kind of parallel life to Max, who had (unlike Max) opted early on for Bolshevism and for the return to Russia and who was, as the Soviet foreign minister, to become one of the most prominent and influential figures in the Soviet Union. Still, it is precious little to go on, not least because Mitrov was not even a Bolshevik, and so one has to say that the evidence for Max associating with the Bolsheviks in London before the First World War is limited, and as for spying for them, nonexistent. He really does seem to have spent most of the time after 1909 selling typewriters in Russia. There is a fading photo of him standing outside a Kirghiz yurt in 1914; there is a set of hand-tinted postcards of Japanese geishas, which he always kept and which he may have bought during a holiday there during his travels. If this was all cover for the work of a secret agent, it was extremely effective and he hid his tracks well.[2]

Max's later connection to the Russian cooperative movement, on the other hand, is demonstrable. In 1919 his joining it had been merely precautionary. But in the early 1920s, before formal diplomatic relations were established between Britain and

Soviet Russia, the cooperative movement became, as he had predicted to his bosses at Yost, the main mechanism for political interaction between the two countries, and it became especially important in Anglo-Russian relations with the establishment in London of Arcos, the Soviet cooperative trading arm. Arcos was always suspected by British intelligence of being a nest of spies, and the police mounted a ham-fisted raid on its premises in 1927, which ruptured relations between the two countries for a time, although little enough was found to warrant the intervention.

Max did have contacts in Arcos because several former Bundists were high-ranking officials there. There was even a young Grodno relative of his on the staff, Isaak Jezierski, who had been stranded in London by the Russo-Polish War. In the summer of 1920, the penniless Jezierski bumped into Max on Oxford Street: to the younger man's surprise, the uncle he remembered as a hard-up revolutionary appeared to have become a wealthy man. Happy to repay the debts and kindness Jezierski's father had shown him in the past, Max supported Isaak financially until he landed the Arcos job. Did Max benefit from his work in Arcos? Since Jezierski was a young accountant, and not a communist, the truth was probably much more banal. That Anglo-Soviet trade in the early 1920s ran through Arcos certainly did not mean that all the people or firms associated with it were engaged in intelligence work. The Arcos officials who had been in the Bund, and may well have known Max, were not necessarily spies, and any London-based businessman trading in Russia, as Max was, would naturally have gone through them.

What I have come to believe is that after the revolution, Max almost certainly sought, so far as possible, to draw a sharp line between his business activities and any other kind of contact with the Soviet authorities for the simple reason that he still had family and friends back in the USSR who had not, and never would, join the party. And because it was hard to tell who was really doing what among the pro-Bolsheviks in London, he would have been inclined to keep his own counsel and stay away from people he did not know or trust. Another longtime Hampstead Russian, Nicolai Klishko, was a Vilna-born civil engineer who had worked for Vickers before the war. He and Max would appear to have had many things in common, not least the fact that at one point Klishko was living only a few doors down the road from him in South End Green. Yet after the war Klishko was a member of the Cheka, an organizer of Soviet espionage in Britain, and the conduit for Soviet funds to the new Communist Party of Great Britain—in the early 1920s he was in the thick of things. When I went to the National Archives to see whether the MI5 file on Klishko indicated any contact with Max, I again drew a blank. There was plenty on Klishko dating back to before the war. MI5 had been reading his correspondence, and his wife's, but combing through half a dozen thick card folders with their record of intercepted letters, conversations, and surveillance over many years, I found no mention of Max at all, nor of anyone he might have known. All this suggested that Max's instinctive suspicion in such matters had been reinforced by the events of 1917 and that whatever circles he had moved in before the war, once he was back in London he kept his distance from anyone too closely associated with the Bolsheviks. He had known them too well, and for too long.

CHAPTER SIX

Wood End

Time lets out its line and then reels it in again. In the early 1970s, some old family friends lived in the village of Wood End in Hertfordshire, an hour's drive from London, and we would go out for a day in the country. Occasionally Dad would disappear next door to see their neighbors; the husband was a historian with an eye for offbeat, intriguing themes — one of his books was about millenarian cults, a later one was on ancient myths of cosmic order — and the son, still in his twenties, was already a fearsome rock journalist who had written a study of pop called *Awopbopaloobop Alopbamboom*. What I didn't realize until many years later was that the historian's wife, Vera, had been the novel-devouring girl who along with her mother had accompanied Max when they fled Russia.

Nor did I then have any idea of just what a remarkable few years had followed in Vera Broido's life. After studying art in Paris and Berlin, she found herself at the heart of Weimar's fashionable avant-garde as the muse of the dadaist Raoul Hausmann, who paraded her around Charlottenberg to the growing irritation of his friends. He photographed her obsessively in the years that she lived in a ménage à trois with him and his wife. Eventually tiring of being a modernist pinup, Vera moved to England in the early 1930s. Her brother and father also ended up there; her mother, the perennial activist, returned to the USSR to revive the Menshevik cause but never reemerged and was shot in 1941, the same year that Vera married her historian, Norman Cohn. In the years before her marriage, Vera and her brother had been living in London, and their shared revolutionary past had kept the Broidos and the Mazowers in each other's lives. It turned out Dad had known her since his childhood. But it was not until she was in her nineties that I finally got to meet her.

It was all thanks to a long-lost cousin of Dad's who had resurfaced quite unexpectedly after the collapse of communism. This was Iosif, whom the family called Osya, and he was the son of Max's youngest brother, Semyon. He had lived his entire life in Leningrad. (St. Petersburg was renamed yet again, this time as Leningrad in 1924 after Lenin's death. It did not become St. Petersburg again until 1991.) When he came to see us in England, he was nearly eighty and it was the first time he had

ever left Russia. Dad thought he'd like to hear Vera's memories of the old days—she was older than either of them and had
many memories from before the revolution—and she invited
them to Wood End. I was their driver.

There was an uncanny physical resemblance between Dad
and Osya, and there were other family similarities too. As we
motored north along the A1 out of Edgware, leaving behind
the unglamorous suburbs, the golf courses, and the roadside
pubs, I noticed that what they both exclaimed at were not the
vistas provided by the gentle arable countryside that began to
stretch away either side of the motorway but the aging concrete bridges that spanned it every few miles. Dad's engineering training had been short-lived, but Osya knew how to design
gun towers for warships and later on turned to harbor cranes
as well. He had come to London proudly bearing a catalogue
with pictures of the cranes he had designed, giant construc-
tions looming over tankers in Soviet docks as if to remind us
that despite the USSR's ignominious collapse, his country had
once stood for the future. There was something revelatory
in his pride. It was easy to forget what the Russian revolution had really meant for people who would never, under the
tsars, have been allowed an education at all. Semyon had been
poor, ill, and Jewish, and in the old days, the obstacles to his
son becoming an engineer would have been immense. Before
the United States, it was the Soviet Union that had epitomized
upward social mobility: It was thanks to the industrialization
drive under Stalin that Osya's family had enjoyed the kind of
life—with a car and a small cottage in the country—that had
previously been unimaginable.

Yet their suffering had been immense too. The Leningrad
Metal Works where Osya had started out was an icon of social-

ism. Not many factories in Stalin's Russia had enjoyed the prestige of this mammoth plant, which had been responsible for
much of the country's electrification as well as for equipping
many of its tanks, submarines, and warships. Osya had been a
foreman on the factory floor when the siege of Leningrad by
the Germans began in 1941. He had lost thirty kilos in weight
and come down with tuberculosis. It was impossible to imagine
what it had been like to live through the ceaseless bombard-
ment, the freezing cold, the hunger, the corpses in the streets,
the day in the summer of 1942 when loudspeakers on street
corners had drowned out the Wehrmacht guns by broadcast-
ing the new symphony Dmitri Shostakovich had composed in
the city's honor. Osya and his family had borne their share of
the tragedy. In the first winter of the siege his younger brother,
Ilya, died trying to cross icebound Lake Ladoga on what they
called the Road of Death. He had left with a group of workers from his factory who were being sent to Sverdlovsk, but his
body had been so weakened from starvation that he had not
even made it to the lake and had expired, a twenty-five-year-old
man, at the Borisova Griva station, where his comrades had left
behind his frozen corpse, his backpack, and his suitcase. A little
later he was followed by his father, Semyon, who had been in
poor health for years. Osya had been successfully evacuated to
Perm with the factory, and when he returned to the city, only
his mother remained.

In 1949, a letter had come from Highgate. Frouma had
wanted to let them know the family news. With Stalin's paranoia at its height, the kind of correspondence that had been
intermittently possible before the war could now cause you
to lose your job, or worse, and the letter got Osya dismissed
from the factory. Luckily his work and wartime record spoke

in his favor, and he quickly found new employment in the nearby Kirov plant. He was still there, well past the age most people in Western Europe would have retired, when Mikhail Gorbachev came into power. By then his mother was long dead and so were Dad's parents. But Osya had not forgotten his uncle's family in London, and somewhere in his Leningrad flat he must have kept the letter that had caused him so much trouble because he used it to get in touch with us. In May 1991, Major Colin Fairclough of the Salvation Army's Family Tracing Service wrote to my brother David in London. He had found our name, he said, in the London phone book. Were we by any chance relatives of a commercial traveler called Max Mazower who had lived at 20 Oakeshott Avenue, London N6, in 1949? In this fashion, the cousins were reunited.

In the car Dad and Osya chatted in the fluent Russian my father remembered from childhood. It was one of those warm early-summer mornings that show England at its best. The fields were implausibly green. We parked in the shade outside the old cottage at Wood End where Vera lived and went into the darkened living room for tea. I remember the wooden floors, the feel of a dacha in the Hertfordshire countryside. She was happy to tell us her stories of revolution and soldiers and smugglers, but they seemed far away, the snowbound past irretrievably gone.

CHAPTER SEVEN

The Afterlife

When Max arrived in Vilna at the start of 1920, the city's fate was being debated at the League of Nations and would not be settled for another two years. It was one of the first subjects to be discussed in this new forum for international government, and in the face of Lithuanian and Russian claims, and amid an ongoing war, the Poles were keen to assert their authority in any way they could. Borders were being drawn and redrawn, and passports were a newly desirable commodity. As Max had been born in Grodno, which was now inside the new independent Poland, he was entitled to Polish papers, and it was with these that he made numerous business trips across Eastern Europe over the coming decade; he did not become a British subject until 1935. He was a man of loyalty—to his family, to his political beliefs, and to a certain vision of Russia too. But there is no indication that this loyalty extended to the country that was now claiming the territories where he had grown up. He could speak the language, but to be Polish was, for him, basically a flag of convenience.

Yet Max possessed the ability, uncommon in those with strong ideals, to assess the political outlook unsentimentally. Despite having inclined in the old days towards Russia rather than Poland, he could see that the Tsarist empire was finished. After staying with his brother, he stopped off at Grodno and obtained official written confirmation that he had been born there, a wise and necessary precaution in an era in which statelessness meant vulnerability. No close family was left. His parents were both dead, and the half brothers and half sisters from his father's first marriage—not that he had ever been close to them—had mostly emigrated before the war. There were distant cousins around the world: In Cook County, Illinois, a certain Abe Masover was by this time a prominent local attorney; there was a rabbi in Palestine; a couple of seamstress sisters in Buenos Aires. Apart from his young cousin in London, none of them meant anything to him.

His beloved Bund—the larger family that had in a way supplanted his own—was a shadow of what it had once been. The new borders of Eastern Europe now sliced through its old heartlands: Vilna and Grodno lay on the Polish side of the frontier, cut off from Minsk, Petrograd, and Moscow. As the movement fractured, old ideological rivals like Zionism became more popular. In Poland the Bund did reemerge between the two world wars and became a force of some consequence there, but it was now the voice of an ethnic minority in an anticommunist nation-state and its ambitions were chiefly confined to the Jews of that country.

Within the USSR Bund members faced the dilemma of denouncing Bolshevism or joining it. By 1925 slightly more than two thousand of them had moved into the party; that left the majority outside it. Lip service was paid to the Bund's revolutionary past by the country's rulers, and it was never an unsurmountable barrier to advancing within the *nomenklatura*: Two of the three key figures inside Stalin's office serving the general secretary of the party had previously been in the Bund.[1] Even so, to have remained a Bundist after the split in the Russian

Social Democratic Workers' Party in 1903 could raise eyebrows, and to have delayed joining the Bolshevik party after 1921 carried the suggestion of unsoundness. Because Semyon—Max's youngest brother—never joined, for example, he was repeatedly turned down by the party for a pension despite everything he had done and endured for the revolutionary movement under the tsars.

Distinctions that have some meaning at one time can lose it later. Once the Terror came, the charge of "idealization of the Bund" led straight to the Gulag, and by the mid-1930s it made little difference whether you had thrown your lot in with Lenin or not. The fate of many of Max's comrades was grim. Zhenia Gourvitch, one of the co-participants at the 1903 Geneva meeting, was exiled to Siberia and never returned. Another, Mark Liber, was arrested and died, probably shot, in 1937. The veteran Bundist Anna Rozental settled in Polish Vilna in the early 1920s, but when the Red Army occupied the city in 1939, she was arrested by the NKVD and deported to the USSR, where she died in a Soviet prison. The revolutionary Yiddishist Esther Frumkin, who did join the party in 1921, was shot in 1943. Moses Rafes, whom Max had known in Vilna for years, was a Bundist representative to the Petrograd Soviet of Workers' and Soldiers' Deputies in 1917 before switching over to the communists. In 1923 Rafes published a rich history of the Bund that portrayed Bolshevism as the "Bund's heir," a view that was quite common then. Six years later, he changed his tune, publishing a new version that cast Bundism as an ideological deviation, but it was not enough to save him and in 1938 he too was arrested and died in northern Russia.

The final break between the Bund and the Bolsheviks came during the Second World War. In early 1943, a young Bundist

called Lucjan Blit arrived in London with disturbing news that
he soon communicated to Max and others. Passing through
the central Russian town of Kuibyshev on his circuitous way
out of Europe, he had shared a hotel room with two leaders of
the Polish Bund, Henryk Erlich and Viktor Alter. Max would
have known them both, distinguished figures who had turned
the movement into a powerful force in Poland between the
wars. Fleeing the Germans in 1939, they had been arrested and
interrogated over many months by the NKVD. Erlich, the older
man, had been harshly treated, but he had also found the Soviet
secret police oddly interested in his views. At their prompting,
he spent weeks in captivity composing a history of the Bund,
and another of the Polish labor movement — extraordinary documents that survive to this day in the Russian archives.

Erlich had been held for more than a year when he was called
in for conversations with senior NKVD officials, including their
chief, Beria. They were curious about how he saw the course
of the war. It was the spring of 1941, some months before Hitler launched his surprise attack on the Soviet Union, but Erlich
did not hide his opposition to the Molotov–Ribbentrop Pact,
nor his view that an alliance between the USSR and the Anglo-
Americans was mankind's only hope. The secret police seemed
interested in his assessment of public opinion in the West and
how it might respond to such a development. Their interest
was not just academic, because in the aftermath of the invasion
that summer, Erlich and Alter were suddenly released, and told
their imprisonment had been a mistake. Stalin — a long-standing
enemy of the Bund — was now seriously thinking of using them
to head an international Jewish mission to build support for the
USSR abroad: he believed the Bund still commanded respect in
the American labor unions in particular. The last chapter of the

Bund's long, tormented history with Bolshevism thus looked as if it might be written as a story of wartime cooperation. Instead, the tyrant changed his mind: The two men were suddenly summoned by the NKVD — Blit had been dining with them on the day the call had come — and then simply disappeared. Not until 1943 did the truth emerge: Erlich had hanged himself in his cell, and Alter had been shot. The Kremlin's absurd justification was that they had been trying to undermine the war effort. Cynically releasing the news as the world was celebrating the Soviet triumph at Stalingrad, Stalin ensured that there was little outcry: Few in London or New York wanted to focus on this awful story. But for the surviving Bundists such as Max, the tragic end of their comrades was the final proof, if they needed any, of the chasm that divided them from communism.[2]

Max never returned to Russia after a last business trip in 1923. But he remained faithful to his past, and the house at 20 Oakeshott Avenue became known as a place where an old party comrade could count on a welcome. Max himself left no record of any later political activities, but one or two sources indicate that he supported the London Bundists and a group they set up, the Jewish Socialist Organisation, which funneled money to comrades in Poland and helped in the East End when Oswald Mosley's Blackshirts made it seem as though anti-Semitism and fascism were gaining a foothold.[3] On the fortieth anniversary of the Bund's founding there was a large celebration in London, which several leading Polish Bund members attended. The Mazowers had a reputation for being a "good Bundist family, always willing to lend a hand," and Max's obituary talked about "his warm, cultured home...a meeting place for colleagues and

Bundist workers." It was as though the domestic space he had never really known as a child emerged late in his life to help shelter the remnants of a movement that had found history against it. A culture of caring for history's losers seems more attractive to my mind than an easy identification with its winners—not least because in the end no one really wins. Few people had better reason to understand that the cult of success is only another form of escapism than the Bundists of Max's generation.

Their ethos of solidarity lingered on to the end of the century. In 1997, celebrations marked the Bund's centenary, and there was a lively daylong meeting that took place in a modest college hall on Holloway Road in North London. The old-timers were now the surviving representatives of the Bund from its interwar Polish incarnation rather than the original Tsarist organization that Max had joined, but of course deep allegiances and commonalities of outlook joined the generations.

I spoke to several of them who had been involved in the Bund's work immediately after the war. Meir Bogdanski was there — a Polish Bundist who had arrived in London in 1946. He remembered Max — the brown suit, the ballpoint pen in the pocket of his white shirt, his sharp brown eyes. Perec Zylberberg, a younger man who had passed through Oakeshott Avenue on his way to Canada, recalled "a warm, socialist home" and Frouma's conversation, which was such a contrast with Max. "[He] talked much less than your mother," he told Dad. "In fact he just used to sit there quietly listening...just a man listening. If he talked, it was a word or two." How did he talk? "Not loud, not at all bombastic or rhetorical. When he spoke it was matter-of-fact. If he said something, you knew he had thought about it." Zylberberg confessed that he had been puzzled by this paucity of words, which seemed to him to indicate some inexplicable abdication of will, and yet, he said, "I looked up to him."

CHAPTER EIGHT

Zachar

Max always kept this last letter from his brother Zachar. It had been sent from Vilna on May 20, 1940:

> Dear Frouma and Max! If your stingy writing habits were unable to kill my familial attachment in peacetime, the chance for it is even smaller now in wartime. I hope you received my letter: I still have not heard from you. Inform me immediately: How did you survive the winter? We had an incredibly harsh one. How are you feeling now? How is your health? Do you live in London now or someplace farther away? How do your children react to events? To sum it all up: write about everything and immediately. Everything here is the same as usual: to be more precise, the situation keeps deteriorating…I had news about Semyon a couple of months ago—that he had been bedridden for a couple of months, but then, it seems, recovered. Stay healthy and unharmed and write to me without fail.

He had signed off "Z. Mazoveras" in the Lithuanian style, because the Lithuanians had taken over Vilna the previous October in a deal with the Russians: They were converting the city as fast as they could into a new national capital, targeting both the Poles, who had run it for the past two decades, and the local Jewish inhabitants as well. It was a completely futile effort because less than a month after Zachar's letter was sent, the Red Army marched in, the city became the capital of a brand-new Soviet republic, and tens of thousands of its inhabitants were arrested by the NKVD. One year later, the Germans launched their invasion of the Soviet Union, and for Zachar and his family the time of writing letters was over.

Max in London; Zachar in Vilna; Semyon in St. Petersburg: Three brothers and three choices, or better—since choice does not feel quite right—three wagers on fate is how it might seem. In hindsight, time becomes a series of might-have-beens, history a slalom course, a battle of wits with whatever lies round the next corner. When Max passed through Vilna in early 1920, on his way out of Russia, Zachar's address was 5 Portowa Street, a large building on a wide street where he and his family rented an upper-floor apartment, number 18. Apart from an old people's home in a fin de siècle block nearby, there were few other traces of communal Jewish life, for this was not at the heart of the old Jewish quarter. We know his address from the application Zachar made for a Lithuanian passport and from Max's simultaneous application for Polish papers. We know too that Zachar had by then become a dentist. He had a ten-year-old daughter, Rebecca, and he was married to a woman called Perel, or Pearl. And that is about it.

Some while ago, when I was trying to find out more about Vilna, and about Portowa Street in particular, I came across the memoirs of Litman Mor: I had never heard of him but he turned out to have been in the Zionist youth movement in interwar Belorussia and had ended up as a civil servant in Israel. The crucial point was that for the first year or two of the Second

World War, Mor had stayed in the same apartment block as Zachar. In October 1939 Mor had come to Vilna to escape the Russian troops flooding into eastern Poland. The parents of one of his friends owned the building at 5 Portowa Street.

Thanks to Mor's memoir, we know that one night shortly after the arrival of the Wehrmacht in the summer of 1941, Lithuanian police acting on German orders searched the building from top to bottom and took away all the Jewish men they found. Mor and his friend were hiding in what the police thought was an unoccupied flat, and they heard screams as the men were forced to leave, and the cries and yells of the women and children left behind. When the raid was over, they stayed on for a time in one of the apartments. But when the ghetto was established that September, the remaining Jewish residents of Portowa Street had to leave the building and find lodgings within the ghetto, and Mor and his friend collected their belongings and entered it voluntarily. Soon the rumors reached them that people were being taken to the nearby Ponary forest, a prewar picnic spot a few miles out of town, to be shot. "All roads lead to Ponar now / There are no roads back," run the words of a lullaby written by an eleven-year-old boy in the ghetto.

Growing up in North London in the 1960s and '70s, I think we always felt fortunate that our sense of our family background was not defined by the Holocaust, not bound up with the kind of obsessed fascination with the death camps that was fast becoming part of public culture on both sides of the Atlantic. In thinking about ourselves this way we did not ignore Zachar's story; it simply did not impinge on us. Actually we did not even know who this long-forgotten uncle of Dad's was.

When I started to search among the databases, quite numerous it turned out, of Holocaust victims, I came across some information in a list in the Yad Vashem Archives. It contained a surprising number of Mazowers or Mazovers, although almost none of them, so far as I could tell, counted as close relatives. There was one reference, however, to a Zachar Mazover. It came in the file of Riva Zilberbach, who was listed as having died with her baby, a girl called Tonia, in 1942 in Vilna. No mention was made of the fate of her husband or her father. But the Mazower connection is specified as Riva's maiden name was Mazover and her father's first name was given as Zachar, and her birth date is given as 1912, close enough to the information on an earlier Lithuanian file for Zachar's daughter's birth date as 1910: Riva is an obvious abbreviation for Rebecca. An adjacent file referred to someone who was probably her mother, Pola, listed similarly as having died in the ghetto in 1942. Was she Zachar's wife, the same woman named on an earlier document as Perel? As very few Mazowers lived in Vilna between the two world wars—to judge at least from the telephone directories of the era—almost certainly what I had found was a reference to Zachar and his family, his grown daughter, about thirty and newly a mother.

Unexpected confirmation that I was on the right track came a little later. In Paris my French cousin Patrick handed me two plastic shopping bags. The envelopes inside contained a trove of family correspondence—dozens of letters in Russian, mostly from Frouma over a span of twenty years to her brother and sister in Paris. In one of them, dated late July 1945, Frouma reported that they had just been visited by a young Polish Jewish refugee couple from Vilna: Markus Klok, who was a Bundist, and his wife, Syma. The Kloks had managed to flee the city at the start of the occupation, thanks to the papers issued by a very remarkable man, the Japanese vice-consul in Lithuania, Chiune Sugihara. The so-called Sugihara visas, mostly given out in defiance of the orders of Sugihara's superiors, entitled the bearer to cross the Soviet Union, and enabled thousands of Jews to escape the Nazis, among them the Kloks. They had made the epic journey along the Trans-Siberian Railroad to Japan and Shanghai, before managing to find a ship to Cape Town and finally reaching Britain at the end of 1942. England became their base for the rest of the war and they often stayed in Oakeshott Avenue; in official documents, they would give the Mazowers' address as their residence in England. They were friends.

The Kloks would have been able to tell Max much about the city he knew so well and about what had happened there in the years leading up to the war. In the summer of 1945, they also learned what had happened after the Germans had taken over because Markus met some survivors from the Vilna ghetto while he was working in a former concentration camp in Germany. They broke the news to him that his family had been killed, and so had his wife's. And there was more—they reported that Max's brother had been in the ghetto as well. Shortly after, Markus returned to London and told the Mazowers. "It means that [Zachar] died," Frouma wrote, "because the Germans only transported out 1,700 men and 1,700 women, aged 18 to 30, and the others were wiped out...I cried so much for two days as I haven't in a while."

A photograph taken by Syma on the day they shared the news, or very shortly after, shows Max, Frouma, and Dad on the doorstep of 20 Oakeshott Avenue. The hydrangeas are in bloom in the front garden, contrasting sharply with the darkness of the hall behind them. Dad is as smartly dressed as his father, and both of them have a quiet, courteous smile for the camera. Frouma does not: She looks pensive and her arms are emphatically folded. Standing between them, she seems to me an embodiment of strength, the protective deity of the household. On either side, her two men, the aging Russian past and her English future. I came across the picture more or less by accident, while I was searching through a collection of Syma's papers online; her married name had changed by the time her papers had been catalogued, she had died, and the picture was filed under a misleading heading. Yet there it was, rising unexpectedly out of the sea of the Internet. I stared at it a long time. It seemed then, and still seems to me, to contain within it some essential aspect of the household in Highgate, a kind of marker of where the three of them stood in the world, a family and a home, a hard-won achievement.

It is almost certain therefore that Zachar's family was among the tens of thousands of the Jews of Vilna who either died in the ghetto or were shot by executioners in the sandpits amid the pine trees at Ponary. Any who did not die there met their end in Sobibor, where the elderly survivors of the ghetto were sent—Zachar would have been sixty-five in 1942. The only other possibility, but it is remote in the light of Frouma's letter, is that the Yad Vashem files referred to someone else entirely with the same name, and that Zachar and his family were not in Vilna at all when the Germans entered. At various times, Dad seems to have thought they had ended up in the port town of Sopot or in Riga; neither offered better prospects for Jews than Vilna. What is certain is that after the war Zachar and his family were never heard from again.

The thing that really surprised me in the whole story was Dad's lack of clarity about something as fundamental as where his uncle had been living when the war came. Evidently the subject of Max's brother had been mentioned so seldom in Oakeshott Avenue that even though Dad had almost certainly been at home on the day the news from Vilna came in, he most uncharacteristically did not remember the details. Perhaps one's capacity to forget painful news can be trained, a kind of defense. Or it may have been a choice on his part, an opting for the future over the past—the future of his homeland over the dismal news from a country he had never seen. The Kloks' visit had coincided with the Labour Party's historic victory in the first general election after the war. Dad, who had just joined the party, had been working hard locally. He and a group of friends had been on the streets getting out the vote, and he had been jubilant when the results came in. It was a moment in which to look forward, and while the figure of Zachar floated inchoately in his memory, the summer of 1945 always meant for him that great feeling of excitement and hope.

The original silence must have been Max's, I suppose, and if so, it was certainly not an expression of indifference. Max's brothers were both younger than him and he had looked after them after their father died. They had shared an allegiance to revolutionary Jewish socialism and the experience of being targeted early in the century by the Tsarist authorities. Zachar had joined the Bund after Max but he had suffered no less, enduring years in exile before returning to Vilna in 1913—one Okhrana letter mentioned him as the Bund's "librarian" there—and settling down with his wife and baby girl. Once in London Max had continued to care about them. With Semyon in Petrograd, contact had been difficult. But Max was in touch with Zachar for some years more, sending money and possibly seeing him on trips abroad; he only stopped visiting Poland in 1931. Around 1926, to help his brother out, Max had set up a trading company exporting goods from England to Poland so that Zachar could market the goods and share in the profits. When that did not pan out, Max did something more. He sold his house and moved to a smaller one round the corner, at 20 Oakeshott Avenue, where the family would live until his death, thus freeing up money to send to Zachar. In this sense, the very presence of the Mazowers on Oakeshott Avenue testified to the closeness of the bond between the two brothers.

Although Max had not been to Poland for nearly a decade when it was invaded in 1939, he was following the news coming out of there closely. Yet when the fighting and the killing ended and there was no more to be done, he put that last letter away in a drawer, kept the tiny photos it had contained of Zachar and his wife, and retreated into silence. This may have been out of a sense that talk could do no good; it may even have been, in some less articulated way, a kind of gift to those around him, a desire to allow them the space, Dad in particular, to form their own relationship to past and future rather than to impose some kind of duty of grief upon them. After Max died in 1952, Zachar's memory faded with him. And this silence was emulated by Dad, who never met his father's brothers, and as a result, to him they were little more than names.

CHAPTER NINE

The Expanding Silence

During the Second World War there were not many people in London better placed than Max to have made a knowledgeable assessment of the prospects facing the Jews in Nazi-dominated Eastern Europe. In the postal censorship service, where he worked during the war, he was valued for his expertise in German, Polish, French, and Russian, not to mention his precision and discretion. But he possessed a far more important source of information than that. Beginning in 1941, Leon Feiner, a leading Polish Bundist, was sending top-secret reports on the Nazi treatment of the Jews from German-occupied Warsaw to the Bundist representatives with the Polish government in exile in London. Feiner's conduit was the astonishingly courageous Polish officer Jan Karski; Feiner had actually helped Karski to enter the ghetto through the Warsaw sewers to see conditions there for himself. Their reports provided the earliest precise intelligence to reach the Allies on the extent of the killing.

Max would have known about much of what those reports contained because he was on intimate terms with the leading Bundists in wartime London, notably with the man to whom Feiner was sending his materials—the party's main representative in London, Shmuel Zygielboym. Zygielboym was one of the many Bundists whose stay in the gray, unfamiliar British capital was cushioned by Max and Frouma's hospitality in

Oakeshott Avenue. He had been born in Vilna at about the time that Max was beginning his socialist work there and had served on the Bund central committee since 1924. In December 1939 he had been smuggled out of the country, leaving behind most of his family, and after a long and roundabout journey he had reached London in March 1942 where he joined the Polish government-in-exile as one of its two Jewish members. Two months later, he received a report from Feiner that detailed the extermination site at Chelmno and the use of gas there, and estimated that 700,000 Polish Jews had already been murdered. Zygielboym managed to get articles based on this published in British newspapers and to speak about it on the BBC. The details were strikingly accurate and appeared just as the German leadership was finalizing its plans for the complete extermination of Poland's Jewish population.

GERMANS MURDER 700,000 JEWS IN POLAND

TRAVELLING GAS CHAMBERS

DAILY TELEGRAPH REPORTER

More than 700,000 Polish Jews have been slaughtered by the Germans in the greatest massacre in the world's history. In addition, a system of starvation is being carried out in which the number of deaths, on the admission of the Germans themselves, bids fair to be almost as large.

The most gruesome details of mass killing, even to the use of poison gas, are revealed in a report sent secretly to Mr. S. Zygielboim, Jewish representative on the Polish National Council in London, by an active group in Poland. It is strongly felt that action should be taken to prevent Hitler from carrying out his threat that five minutes before the war ends, however it may end, he will exterminate all Jews in Europe.

It was the avowed intention of the Germans from the early days of the war to exterminate the ... population on Polish

... trace of them has been lost. About 2,000 more were put into barracks in a Lublin suburb. Now there is not a single Jew there.

In Cracow during March 50 men on a proscribed list were shot outside their homes. A similar number of men and women were killed outside ...

Zygielboym's wife and two sons were among those trapped inside the Warsaw ghetto, and he was in a terrible predicament and consumed with guilt for having abandoned them. Feiner's instructions were that he should use the information to get the Allies to do something to stop the killing, but the failure of the Bermuda Conference, which was called to address the issue of Jewish refugees in April 1943, depressed him deeply. It was clear that there was no political will on the Allied side to act with the speed and on the scale required. On May 11, in his West London apartment, Zygielboym took his own life. He had hoped news of his death would shame the Allies into action, but it did not.

There were dozens of mourners at the Golders Green crematorium later that month, among them, it seems probable, Max and perhaps Frouma, in a gloomy hall filled with the dark overcoats and sad faces of the survivors paying tribute to their comrade. Eleven years later, in 1954, two years after Max died, there was another memorial service and this time it was Dad who attended. He listened as the speaker, another veteran, mentioned Max and the support he had given the Bundist leadership in those wartime years. Max's obituary in the New York Bundist press had said the same thing: "His welcoming home became a meeting place for colleagues and Bundist workers who performed important tasks to aid the Jews in Poland." It was not only Zygielboym: Leon Oler, the man to whom Zygielboym addressed his farewell letter before his suicide; Emanuel Scherer, who took over from him after his death as the Bund delegate to the Polish government-in-exile in London—these and other leading Bundists, strangers in London, wanderers, all passed through the front door of Oakeshott Avenue and sought some respite there as they grappled with the negation of all that the Bund had ever stood for.

So it would not be odd if after the war Max, who had never been one to waste words, felt nothing remained to be said or done on the larger issues for which he had once risked his life. A significant portion of Soviet Jewry survived the war but remained in the hands of men whose views and temperaments he had known at first hand for more than half a century. In Poland, only ruins were left. The forests he had once traversed on clandestine Bund business had seen atrocities on a scale no one in those days had imagined possible. In his birthplace, Grodno, the Gestapo chief had made the head of the Jewish council don a top hat and tails and then paraded him through the streets seated upon a barrel of excrement. He had made town elders clear away the snow with teaspoons. He had hanged children. Vilna, Łódź, Warsaw—the once flourishing cities where Max had lived and played a role of some import—were vestiges, unrecognizable. As for the triumph of Zionism in the Middle East and the creation of an independent Jewish state, this represented the antithesis of everything Max had believed in, and there is no evidence that I have come across that Israel's founding moved him in any way. Silence and loyalty were all that remained. In 1947 he had a bout of jaundice and in the photos taken then he looks suddenly aged, stooped, and thin-cheeked. He became increasingly withdrawn and listless. There were a few more trips across the Channel to the Normandy coast he loved but no traveling beyond that. Other ailments followed and the life went out of him. After a period of illness, he died in the spring of 1952, taking most of his secrets to the grave.

CHAPTER TEN

André

Max's silence hid many kinds of secrets, not only political. In early 1920, when he escaped the Bolsheviks and returned to London, he had not yet made the acquaintance of Frouma Toumarkine, the woman who would become his wife and Dad's mother. Nevertheless, he already had an eleven-year-old son awaiting him in London. His name was André.

The black sheep of the family, Dad's older half brother was a shadowy and constantly shifting presence who was all but invisible to the Mazowers for most of his life, flitting in and out of Oakeshott Avenue in the early days, never saying where he had come from or where he was going, a man so absent from the record as it was passed down to us that I have been able to find only two or three photographs of him, one of these on the jacket of a book. I never met him and cannot say with any assurance what he looked like, how he dressed, what kind of taste he had in the things that count. For a long time I was not completely sure even when he was born, or got married, or when and where he died. Trying to understand where he came from and where he went has felt, and still feels, a bit like chasing a ghost.

André's life was from its outset one of wandering and metamorphosis. By the time he could read, he had lived in at least five places. In the course of his ninety-five years, he went through three or four nationalities, changed his name officially at least once, and wrote under at least one name more. The idea of the family, which was fundamental for Dad, seems for André to have been for much of his life something to escape. To us children, he was scarcely part of our world at all, nothing more than the name of someone we learned later on had figured in Dad's childhood but who never materialized or left the slightest trace on our way of life apart from a single book that he had written on Spain that always sat on the living-room shelf. Or at least so we thought. But as I look into it more closely, guided by the reminiscences Dad once shared with me—and I remember it was not a topic he wanted to dwell on because I had to persist and keep bringing him back to it—it strikes me now that in searching for André what I am really trying to flesh out is not so much the real André, whoever he might have been, as the absent figure who defined in Dad's mind the kind of man *he* resolved never to become. The occasional references to him that we heard were not positive. But children, who can be so curious about the world, also have a capacity to take things without question. We never thought to ask what had happened to André or why. Was it that we detected subliminally some sadness or pain that was best kept out of sight?

I once consulted a booksellers' search engine to see what would come up under his name. "André Mazower" revealed nothing, which was a disappointment but not really a surprise. Under "André Marling," the name he had adopted during the war, there were several copies for sale of the book I knew about, *Spanish Fare*, a set of sketches of life that he had published in the

early 1960s when he had been living in Madrid. But then, at the
end of the listings, came something else:

> *Civiltà* — Number 1
> André Marling (Andrei Krylienko)
> 1987: Short-lived, 1 issue only. Journal privately printed
> for private distribution. Anti-Semitic sentiments.
> Traditional Catholicism.

Further research suggested that an "Andrei Krylienko" or
"Krilenko"—he seems to have used both spellings—was also
the author of an anti-Semitic tract called *The Red Thread* that
appears to have circulated among New World Order conspiracy
theorists in the United States. Its publisher, Omni, a California-
based press, has been described as "a leading purveyor of radical traditionalist Catholic materials, including a cornucopia of
rabidly anti-Semitic and conspiratorial writings." *The Red Thread*
is held in only two libraries: WorldCat—the online database of
libraries around the world—categorizes it as "controversial literature." When a copy came up for sale in a Midlands bookshop
specializing in the far right, I bought it. *Spanish Fare* sat promi-
nently on our bookshelf in the living room but Dad had never
mentioned anything else that André had written, let alone
something of this sort. I think he had known nothing about it.

When I also found copies of what seems to have been
André's first pamphlet, *Money and the Modern World*, which
had been published in 1969 by an obscure London-based press
called the Plain-Speaker Publishing Company, an entire political milieu began to take shape in my mind. Plain-Speaker's
authors included exiled Russian monarchists, sympathizers
with General Franco, and other counterrevolutionaries. They
tended to be for white Rhodesia and what remained of the

British Empire, against immigration from the former colonies, and — to judge from the in-house journal — were viscerally opposed to what they called race mixing even while denying that this made them racists. They were to a man anticommunists and many of them were obsessed with history and where and why it had gone wrong. Hatred of Freemasonry was ubiquitous. And of course there were the Jews: Hitler had, according to one author, apparently been the puppet of a small cabal of Jewish masterminds who had tricked him into declaring war on Russia. It was like an extreme version of the kind of paranoid fantasizing that had gripped the imaginations of some Nazis between the wars. Only this was postwar England and the Plain-Speaker's publishing address was the residence of George Knupffer, the son of a White Russian officer who had settled in placid Chiswick in southwest London and made his living as an inventor of oil-fired boilers while publishing screeds against world conspiracy and memorials to the deposed monarchs of Eastern Europe. He was known to MI5, which liked to keep an eye on people like him. In publishing with the Plain-Speaker, André found himself in the company of figures such as Arnold Lunn, a well-known champion skier and (less well known) ardent supporter of Franco; and a New Zealander, A. N. Field, a propagandist for white supremacy. And there was Pedro del Valle, a retired general of the U.S. Marine Corps, who was firmly convinced communists were taking over the United States. Del Valle had contributed a brief introduction to André's pamphlet, describing the author as "a man of courage, a good Christian," who was unafraid to take on the "moneychangers" and provided "a great light to guide us in our War of Liberation against the Satanic Powers which now hold sway over Christendom."

Civiltà had been composed by André twenty years later. The forty-three typewritten pages stapled within a red paper cover looked like something one would expect to have been produced by a bunch of enterprising high schoolers. But inside there was a stern motto in capital letters: VETUSTATIS NORMA SERVE-TUR — "Keep the ancient rule" — and there were warnings of the imminent collapse of Christian civilization and forecasts of the approaching climax of the "6,000 year struggle between the forces of good and evil." The author hoped his writings would lead to the formation of small groups of like-minded Christians, the nuclei of a spiritual revival. And there was a darker side: In the struggle between God and the Dark Powers that tried to frustrate His plans for the happiness of men, there was the usual archenemy.

By the time "Andrei Krylienko" came to write the third work, *The Red Thread*, his obsession with Jewish power had intensified. Now in his eighties, he presented the events of the past two millennia as the machinations of a secret conclave of Jewish elders, an enduring occult conspiracy that was the "red thread" of the title running from ancient Rome to the Rockefellers. If there was a thread, it was one woven from the intellectual influences that linked such ideas to the Tsarist secret-police forgery, *The Protocols of the Elders of Zion*, via a series of long-forgotten anti-Semites, men like the White Russian Count Cherep-Spiridovich, the author of *The Secret World Government, or "The Hidden Hand,"* and the Argentinian Hugo Wast, Jorge Luis Borges's fascist predecessor as the director of the country's national library.[1] Although the material was secondhand, that did not mitigate the shock I felt on reading it. I wondered how it was that Dad's older half brother, the son of a Russian Jewish socialist, could possibly have moved so far to the Right.

The story that had come down in the family was that when he was a baby, André had been brought by Max to London shortly before the First World War after André's mother, Sofia, a fellow revolutionary, had died. In the absence of a birth, marriage, or death certificate, it was hard to be sure. Max had preserved an almost total silence about how or why this had come about, and he never mentioned the subject to Dad.

What we can establish with reasonable certainty is that Max was living alone in London at the time of the 1911 census, and that André was with him beginning sometime in late 1912 when Max took lodgings for the two of them in a large Victorian villa called Ingleholme, on the corner of Bishopswood Road and

Hampstead Lane in Highgate. This house became Max's London base and was where André resided from the age of three and a half. Ingleholme housed a small school run by a Quaker couple, Joseph and Marion Hudson, and as Max was away on business nine months of the year in Russia, the Hudsons effectively became André's surrogate parents for nearly a decade.

The Hudsons had evidently been chosen by Max with some care because they were serious educationalists: their "home school" was a progressive, almost avant-garde experiment in learning. Most of the house was given over to the school, which had around a dozen boarders along with a cook and three maids. "In a fine old mansion," wrote a visitor, "in one of the healthiest suburbs of London, surrounded by trees and lawn and garden live Mr. and Mrs. Hudson with their own children and several others besides, under conditions for child culture seldom equaled. Nature, art, music, literature, history, work, play and mother love all unite to do their best." The children cavorted about the garden in smocks and made their own medieval costumes. It was an unlikely start for a future right-wing conspiracy theorist.

Joseph Hudson was a pedagogue with radical sympathies and wide interests, a student of the American philosopher John Dewey who was on the school's advisory committee. Marion Hudson had trained at the renowned Froebel Institute in South London, a pioneer of kindergarten education. The Hudsons looked after André well, and he became friendly with their son, twelve years older than him and a pacifist. Although the school vanished long ago and with it its records, a few scattered traces survive of their relationship. I recently came across a two-volume edition of Lewis Carroll on a shelf in Dad's study. When I opened up the first volume, I found that it contained a dedication from the Hudsons to André, dated on the eve of his eighth birthday, March 2, 1917. It was the middle of the war, and he was apparently there without either of his parents, and the Hudsons must also have been feeling bereft because their son, Charles, was in France on the western front with an ambulance unit.

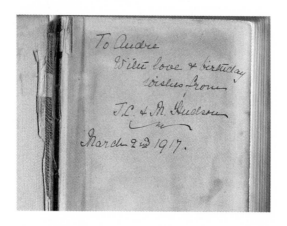

Max was working in Russia for the Yost Typewriter Company throughout the war, and when he returned in the spring of 1920, André had just turned eleven and Max had probably not seen him since he was five or six. A photo taken at the moment of their reunion depicts the two of them standing in a garden. It is hard to read and because it is small, no more than a snapshot, it cannot easily be magnified and their expressions remain elusive. Man and boy have the same slight declension of the head, but they stand at a remove from each other. Max is self-contained, as usual, and he seems subdued—his buttoned-up jacket gives nothing away. André leans off at an angle as if seeking already to distance himself from this semi-stranger. I know it is him because he has his right hand lodged firmly in his jacket pocket, in exactly the same way that he

holds it in the picture that adorns the dust jacket of the book
he published four decades later.

Max must have kept this—there are no others from these
years—which suggests to me that it had been a moment he
wanted to preserve. As to what André felt, there is nothing but
the image to go on. Photographs are ambiguous and it may
be a mistake to read into this one the sense of estrangement
that was going to emerge in the coming years. It is impossible really to know what André made at this point of the gaps
between Max's visits or of his mother's absence. He was surely
lonely. Did he also feel that something shameful hung over his
mother's absence? Max and Sofia had never married and Dad
thought André had suffered throughout his life from the taint
of illegitimacy, a source of shame much stronger at the start of
the last century than it is today. But in 1920 André may not have
known about this and in any case the Hudsons do not sound
like a couple to have been bothered by such things. When they

retired and moved out to the Essex countryside, André went with them and got into one of the country's leading grammar schools, the King Edward VI School in Chelmsford. He did well, finished up at an old Quaker school not far away, and won a place at Cambridge.

By then, the tension and pain in André's relationship with his father had become unmistakable. Max was spending much more time in England after the spring of 1920 but he did not bring André back to London to live with him. And as his schooling was nearing an end a few years later, André got a real shock: In the summer of 1924, Max returned from one of his trips to Eastern Europe in the company of a thirty-two-year-old Russian widow—Frouma—and Ira, her eight-year-old daughter from a previous marriage. They had fled Moscow with little more than a suitcase and Max announced to André that he and Frouma had gotten married in Riga and that he now had a stepmother and a half sister. They had met in Moscow two or three years earlier, but tight-lipped as always Max had not said a word to André beforehand. With Frouma in charge, a family household was established on the Holly Lodge Estate and there was always a room for André. But Dad's arrival on the scene in 1925 would have been hard emotionally for André too, and to judge from Frouma's letters, his relationship with his father never recovered. In 1926 he spent the summer at a Quaker college, did some traveling in Germany, and then went on to Corpus Christi College, Cambridge.

College became, in André's words, "a second home," freeing him of "the previous necessary but tiresome interventions of parents and school-masters." Advised by a tutor that he should study economics, he dreamed of becoming a poet, rowed in a college eight, and ended up with a degree in English. He had fond memories of his time at Corpus Christi and became attached to the father figures at its helm.

Life in college in those days was not extravagant—Corpus had little of the ostentatious Christ Church partying idealized by Evelyn Waugh in *Brideshead Revisited*—but it was full of social distinctions all the same. There were the public school-boys and those from grammar schools, boys from the gentry and those like André whose fathers were in trade. An exclusive dining club—the Chess Club—was for the college upper crust; naturally, they did not play chess. Corpus was a small place, intimate, and more than in most places, life revolved around chapel. Two pounds a week—a sum that amounted to André's entire income seven years later—bought the services of a man who would wake you, light the fire, choose and lay out your clothes, and bring breakfast to your room. Dependent upon remittances from Max, André was not well-off nor was he a public-school man.[2]

One of the friends he made that first year, a man he kept up with for some time afterwards, was an Etonian called Henry. Captain and opening bat of the unbeaten Eton XI of 1926, Henry's full name was Henry Edward Hugh Pelham-Clinton-Hope, the Earl of Lincoln and the future 9th Duke of Newcastle. The young earl had problems of his own, of a rather different kind than André's. He had inherited a stately Italianate home in Nottinghamshire called Clumber House, a kind of Brideshead on steroids set on an estate of nearly four thousand acres on the edge of Sherwood Forest, with terraced gardens, the longest lime avenue in Europe, and a lake large enough that in its heyday a frigate and a yacht had been kept on it for guests. All this had strained the family fortune and the earl was the first in his line not to live there. Eventually it was demolished leaving behind little more than the stables, the garden temples, and the 7th Duke's chapel. (Further indignity was visited upon the estate during the war when a top-secret weapon, a seventy-seven-foot 130-ton mechanized trench-digging monster, nicknamed Nellie, was tested on the grounds in the presence of Winston Churchill, who had hoped to use it in some imaginary replay of the First World War. Never deployed, it churned up swathes of the Clumber turf as if in some Waughian nightmare the new machinery of modern total war was literally uprooting the old landed ways.) It is easy to see how the illegitimate son of a Russian Jewish businessman living in mock-Tudor Highgate might have felt the precariousness of his social standing, might have started to keep his friends and his family apart, and might have dreamed of the kind of lineage—and faith—that would be a source of pride rather than shame.

The main clue we have as to the direction of André's thoughts at this time comes from an unexpected quarter. On the eve of the Wall Street crash, none other than T. S. Eliot wrote to a friend in banking that he had been visited by a recently graduated Cambridge student called André Mazower, the son of a Russian refugee with "some small business in the Midlands." The boy apparently knew no Russian and his French was "a little rusty"; his English, however, was fluent, and Eliot, slightly baffled, concluded that his nationality "is rather uncertain." André had some poems to his name, and though Eliot did not think much of them, he did what he could to find the young man some work.

The connection was less fortuitous than it might appear at first sight because Eliot had close ties with André's college.

One of Eliot's friends there was the historian Kenneth Pick-thorn—reputedly the rudest man at Cambridge—who would invite him periodically to dine with the fellows, and it was Pick-thorn who had recommended André to Eliot. In the summer of 1928, when André first contacted the poet to seek advice about his future, he told him he was thinking of going to Harvard to study for a doctorate in English. He had been born in Paris, he said, and hoped this would get him one of the places the university offered French students, but added he would need financial support since "he was not in a position to accept an allowance, even if it should be offered him, from his parents." The Harvard idea came and went, as many of André's ideas would, to be replaced by the thought of finding work in Paris, a fashionable destination for Cambridge undergraduates in those years. But Eliot evidently saw something in André, or felt sorry for him, because he did not give up trying to help him.

What was it that attracted Eliot's solicitude? Was it André's obviously thorny relationship with his father, which may have reminded the poet of his difficulties with his own parents? Or perhaps a seriousness about faith and an ambivalence about Judaism, which is signally unmentioned in André's account of his "Russian" background? These were the years in which Eliot was received into the Anglican communion and started to describe himself as an Anglo-Catholic, and his example provided both a positive impetus to seek solace in the idea of the church and a negativity about Jews that it is hard, in the light of André's later writings, not to see foreshadowing what was to come. In his correspondence with Pickthorn during these years, Eliot slips easily and quite often into a kind of casual anti-Semitism. There are also his 1933 lectures, *After Strange Gods*, an unpleasant fusion of spiritual anxiety and snobbery, with their praise of the "blood kinship" of "the same people living in the same place," their emphasis on the social value of a "unity of religious background" and the judgment that the presence of "any large number of free-thinking Jews" is "undesirable." It was at Corpus that Eliot was to deliver his better-known lecture "The Idea of a Christian Society" in March 1939 — a call to treat Christian values with intellectual respect, to appreciate that modern democracy was as much in crisis as fascism or communism, and to change the way economic life in particular was organized so that it might facilitate rather than impede a life of devotion.

Eliot felt at home at Corpus, a place where the fellows had to be of the Christian faith, and where many of them took their Christianity seriously. Indeed, the college was in those days something close to what one of its products describes as a "conservative-Anglican plot." Caustic and demanding, Pickthorn, who was later an MP, was a college dean and a dedicated

mentor to his young men. Two history dons — Geoffrey But-
ler and his nephew Rab — were superbly connected within the
Conservative Party and keen to revitalize it. And presiding
over all of them was William Spens, a brilliant if Machiavel-
lian educationalist who became master during André's time in
Cambridge. Spens was much in the public eye, prominent in
debates about the direction of the Church of England and its
relations with Rome. All three of these distinguished conservatives — Spens, Pickthorn, and Eliot — in one way or another
extended their sympathy and friendship to the politely spoken,
talented young undergraduate.

Eliot had had understandable difficulty figuring out André's
background. Downplaying his Jewish connections, as one would
have been likely to do in that milieu, André had emphasized his
links to France, his birthplace. And he had flaunted his estrangement from Oakeshott Avenue by underscoring his resolve not
to accept any financial support from his parents. In reality he
remained for a long time more dependent upon his father and
the whole Mazower household than he had admitted to Eliot.
But his ambivalence towards it and his desire for distance could
not have been made clearer: The thing he wanted, whether it
was Harvard or Paris, was to get away.

Money was a bit of a problem, as it would be always, I
think, for the future author of *Money and the Modern World*. In
the summer of 1929, after graduation, he spent a month working as a temporary clerk at a bank in Paris, probably thanks to
Eliot, and stayed on a few months more in the French capital
before he had to go back to Oakeshott Avenue. In 1930 he had a
longer spell in Paris, working for the White Star shipping line,
but when that ended in the autumn of the following year, he
returned to England penniless. Eventually, he made enough

from binding and repairing books to rent a room on the fringes of Fitzrovia, heading back to Oakeshott Avenue again when things were bad to run errands for his father.

His nationality is rather uncertain. The truth is that André was stateless. He had entered England in 1912 on a Russian passport, and it was as the subject of a defunct empire that his details were entered on the Central Register of Aliens. To be an alien was a demeaning business. The file the Metropolitan Police Service kept on him was supposed to record every change of address or employment, every trip abroad, and he was obliged to notify them regularly. His irregular status did not prevent him from traveling but did make coming and going more fraught. Because he had been born in France, he found that he was entitled to French citizenship and in 1932 obtained his passport through the consulate in London. But although this regularized his status, it also rendered him liable to conscription into the French army, and so he applied to the Home Office for naturalization as a subject of King George V. With Spens (who was now the vice-chancellor of Cambridge), the earl, a headmaster, and the Hudsons' son among his guarantors, he had no difficulty. The police reported that he seemed respectable and did not frequent extremist circles; MI5 had no objections. One of his testimonials referred to him as a "charming, highly intellectual man, deeply devoted to old England." Vice-Chancellor Spens described him as a friend who came to visit him and his wife "at every available moment": André was then twenty-three, and Spens was fifty.

Highgate had become a last resort. Showing up on the doorstep in Oakeshott Avenue one day he seemed "starving" and "penniless." Although he was just about making ends meet, he remained dependent on Max financially for long stretches of time. Otherwise there was little contact: By the early 1930s he wanted to keep the Mazowers firmly separate from the rest of his life. He came, Frouma wrote, without telling them where he had been and left without saying where he was going; if they wanted to get in touch with him, they were told to write to his bank. "He was like a sort of specter in the background," was what Dad remembered.

The author of one of his testimonials told the Home Office that he believed André had been neglected once Max remarried, and this was without doubt what André himself felt. His relations with Max were so thorny that Frouma feared to leave them alone for very long, and her letters convey the tension that his visits brought into the house. "Family seems to burden him," she wrote. He needed the family but he also resented it. It is hard to imagine that he ever got much overt sympathy from Max, who not only found it more or less impossible to express feelings of tenderness but had been obliged to earn money from boyhood to help his own family and had paid for André through school and college even as the Depression deepened his own financial difficulties. Might not Max have read into André's seeming failure to make something of himself — to contribute in any way that Max recognized — a deeper failure of his own, in which the psychic costs of having turned his back on active revolutionary politics were shot through with disbelief at how he could have produced such a politically conservative and impractical son? André's evident shame at his parentage cannot have been easy for Max to bear because he was a proud man, and he does not seem to have ever regarded his own lineage as something to be rejected. Each was already writing the other out of the script of his life.

There was a mutual turning away. The last of only two photos of André in family albums filled with innumerable pictures

of everyone else must have been taken by Dad in the back garden at Oakeshott Avenue sometime in the mid-1930s. Unwilling
to face the camera, André stares off to his right, hands as ever
wedged in his pockets, as formally dressed as his father tended
to be, and like Max wearing his jacket tightly buttoned. It is an
image of a man wishing things were different, wishing he were
anywhere but there.

When the war broke out, André was determined not to let
his unusual name prevent him from joining up. Rebuffed initially by the navy on account of his foreign birth, he served in
the Auxiliary Patrol, working bravely through the Blitz amid
the flames and debris of burning buildings along the Thames,
before going to Dunkirk to help evacuate British troops and narrowly escaping being stranded there himself. It was then that
he decided to change his surname to Marling. A German invasion seemed imminent, and many immigrants were doing this,

alarmed at the surge in anti-Semitism that took hold in wartime England. On the same day as André gave up Mazower, Ernst Rosenwald of 72 Belsize Park Gardens became Ernest Ronald; Jacob Finklestein of Alvington Crescent Dalston became Jack Marks; Solomon Smelovitch of Bridge Road Leyton turned into Sidney Somers; and Wolf Hecht became William Hart. Did they do this in order to appear less foreign in the eyes of their fellow Englishmen or for fear of being arrested when the Germans landed? One cannot imagine the Gestapo, which had already drawn up its search lists of wanted Englishmen, being fooled for long: All they needed to do was to peruse the pages of *The London Gazette* where these changes were formally announced.

His first name, on the other hand, was left untouched. If André was motivated principally by fear of a German invasion then why did he not go the whole hog and become a properly English-sounding Andrew? I think the answer is clear enough: It was not so much to get away from the Germans that he changed his name as to establish his distance from Oakeshott Avenue and his father. Whereas Mazower pointed east to the Polish-Russian borderlands and was at best unclassifiable and at worst suggestive of Jewish origins, André had different connotations, French above all and shifted easily into and out of a Russian variant—Andrei—which was Christian in its associations, not Jewish. Or perhaps the real desire ran deeper than that: Was not his first name one of the very few ties that he had to his mother, the name by which she knew him and that she had chosen, perhaps for its Tolstoyan connotations?

The surname Marling reassured naval minds unnerved by the suspiciously alien Mazower, and in May 1941 André became a temporary lieutenant in the Royal Naval Reserve. He was

probably on the HMS *Enterprise* when it took part in a celebrated clash in December 1943, engaging a group of German
destroyers and torpedo boats in the Battle of the Bay of Biscay,
and sinking several of them. On board the aircraft carrier the
HMS *Vengeance* the following year, he passed through very different seas, sunnier and warmer, catching a glimpse of Spain,
the country that was soon to become his first true home, then
sailing through the Mediterranean—now safe for British shipping—and on to the Pacific, docking at Ceylon before reaching
Sydney where the aircraft carrier was fitted with more effective
guns for protection against Japanese kamikaze attacks. He must
have found the return of peace difficult and austerity Britain
drab. At thirty-eight he was old to find a new career and moved
around Marylebone to a series of rented rooms while searching
for a way to make a living before deciding to leave the country. He spent a few weeks in the spare bedroom in Oakeshott
Avenue and then, on Christmas Eve 1948, he was at the port of
Southampton embarking on a rackety steamer bound for Spain
and South America. Most of his shipmates were Polish refugees and their families, leaving the devastation of Europe and
its displaced persons camps for a new life in South America. It
must have been a lonely exit from the country in which he had
grown up and for which he had fought with courage. Hence-
forth he was only to return for visits.

A new phase in his life now began—in Spain. The country was
slowly recovering from the ravages of the civil war under the
dictatorial rule of General Franco, and André rented a small
flat in the old Moorish quarter of Madrid. He found a job as
a night watchman at the British embassy and then, for more

than a decade, worked in the English-language service of the national radio station. He became fluent in Spanish, knowledgeable about the country, and increasingly drawn to its antiquated ways. Spain's isolation from the rest of Europe, its slow industrialization, and the conservative values and religious rhetoric of the regime seem to have made him feel at home, and it was while he was there that he converted to Catholicism. Christianity would play an increasingly overt part in his life and thought.

He would come back to stay at Oakeshott Avenue occasionally, usually for a week or two around Christmas, but relations between him and his ailing father did not improve. Opting to live in Franco's Spain was a powerful statement in itself—the Mazowers had been staunch antifascists during the Spanish Civil War—but André's conversion to Catholicism seems to have been something Max found really shocking. One episode stuck in everyone's mind. During a visit, presumably after a difficult exchange with his father, André became so frustrated that he seized the ax they used for making kindling, marched out into the garden, and started hacking down a horse chestnut tree. As his stepmother protested, he was defiant: "I planted this tree, it's mine, I can chop it down if I want." Dad never forgot André with a set look on his face going out and chopping the tree down. "That was rather typical, from what I remember. He was quite erratic." (In fact, as we shall see, there may have been a specific reason, of which Dad was unaware, behind this outburst.) In the entire course of my childhood, I cannot remember a single occasion when Dad lost his temper with us. He was very slow to anger and when he did, it almost always manifested itself in other ways. It is as if André was a kind of polar opposite—unsettled, self-isolating—of the man

Dad was already halfway to becoming. After his departure for Spain, André left almost no possessions in the attic of Oakeshott Avenue, just a couple of boxes with old notebooks and an oil painting in muted grays, browns, and blues of a thin man smoking a pipe.

In Madrid he married a younger woman who had fled Stalin's Russia, and they had a son. And in 1963, he published *Spanish Fare*, a series of sketches drawn mostly from the radio talks he had given. The book conveys his affection for the country and its people, and expresses an easy intimacy with their habits. The author does not hide his conservative leanings, and like a modern Cassandra he warns about the perils facing Western civilization, mostly from the materialist barbarians across the Atlantic; but the preaching is held in check by anecdotes and local color. There is certainly nothing like the extremism of the views that are on display in his later pamphlets: Defiant and tenacious in holding these beliefs, he was probably already conscious that they raised hackles and would disqualify him from polite society. Later on he seems to have tried them out on a few writers, scholars, and public figures and been discouraged by their reluctance to take them up, by what he saw as their hypocrisy in being unwilling to preach what they inwardly believed. On the back jacket, there is a photograph of the author, a somewhat stern-looking figure in profile, jacket buttoned and hands firmly placed in its pockets, staring across a terrace from the side of the frame with the Madrid skyline behind him. With his receding hairline and small neat mustache, it is not hard to see a resemblance to Max. It is the image of a proud man, wounded by life but defiant, standing at an angle to the world.

Two years after the book was published, Dad had to go to
Spain on business. Max had been dead a long time and Frouma
had just died. As he was clearing out the Oakeshott Avenue house, Dad found some old notebooks in the attic which
seemed to belong to André so he got in touch and went to his
flat in Madrid. It was ten years or more since they had seen
each other but he found André little changed physically. As
they chatted over tea, however, it dawned on Dad that in other
respects André had changed quite a lot. It was not just that he
said nothing at all about Max's death, or Frouma's; he had left
Dad's world in other ways as well. Dad wrote later to a relative:
"He struck me as slightly mad, certainly politically...very right-
wing and very pro-Franco and anti-Semitic." For Dad, the gap
was unbridgeable: "I just felt we had very little in common. His
fascism rather upset me. Anyone who supported [Franco] and
what he stood for, I really didn't want to have anything to do
with. That was '65."

And that would have been that, except for the papers from
the old house that Dad had brought with him to Madrid.
Another twenty years or so elapsed, and one night in 1987 the
phone rang and who should it be but André. Later on, Dad
recounted their conversation: "'Oh dear, where are you? Are

you still living in Madrid?' 'No, on Lake Geneva, on the French side. I wanted to ask you, Bill, do you remember handing me an exercise book?' I said, yes. He said, 'Did you look at the first page?' I said, 'I can't remember'—I remember there were some poems in it, I really didn't remember, this was [twenty] years later. He said, 'Well, there is some writing in Russian. As I don't speak Russian. I had a friend of mine here translate it. I'll send you a copy.'"

When the translation arrived, there was for once an address: André, now nearly eighty, was living in a small village above Lake Geneva. What he wanted to talk about was the mystery of his birth. The notebook had belonged to his mother, and for the first time we were confronted with the question of who she was and what had happened to her.

CHAPTER ELEVEN

The Krylenko Connection

Among Max's secrets the story of André's mother was perhaps the most tightly guarded of all. That Dad knew anything was thanks to his aunt Niura, Frouma's sister, with whom André had briefly been close when she was living in Paris. Niura had learned that Max had a relationship before the First World War with a fellow revolutionary, a young woman called Krylenko. Dad had grown up under the impression that she died shortly after André was born and that this was why he had been raised in London by Max. There was a famous Bolshevik called Nicolai Krylenko and Niura thought they might have been related, perhaps were even siblings. But what her first name was neither Niura nor Dad knew.

Over the phone, André now delivered a small bombshell: The text at the beginning of the notebook that Dad had brought to Madrid from Oakeshott Avenue back in 1965 indicated, so André said, that Max had not been his father at all. Apparently what it showed was that his real father had been an Austrian military doctor named Dr. Karl von Hörnigk, who had disappeared while on a mission for the Red Cross in Russia before 1914. Max must have been a friend of von Hörnigk, said André, and agreed to act as guardian while his mother went to Russia to search for her Austrian husband. André added that his mother was called Sofia Krylenko and she had indeed been a sister of Nicolai Krylenko, a man who later rose to the uppermost echelons of power in the Kremlin as the Soviet commissar of justice before falling victim to Stalin's Terror himself. (The same Nicolai Krylenko subsequently found immortalization, if that is the right word, as one of the principal villains of Aleksandr Solzhenitsyn's *The Gulag Archipelago*.) André also told Dad that his mother had been married a second time, to a Belgian doctor named von Mayer, before ending up in Moscow where her brother had confined her to a mental asylum. André had communicated with her under her married name of von Mayer right up to the outbreak of the Second World War and had then lost all trace of her. "This came as a considerable surprise to me, as you can imagine," was Dad's laconic summing up.

I remember sitting across the kitchen table from Dad as we turned this new information over and over in our minds and tried to figure it out. Unmistakable in the whole complicated story was André's repudiation of Max's parentage. The rest was really quite odd and confusing: Was the Red Cross actually sending Hapsburg officers to Tsarist Russia on its behalf just before the First World War? Was the doctor, if he had ever existed, likely to have been such good friends with a Russian Jewish socialist that he would ask him to act as his child's guardian, as the document—if it was a document—appeared to indicate? Why would Max have agreed at a very difficult time in his life to care for an infant who was not his? It all sounded unlikely.

Dad's suspicions were heightened when André sent him a copy of what he said was Max's statement of guardianship. The Russian vocabulary used was postrevolutionary and some terms sounded as if they had been badly translated from another language. The handwriting was all wrong too—one thing Dad did know was what his father's always precise hand had looked

like — and there were elementary spelling mistakes and small but
crucial discrepancies in the Russian patronymics. When André,
who did not know Russian, assured Dad, who did, that it could
have been written by Max because his handwriting had changed
as he got older, Dad became fed up with the whole matter. He
had always believed his half brother to be a "highly imaginative
character" — no compliment in Dad's book. But this latest communication of André's puzzled him. The von Hörnigk character
seemed fake. After all, why should his father have been so upset
with André during his visits home if he had not really been his
father? The intensity in Max's feelings suggested kinship.

I doubt Dad would have minded to learn he and André were
not blood relatives. What I think did disturb him was to be
reminded after so many years of the fierceness of his half brother's wish to repudiate their father and everything he stood for,
especially now that André's tendency to fantasy had apparently
tipped over into a kind of amateurish forgery. Dad's inward
judgments could be harsh and uncompromising, but usually
he kept these very well hidden and did not tell people what he
thought of them. However André's behavior touched a nerve
and was impossible for him to forgive. Other letters followed
containing ever more fantastic claims and demands, and at the
start of 1991, Dad broke off the correspondence. Yet the uncertainties gnawed away at him. When he wrote to his long-lost
cousin Osya later that year about what he called "the mystery
of André," he confessed that he was still in the dark: "My parents never spoke about it in my presence. Did your father ever
mention anything about it?"

Dad remembered André's visits home with scant sympathy for his half brother and barely suppressed anger. What
remained with him was how upset these stays could leave his

parents; causing them pain was, in his view, the cardinal sin for a son. Yet for André, to have had to rely on Max and Frouma for intermittent shelter and support into his forties must itself have been a source of anguish; to me, it feels as if he were making an unconscious demand for the repayment of a different kind of debt. Dad was the younger son who had been given the parental love André never had. Above all, Dad had enjoyed a mother's care in its most tender and unquestioning form. The original source of André's emotional deprivation was surely not in Oakeshott Avenue at all, not in the figure of his taciturn father who was unable to express the solicitude that lay inside him. It was rather in the house, the home, that had existed for him only as a momentary glimpse in an uncertain land at an age too young for it to mean more than loss, a home briefly animated by his never mentioned mother, the absence behind the absence that he himself was to become.

André's naturalization papers, which are held in the National Archives in London, offer a chance to test his 1987 version of his parentage against a much older one. "André Mazower, from France. Resident in London"—entered thus in the Home Office register—had applied for naturalization in the summer of 1933. He stated in front of a solicitor that his father was Mordchel Mazower—"of Polish nationality"—and that his mother was "Sofia Vassilievna Krylenko of uncertain nationality." If she was indeed related to the well-known Bolshevik, this was the correct patronymic. (In contrast, André's fake document named her as "Sofia Krylienko, Russian, born in St. Petersburg, Russia, 15 October 1886, the son of Ivan Krylienko and Tamara Kornilova," which was a total fiction and got pretty much everything wrong—including her patronymic and the parents' names.) Although the Home Office file contains much other information, it says nothing more of any consequence about his mother: André declared at that time that all he knew about her was that she was in the USSR and that he feared she was dead. No one in Whitehall, on the evidence of the file, appears to have drawn the connection with her brother Nicolai.

Nicolai Krylenko was by that time an internationally recognizable public figure, and he was known to have had a brother and several sisters—there was Olga, a pianist called Vera, and Elena, who was well-known to historians of the American Left because she had married the legendary radical Max Eastman. But had there also been a Sofia, or was this nothing more than a family myth? I asked a friend of mine, a historian who knows as much about Stalin's Russia as anyone alive, but he had never heard of her and could find no reference to her in any of the standard works.

Then I discovered I was not the only one looking for her: André's son had been doing the same thing before me. One April evening in 1997, ten years after his father's phone call to Dad, he had accessed an Internet site specializing in Russian family histories and, without specifying his own relationship to André, had sought the help of other subscribers for information about his grandmother: "I am doing this research on the behalf of her son (now aged 88) and would really be glad if I could assist him in finding more about his mother (he only met her twice after she left for Russia)."

Was it my imagination or did the wording of that final sentence suggest that before she left for Russia—he seemed to think she had gone back around 1911 or 1912—André had seen much more of her, perhaps even been with her until then?

At that point he would have been around two and a half, too young to have clear memories of that period but old enough to know they had been together, especially since they had met and written to each other after that date.

But if André was living with his mother, it was not yet in England and not with Max. April 1911 was the month of the U.K. census, and Max ("a Russian visitor") was listed on the form as living on his own in lodgings in Gordon Place in Bloomsbury. (He was briefly in London to report back to his employers at the Yost Typewriter Company.) The strange thing is that on the page of the census return for his boardinghouse, Max declared himself a married man with a wife and child. He filled in the number of years he had been married (three) and the number of children he had (one) and then he or someone else crossed them out, since only women were required to provide this kind of information. But his error is a clue. Because 1908 was the year he would have met Sofia Krylenko, the child thus referred to had to have been André. Was he already anticipating bringing André and his mother to England?

2nd, 1911, in this dwelling and was alive at midnight, or (2) arrived in this dwelling on the morning of Monday, April 3rd, not having been enumerated elsewhere. No one else must be included. (For order of entering names see Examples on back of Schedule.)	"Wife," "Son," "Daughter," or other Relative, "Visitor," "Boarder," or "Servant."	"under one month," "one month," etc.		"Widower," or "Widow," opposite the names of all persons aged 15 years and upwards.	Completed years the present Marriage has lasted. If less than one year write "under one."	present Marriage. (If no children born alive write "None" in Column 7).		
		Ages of Males.	Ages of Females.			Total Children Born Alive.	Children still Living.	Children who have Died.
1.	2.	3.	4.	5.	6.	7.	8.	9.
1 Marie Sampson	Head		47	married	14	4	4	
2 Mark Masower	Boarder	36		married	3 yrs	1	1	—
3 John Coxthon Butler	Boarder	31		single	—	—	—	—
4 Arthur Heinig	Servant	18		single	—	—	—	—
5 Agnes Vörös	Visitor		48	married	29	3	2	1
6 Michaela Vörös	Visitor		5	—	—	—	—	—
7 Caroline Chalmers			43	married	27	5	2	3
8 Marie Firth	Visitor		46	married	32	9	8	1
9								

Sofia and André's absence from the U.K. census was consistent with something else. Online, André's son had also mentioned a stay in the Belgian city of Liège around this time. He added that after living there, Sofia had returned to Russia and married someone called "de Mayer"—was this the Belgian doctor André had mentioned to Dad?—and that she'd had "two or three children" with him before she was eventually sent in the 1920s to somewhere called Mas Gorsk, where she died. He mentioned that she had been a Menshevik, which was perhaps, he speculated, why she had been living in Paris and Liège, both prewar centers of Menshevik activity.

There seem to have been no very helpful online responses. But it turns out the essentials were correct: The infamous Nicolai Krylenko did have a sister called Sofia and she was indeed André's mother and she did marry a man called de (or von) Meyer (or Mayer) and have other children. Now that I have been able to piece together a few more fragments of information about her, I can see that it is not surprising André was so in the dark about her: She was an even more elusive and troubled figure than he was, and several people besides Max had good reason to want to draw as little attention to her as possible.

The idyllic Mediterranean setting of Capri has had a long association with the European Left, and in the early summer of 1924 it was the site of an important love affair in the cultural history of modernism. Asja Lacis, a left-wing Latvian agitprop theater director, was staying on the island, which was a holiday magnet for the avant-garde of central Europe despite Mussolini's growing grip on power in Rome. While in the market one day she encountered an unhappily married bespectacled German Jewish intellectual who was having difficulty finishing his dissertation and flirting with the thought of leaving Europe to try his luck in Palestine. His name was Walter Benjamin, and he fell deeply in love with her. Their meeting and subsequent affair has been credited with transforming his thinking, reorienting it away from his earlier interest in theology and Jewish mysticism and towards an engagement with Marxism and the Soviet experiment. People disagree on whether this was for the better or not, but few question the importance of the meeting. Fewer have paid sufficient attention to Lacis who was a remarkable woman in her own right, a friend of Bertolt Brecht, a pioneer of proletarian theater, a beauty, and a survivor of Stalinism; she died in Latvia in 1979. And I would hazard a guess that no one at all has bothered with the figure of Sofia Krylenko, who hovers on the story's margins.

Lacis, it turns out, was a friend of Sofia's, and in *Recuerdo de Walter Benjamin en Capri*, an extract from her memoirs, originally written in Latvian but available in Spanish, she tells us that Sofia was also staying on Capri where they spent a lot of time together. She mentions their visit to the maverick Italian poet Filippo Tommaso Marinetti, the founder of the futurist movement. They were overwhelmed by the magnificence of his garden, his liking for Gabriele D'Annunzio's writings, and the fact that Marinetti's wife, the artist Benedetta Cappa, was dressed only in futurist black-and-white. (Marinetti, whose right-wing sympathies were by then pretty evident, was another captive to the splendor of what he called "the Futurist island.") That is all Lacis tells us. But it is sufficient to give us a glimpse of Sofia, moving in Leftist circles in Continental Europe in the mid-1920s, a woman of culture and independence and means, a modernist, a free spirit.

By this time she had not one but three children, all of whom were being looked after by others, and we know this because when the infatuated Benjamin followed Lacis to Moscow two and a half years later, he called in an idle moment to see Sofia. She was not there but he found another Krylenko—the redoubtable matriarch, Olga—living in a rented, sparsely furnished apartment. The drabness of it impressed itself upon him, as he wrote in his *Moscow Diary*: "If people manage to bear rooms which look like infirmaries after inspection, it is because their way of life has so alienated them from domestic existence."

He could not have been more on the mark. Where Sofia was concerned, alienation from domesticity was something like the leitmotif of her way of being: Benjamin, who knew her slightly in Germany, describes her as stubborn and estranged "but not entirely severed" from her family. As it turned out, she was not in Moscow at the time of his visit, nor even in the Soviet Union, but Benjamin did meet her two daughters—they struck him as slightly sad—who shuttled between their grandmother and *her* mother, "not having seen their mother for years." There is no mention of any de Meyer (or von Mayer). The children, according to Benjamin, were products of "her first marriage to a nobleman who fought on the Bolshevik side during the civil war and died." By coincidence, while Benjamin was there, Sofia's younger daughter was opening a letter from her mother who wrote from Germany that she was in some difficulties and might have to leave. Her "illegal work"—presumably for the underground Left—was responsible. And then Benjamin adds some enigmatic words that convey the family's reaction: "she is a calamity and her mother is visibly upset."[1]

Why? The reasons were evidently political, although against and for whom Sofia was working was not clear to me when I read Benjamin's remarks. But she had evidently never made the turn to familial life that Max and other prewar revolutionaries had. She had remained an activist and castigated others for their compromises. Like her son, she was a person who preferred communicating with her family by letter, and she lived on the edge and was involved in activities that alarmed them. Yet she apparently had good enough relations with them to make it plausible that she would have considered one day returning to Moscow where her daughters were living. Overall, Benjamin's account made André's story seem more rather than less likely. For if Sofia had indeed once been a Menshevik, as he seems to have thought, then her presence would have over time become very much more than merely inconvenient to her family in the Soviet Union, since her brother Nicolai, as the prosecutor general of the USSR, was hunting down opponents of the Bolsheviks and would later be entrusted by Stalin with the trial of the so-called Menshevik conspirators in a show trial in 1931.

Benjamin and Lacis are not the only figures on the Left to offer us a glimpse of Sofia. Closer to home, there was also her younger sister, Elena. In the early 1920s Elena had met the prominent American radical Max Eastman and had begun an enduring relationship through which Eastman came to know the entire Krylenko family.

In 1924 Elena and Eastman left the USSR and three years later moved for good to the United States, where Elena became an accomplished painter, a dancer, and the confidante to many leading figures of interwar American progressivism. What I did not know was how much she had been able to stay in touch with her family in Russia after she had reached America. Since her personal papers are held along with Eastman's in the Lilly Library at Indiana University in Bloomington, I contacted the archivists. And there I found the answer. On February 25, 1956, three years after Stalin's death, Nikita Khrushchev, the first secretary of the Communist Party, had electrified the world by delivering a speech in which he criticized Stalin and the crimes of the Terror. One of the consequences was the rehabilitation of many of his victims, among them, ironically, Nicolai Krylenko. Elena, who was already suffering from the cancer that was to kill her, wrote to Nikolai Bulganin, the premier of the USSR, that September from her home on Martha's Vineyard.

> Dear Sir,
> Since my brother Nikolai Krylenko has been rehabilitated I venture to ask you to tell me of the fate of the other members of our immediate family — my sisters, Olga, Vera, and Sophia, and their children, and also my second brother, Vladimir

Krylenko, a mining engineer. My last news of the family came from Olga in 1935. Since then I have received no letter and no word or news from any one of them in spite of my repeated attempts to get into communication by mail.

Another note in the same file confirmed the existence of a husband called Meyer and their daughters, André's half sisters: "Sister—Sophia MEYER [née Krylenko]. Had two daughters: Natalia and Caterina."

Because André's British naturalization papers stated that he had been born in Paris, the next thing I did was to order his birth certificate from the French authorities, hoping it might shed light on the question of his paternity. It did and it didn't. Late at night on March 3, 1909, it said, the "student" Sofia Krylenko had given birth to a son at a lying-in hospital, the Clinique Tarnier, beside the Jardin du Luxembourg. And the father? *"De père non denommé."* As was customary in cases of birth outside wedlock, he had not been named, a further indication that André had indeed been illegitimate. There had been no wedding and the Hapsburg-officer story that André had tried on Dad was a myth.

In the file, appended to the certificate, there was also a note, written more than twenty years later, on which the heading "Krylenko" was scored through and replaced with "Mazower." Max (named here as "Morchel Mazower") had presented himself to the French consulate in London on February 24, 1930, in order to acknowledge his paternity—this was the time when André was applying for a French passport—and when the *mairie* of the sixth arrondissement received a copy, an official placed it next to the birth certificate.[2]

The real mystery remains how, where, and when Sofia and Max met. We simply have no idea because nothing has survived to say, and apart from André himself—and perhaps in more oblique form Max's crossed-out entry on his census form—their encounter has left no traces at all. Neither of them did enough to attract the attention of the Sûreté and I have found nothing in the police files in France. Because the period between Max's escape from Russia sometime in 1907 or 1908 and his move to London in late 1909 are a blank, it is not even certain that Max visited Paris at the time when André was conceived, and he and Sofia may have met in Switzerland or Germany. But the circumstances are not hard to imagine. Both Sofia and Max were connected to the Russian Social Democratic Workers' Party, and both were in exile from the Tsarist regime. The Krylenkos were not Jewish, but religious background counted for little on the Left. Max had numerous Menshevik friends, while Sofia's brother Vladimir was to marry a Jewish woman from Vilna.

What we do know about Sofia is that she was a generation younger than Max and an ardent revolutionary. She came from the intelligentsia, the eldest of six children of moderately well-off parents with radical sympathies dating back two generations. There was a Decembrist grandfather, and a father who'd had his own youthful run-ins with the Tsarist police and became a liberal newspaper editor in Smolensk before he was forced to give it up. The family background was bookish and cultivated, and Sofia had been encouraged in her studies, attending the St. Petersburg Higher School for Women, an exceptional institution that held out against the deep conservatism of the Tsarist authorities to offer university-level training for women. The school was known for the radicalism of its students, and by 1905 Sofia was an active social democrat, heavily involved in local party work, disseminating revolutionary literature, and organizing agitation among workers, peasants, and army conscripts. In an iron chest in her room, she had stored hundreds of copies of illegal proclamations, newspapers, and pamphlets as well as internal party documents. After the revolution, when the police in St. Petersburg staged a raid on her circle, they found this cache and called her in for questioning. Her response was to flee via her family home in Lublin, which was conveniently located in western Russia for border crossings with the Hapsburg Empire. We know from the memoirs of Lenin's wife that the Krylenkos—particularly Nicolai—knew how to smuggle people across the frontier in a hurry, and by 1908 Sofia was in France. Sometime in the summer of that year she became pregnant.

I have found only one photograph of her, taken before her flight. In her file, the Russian police describe her as dark blond, with her hair parted in the middle, with dark gray eyes, of medium height, and lean. She was reputed to be fiery and striking and the photograph does convey her uncompromising nature. It is a strong face, the face of someone determined and used to getting their own way, but not one lightened by humor, and with little or no trace of the skepticism we find in Max's eyes. Benjamin talked about "the astonishing narrowness of her stubborn character," and this insistence on hewing her own path and remaining faithful to her political ideals, not at all uncommon among revolutionaries of her generation, was to blight the lives of her children and to have tragic consequences for her.

Софія Васильева КРЫЛЕНКОВА

The French police reckoned that there were at least fifteen hundred Russian radicals in Paris around the time she arrived in the country, many of them in lodgings in Montparnasse. Rue Lalande, the street mentioned on André's birth certificate as Sofia's address, was located next to the famous Cimetière du Montparnasse, north of the intersection with rue Daguerre in a neighborhood known to be frequented by Russian students.

One hundred yards down the road on the corner was the house where Leon Trotsky had met his second wife a few years earlier. Number 22 had been under the surveillance of the Russian secret police for years and associates of the famous anarchist Prince Kropotkin used to stay there.

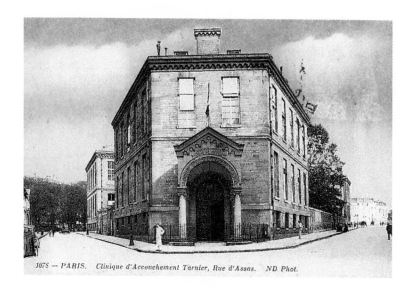

1078 — PARIS. *Clinique d'Accouchement Tarnier, Rue d'Assas.* ND Phot.

Situated at the quiet end of the street, above where the beauty parlors and the fitness centers peter out, 22 rue Lalande is today a surprisingly imposing and neatly maintained Second Empire building. Even allowing for changes over the years, its elegance suggests that while Sofia Krylenko may have been in exile, she was not starving. The Clinique Tarnier where André was born is less than a mile away. Late one September afternoon, I meandered through the cemetery to boulevard Raspail, then along rue Vavin and into rue d'Assas, tracing most of that long street southeast in the direction of Port-Royal, in order to find the Clinique Tarnier. There were only a few cars moving past on their way towards rue de Rennes. The shuttered windows of the apartment buildings, the approaching fall, and the sounds of a student party farther down the road all made a melancholy impression upon me. The Tarnier still looks uncannily as it does in a photograph of the era, solid and well-built—it had been constructed just a few years earlier as a maternity hospital for the Paris medical school. But the revolutionary idealism of four generations ago seemed a dim memory, Paris itself diminished by the energy draining out of its once proud republican spirit over the past century, its mood defensive and soured, the French Left no longer a beacon for the country, let alone the world.

In 1909, when André was born, Paris had regarded itself as the center of civilization and the future belonged to the Left. Or so many on the Left believed. It was the era of Joseph Conrad's *The Secret Agent*, of terrorist bombings and the assassination of empresses and presidents, and the police across Europe were nervous and looking out for anarchists. The Belgian police were especially well organized, and thanks to their files we know that after André's birth Sofia did indeed move with him to the industrial fortress city of Liège. Not an unusual choice: It was a major steel producer and home before the First World War to many Russians, most of them attending its mining and engineering school. Sofia's younger brother Vladimir was studying there and his presence may have been one draw for her. But Liège attracted Russians for another reason as well because it was a supplier of small arms for the revolutionary underground and the local police kept a "Russian" file for those they had under surveillance. Sofia's name is not listed there, but other records show her changing residence several times as she moved from

Montparnasse to prosperous Boulogne-sur-Seine, where she spent some months, and then across the Belgian border to the village of Tilff, a riverside rural retreat just outside Liège, where she probably rented rooms in a suburban villa. Given the depth of her political involvement in St. Petersburg, and from all we know about her later activities, I find it hard to imagine she was not still frequenting émigré revolutionary circles.

In these archives, I was also able for the first time to find out about the figure of de Meyer, and to my surprise, the man André thought was a "Belgian doctor" turns out to have been neither Belgian nor a doctor but a fellow Russian with a police file larger than Sofia's. Fittingly, his name shifts across archives and alphabets—sometimes de Mayer or de Meyer, sometimes von Meyer, and sometimes, in proletarian Russia, simply Meyer. Twenty-three years old in 1909—two years' Sofia's junior—Konstantin von Meyer (identified thus in his Russian papers) had been born into military nobility: His father was a retired general whose passion in life appears to have been painting dogs and hunting and battle scenes. Konstantin had moved to Belgium in 1909 and two years later—about the time when Max was listing himself in the U.K. census as a married man and a father—he was living openly with Sofia and her little boy. He had graduated from the St. Petersburg commercial college in 1907, or so he told the Belgian police, and left Russia the following year for Paris with an allowance from his father. In the spring and summer of 1909, he and a couple of blue-blooded friends had been on a bicycling tour in Spain when they had been detained and held in jail as anarchists. They had found themselves in the middle of a full-blown insurrection that had exploded in Barcelona; martial law had been imposed and for weeks afterwards the country had been under lockdown, with checkpoints everywhere. Was their presence there at that time a coincidence? It is hard to say. If so, was it also a coincidence that the address Konstantin gave for his stay in Paris the year before was a hotel on boulevard Saint-Marcel that happened to be where Lenin and his entourage would lodge briefly a few months later?

What clinches it surely is one last scrap of evidence. From Spain he had gone briefly to Geneva to drop off his bicycling companions. What was the address there? the Belgian police asked him later that year: 27 rue Caroline, he told them. As we know from other sources, this was the address of the Imprimerie Ouvrière, the main press used by Bolsheviks and other revolutionaries for their clandestine literature. The likelihood is thus that von Meyer was caught up in the activities of the Russian Social Democrats abroad and was the more valuable because he had not come to the attention of the police back home. He may have been doing someone—Sofia perhaps?—a favor by distributing illegal pamphlets in Spain, a well-known center of radical ideas with one of the most powerful anarchist movements in Europe. In any case, after their release, he said good-bye to his friends in Geneva and went to Liège, where in October 1909 he began studying at the university. In the autumn of 1911 Sofia became pregnant by him and moved with him into an apartment in a little brick house in town with a nice view of a suburban park, awaiting their baby. Three-year-old André was with them.

A few weeks before Sofia was due to give birth, her highly energetic and efficient mother came out from Russia to help. This was the redoubtable Olga Krylenko, whom Benjamin was to meet under very different circumstances in Moscow more than a decade later. Olga got there in time for the arrival of a little girl called Natalia, her first granddaughter, in June 1912. The following February, when she was old enough to travel, Natalia was taken back to Russia. Since we know that Sofia, Olga, and Konstantin also returned, it is probable that Natalia went with one of them. The really odd thing is that André did not. Instead, on December 9, 1912, he was brought to London — I do not know by whom — where he began his new life in England. He was three years and nine months old, with a stranger for a father and a dimming recollection of speaking French that explains why he regarded it later on as his mother tongue. It is a frustrating age, old enough to have fleeting memories — a vision of snow in a garden, a woman bicycling down a street — but too young to be able to make sense of them properly. He was never to live with his mother again, and he would only see her briefly on two occasions many years later.

Back in Russia, Sofia and Konstantin remained together. They had a second daughter, Katerina, in July 1914, and then got married that November, a couple of months after the outbreak of war, in a small church in St. Petersburg. I am guessing, since Sofia like many revolutionary activists of her generation did not attach much importance to marriage, that they did it for the children because Konstantin was on his way to the front. Or perhaps taking his name in some way facilitated her residence in the city. One of her witnesses at the ceremony was later a Bolshevik commander in the Caucasus, so she at least, and possibly her husband too, were faithful to their Leftist affiliation, even in church. Thereafter, Konstantin von Meyer disappears from the scene and all I have been able to ascertain is that he fought on past the collapse of Tsarist rule. As so often, on which side is unclear. The Krylenko family version that they gave Benjamin in Moscow in 1926 was that Konstantin had died fighting for the Bolsheviks, but by then they needed to say that. It is equally possible, given his family's background, that at some point he joined the Whites. His father, the painterly general, is said, according to one source, to have survived the revolution and ended up in Paris.

The First World War utterly transformed the prospects not only for Russia but for the Krylenko family when Sofia's younger brother Nicolai, who had until this point been studying law and serving occasionally as Lenin's chess partner, was catapulted almost overnight into a position of enormous power. The speed of his ascent is hard to comprehend. In 1916 he was arrested as a draft dodger; by late 1917, he was the commander in chief of the Russian armed forces.

This extraordinary turn of events came about because General Nikolai Dukhonin, his Tsarist predecessor, refused Lenin's order to open peace negotiations with the Germans. Ensign Krylenko, a committed Bolshevik, was appointed to replace him. It must have been one of the fastest promotions in history and its impact was immediate. Arriving at the Russian general staff headquarters at Mogilev with an escort of Bolshevik sailors, Krylenko forced Dukhonin's surrender and had the general brought aboard his train to talk. A large and angry crowd gathered outside, and when Krylenko refused to give him up, Dukhonin was dragged out and beaten to death. (Or, as in another version—eyewitness accounts diverge—he was shot.) It was one of the more egregious revolutionary lynchings and it made headlines across Europe before it was overtaken by the much larger news that Russia was pulling out of the war. As the Bolshevik delegation arrived to parley with the Germans at the great fortress in Brest-Litovsk, Dukhonin's comrades fled south to begin the White counterrevolution. An uneasy peace settled on the eastern front, and in March 1918, Krylenko left the army to set up a new system of revolutionary justice. It was the start of a career spanning nearly two decades at the top of the Soviet legal system that made him one of the most powerful, and most feared, figures in Russia. I wonder now whether the killing of Dukhonin, which he had witnessed at close quarters, in any way influenced his subsequent commitment to establishing revolutionary courts and thereby—as he at least saw it—rescuing socialist law from the taint of mob rule.

Especially in the early days, the Russian revolution had something of the quality of a family affair. Elena Krylenko worked for Maxim Litvinov in the Commissariat of Foreign Affairs. Her younger sister, Olga, was secretary to Politburo member Lev Kamenev. (Kamenev himself was married to Trotsky's sister, whom he had met at a Bundist gathering in Paris more than a decade earlier.) In 1918 Sofia found a position—presumably through her brother—running the office that supervised the new revolutionary tribunals on behalf of the All-Russia Central Executive Committee, the highest organ of Soviet government. She never joined the Bolsheviks, but that was no obstacle: most of her colleagues in the department were not Bolsheviks either. The revolution must have seemed initially to be the fulfillment of everything she had been working towards and she threw herself into it. Eastman described her as an "intemperate rebel"—he knew one when he saw one—who "went in for conspiratorial agitation in its most dangerous forms." On a requisitioning expedition in Kiev for the Bolsheviks, she narrowly escaped capture and execution by the Whites. But then her view of things changed, and changed dramatically. It happened when Bolshevik sailors rebelled against the Soviet regime at the naval base at Kronstadt in 1921 and the government suppressed the uprising at the cost of hundreds of lives. Sofia, like many others both inside and outside the party, was disturbed by this and felt that the violence of the response betrayed authoritarian tendencies on the part of the country's new rulers.[3]

Bolshevism was rather less of a united church than historians make out, and by this time it was not only the opposing parties who were critical of the regime. There were protests from the Left as well and many Bolsheviks openly attacked Lenin for selling the workers out and assailed his New Economic Policy for opening the country up to Western capitalism. They criticized the government's reliance on bureaucrats and experts, and questioned what had happened to the rule of the proletariat. Lenin was not impressed. He slammed what he called the "infantile disorder" of "left-wing communism" but that did not silence the dissenters. Among the most troublesome of the critics was a metalworker from the Urals, Gavril Ilyich Myasnikov, no bleeding-heart liberal but a longtime Bolshevik who in 1918 had orchestrated the Cheka murder of Grand Duke Michael Alexandrovich, the designated successor of Tsar Nicholas II. After Myasnikov continued to denounce the Bolshevik government, his revolutionary credentials failed to protect him, and he was expelled from the party, then arrested, and eventually sent abroad to Germany. There a new party had emerged called the Communist Workers Party of Germany (KAPD) as an ultra-Leftist counterweight to the official Communist Party of Germany (KPD). The KAPD felt that Lenin's USSR was not revolutionary enough—it was a halfway house, insufficiently proletarian: "Insofar as it calls for the expropriation of capitalists, it was a proletarian organization for the suppression of capitalism but insofar as it preserved parliamentarism, unions, the dictatorship of the party and of managers, it was a bourgeois entity created to preserve capitalism and to restore it." One implication was that the Moscow-based Comintern was the wrong vehicle for international Bolshevism: It was contaminated by its counterrevolutionary origins and likely to lead the workers of Europe to defeat. A purer, more revolutionary Comintern was needed—a Fourth International. Sofia's ideas ran on similar lines and she was energetically supporting the KAPD's efforts. If her family was worried, as Benjamin reported, they had cause to be. This kind of work on the extreme Left was not only dangerous for her; it was potentially lethal for those related to her back in Moscow.[4]

Not only was Sofia intransigent and extreme in her views but she was—as this suggests—reckless in a way only the utterly uncompromising could be. Having nearly gotten her sister Elena shot in Kiev in 1919—Elena had been arrested by troops looking for Sofia and was saved only at the last minute—she got her into serious trouble again three years later. Elena was in Italy working as a secretary for Maxim Litvinov, by now the Soviet deputy commissar of foreign affairs, at the Rapallo Conference. This diplomatic meeting is remembered chiefly for the rapprochement Litvinov helped to engineer, to everyone's astonishment, between Soviet Russia and Weimar Germany. It was the moment the USSR came in from the cold, and alarm at the agreement could be found not only in capitalist circles in England, France, and the United States but among the dissident communists as well. For them Rapallo confirmed their worst suspicions about what Lenin was doing—moving away from the true revolutionary path by playing the same old diplomatic games as his predecessors. Sofia asked Elena to use the diplomatic bag to bring a letter from "an old friend" back to Russia.

When the letter was intercepted by the OGPU, it turned out to
be KAPD agitprop. The OGPU was too adroit to overlook a gift
like that, and two years later, when Elena sought permission to
leave Moscow to go to London with Eastman, she was called in
for interrogation and found that what they wanted to question
her about was Sofia:

> I spent four hours in the [O]GPU that day…As I did not have
> much to say, I had to compose quite a discourse — about my
> sister's being critical of the present party leaders, about her
> calling me and my other sister, who were "honest Soviet
> workers," bourgeois and philistine, about her having always
> been in rebellion against anything established. I oiled thick
> all this sort of thing because if I did not, it would seem I had
> things to hide, and because I knew that my sister's psychosis
> made her safe. She was at the moment in an insane asylum,
> and had formed a protective habit of actually going crazy and
> getting committed whenever her rather fantastic conspirato-
> rial activities came near to detection.[5]

Whether or not Sophia was really mentally ill, it is impossible to say; but this is only the first of several sources that make
it quite clear she stayed more than once inside psychiatric institutions, sometimes voluntarily and later against her will. In
the end, Elena was only allowed to leave Russia on the condition that she promised to spy on her sister. She agonized over
whether to make the commitment until Litvinov, a worldly
man, told her not to be stupid: Since she was not intending to
come back to the USSR, she should say she would do it and then
forget about the whole business.

For the remaining family in Moscow, forgetting what Sofia
was up to was not so easy. The OGPU boss Feliks Dzerzhin-

sky was increasingly confident that Myasnikov's supporters
within Russia presented no threat to the Soviet regime. But
he was still worried about Germany, where Sofia was spending more and more time. She had been identified as one of the
links between the KAPD and Myasnikov's Workers' Group
in Russia, and a speech she made in Berlin at an international
conference found its way into their files. To judge from other
OGPU reports, she may also have been involved in funding the
German party.

It was in precisely these years that the teenage André's one
or two meetings with his mother must have taken place, the
years when she was living in Berlin while plotting a revolution
against the revolution, dodging the German police, evading
Soviet spies, and leading a life in which the lunatic asylum could
seem like a refuge. Their main encounter seems to have been
in the summer of 1926, just before André started at Cambridge.
The KAPD had had its day by then: Official German-Soviet
relations were blossoming, dissident communism was being
squeezed in both Germany and the USSR, and the KAPD had
split into competing factions. Sofia met her son in Berlin and
they spent an afternoon together. He was now seventeen and
she asked him whether he would go back to the Soviet Union
with her. To her annoyance, he hesitated. For the English ado-
lescent he had become, a young man who liked rowing and was
passionate about poetry, with a growing attraction to conservatism and as far as we know with no interest in revolutionary
politics, no Russian, and not much knowledge of the country,
the chief consideration must have been working out how not to
disappoint her.

I try to picture his mother, who despite her passionately
held revolutionary views seems to have had much of the grande

dame in her manner, and beside her the hesitant, correctly dressed son, *plus anglais que les anglais*, about to enter Cambridge and the world of Kenneth Pickthorn, T. S. Eliot, and the Earl of Lincoln. After they parted, André went back to England and it is scarcely surprising that he found it hard to settle into the household at Makepeace Avenue, where Dad was an infant, enjoying the care of an infinitely solicitous mother. Sofia was evidently still in Germany at the end of 1926, which was when Benjamin went to Moscow, but some time after that she went back to the Soviet Union and to her family there. From Russia, she may have corresponded with André intermittently into the 1930s, but I wonder what she wrote about because to judge from how little he appears to have known sixty years later, most of her life was a closed book to him. By the century's end, he seems either not to have known or to have forgotten whether his mother had been Nicolai Krylenko's sister or cousin, how many daughters she had, and the nationality of her husband.[6]

In 1935 Nicolai Krylenko, the People's Commissar for Justice, was seemingly at the height of his power. He was the chief sponsor of the Soviet chess federation and the promoter of the great international competitions between the wars, an Esperanto propagandist, an ardent mountaineer whose favorite pastime was climbing in the Pamirs, and a ferocious and pitiless prosecutor who had thrown his lot in with Stalin. But Kremlin court politics were as treacherous as ever and behind the scenes he was locked in a long and bitter power struggle with the OGPU's successor, the NKVD, over the nature of law in the Soviet system. Krylenko sought to advance a system of regularized revolutionary justice whereas the secret police preferred to use more arbitrary and less public methods, and however far-fetched the difference might seem today, given that both served a totalitarian dictatorship, there were real winners and losers within the bureaucracy of government. The Soviet secret police's interest in Sofia thus served a double purpose because the information that it collected on her was also useful to them for targeting her brother, an altogether larger and more important catch.

Krylenko's archrival was the lawyer Andrey Vyshinsky, a former Menshevik and by birth a Polish Catholic—two considerable handicaps in Stalin's Russia for which he compensated by acquiring a well-deserved reputation for harshness. When he took charge of the first major trials of the Terror, his bloodthirsty talk of "mad dogs," "degenerates," and "vermin" made him as notorious as Krylenko had been in the 1920s. The activities of Sofia—and indeed of Elena too—gave Krylenko's enemies plenty of ammunition to use whenever Stalin gave the green light. Nicolai's brother Vladimir, the former mining student in Liège, had already been arrested in the terrible summer of 1937—a portent—and on January 31, 1938, Nicolai was accused in the usual fantastic fashion of sabotage, of creating a subversive organization, of plotting with Nikolai Bukharin to assassinate party leaders, and of paving the way for an invasion of the country by fascist states. Krylenko was said to have been intriguing against his own comrades even before 1917. There followed six months of incarceration and interrogations, confessions, and retractions, during which time the NKVD swept through the Commissariat of Justice that he headed, eliminating dozens of jurists. The Military Collegium of the Soviet Supreme Court decided his fate in twenty minutes at the end of July; the protocol of the proceedings was nineteen lines long and he was shot almost immediately in the Lubyanka. One of the main architects of the Bolshevik show trial, indeed one of its leading legal theorists, thus fell victim to the system he had helped to construct. From what we know of comparable cases, he may have been threatened with the death of his relatives if he did not admit to his crimes. And as in other cases, once he had confessed, the remaining Krylenkos and Meyers, or at least those still alive at that date, were at risk too. As Trotsky's first wife, who suffered in this way, remarked of Stalin to a confidante: "In Tsarist times they did not take away the children...But this one—he wants to annihilate everyone."

The original file on Sofia's arrest and detention, if it still exists, remains in the hands of the FSB, the current Russian security service, and may only be viewed by a close family member without any notes being taken or copies made. But the State Archives of the Russian Federation, which are accessible, contain the rehabilitation file that was opened during the process of de-Stalinization, when, as her sister Elena had requested, Sofia's case was reviewed. From it we learn that in 1935—the year communication had ceased between the Krylenkos and their sister Elena in America—Sofia had been sent to a psychiatric institution to the south of Moscow, the Yakovenko Hospital in the village of Mesherskoye. This was a pioneering establishment that had been founded by a radical doctor at the end of the nineteenth century. Leo Tolstoy had once visited and Anton Chekhov admired it. The hospital was set in a leafy estate with a lake and tree-lined avenues down which the inmates were encouraged to perambulate. Sofia was allowed to rent rooms outside the estate and used to take walks with her dogs to the delight of the village children to whom she appeared like a lady of prerevolutionary days. The timing suggests that Nicolai had placed her there, sensing that his own position was in jeopardy, although whether he did so to protect her, as some in the family believed, or himself, or both, we cannot know. Equally suggestive is the fact that she was released in the spring of 1938, once he was under arrest. Back in Moscow, she was without work. Perhaps the hospital had been a place of safety.

It certainly seems so in the light of what happened next. On the evening of May 6, 1938, she took a shortcut to get from her apartment in downtown Moscow to the nature reserve where she liked to walk. Unfortunately this led her through the camp of the Comrade Stalin NKVD cavalry detachment and she was arrested. It seems a lethal kind of mistake to have made, a bit like walking deliberately into the lion's den. It also seems odd that the distance from her apartment to the forest, Serebryany Bor, was more than ten miles—not so much a stroll as the strenuous walk of someone compelled to exercise for their own peace of mind. Perhaps Sofia was not entirely aware of what she was doing. She had been released from Yakovenko only two months earlier and the NKVD now ordered a psychiatric examination and sent her to the Serbsky Institute, which was the main supplier of forensic psychiatry to the Moscow criminal courts. (The institute had a close relationship with the NKVD and much later, in the 1960s and '70s, it would become notorious for its role in the incarceration of dissidents in psychiatric institutions.) After being held there for several weeks, she was examined by a team of four doctors.

Their report is included in the file and it brings us, in what were obviously circumstances of enormous strain and pressure, closer to her than any other document I have been able to find, because it includes some of the things she said, at least as they were written down. She told the doctors that she had been treated in psychiatric hospitals before Yakovenko, that she had been diagnosed with schizophrenia there, and that "her relatives had mistreated and starved her." She was described as being below average height, with a low appetite. Her "visible mucous membranes" were pale and the heart was enlarged on the left side. There were no abdominal abnormalities, her reflexes were good, and the Wassermann reaction for syphilis was negative. Her examiners reported as follows:

> The subject is oriented according to time and place and considers herself mentally healthy. She exhibits a haughty behavior, answers questions with great disdain, and never answers some questions at all. She believes that her placement at the institute is inappropriate and insists on immediate discharge. She expresses fragmentary delusions of grandeur and persecution…Apparently auditory hallucinations are present—the subject systematically plugs her ears with paper and cotton wool "so that the noise in the unit does not interfere with thinking." In the institute she keeps aloof, sometimes refuses food; she was fed via a feeding tube with great difficulty once. In recent days, she eats only sour cream and cranberries, claiming that "the water is greasy and causes vomiting: everything else clutters and hinders thinking and brings us closer to animals."

The four NKVD doctors concurred that she was schizophrenic—whatever that really meant—and recommended she be sent to a psychiatric hospital for compulsory treatment. She was still in the hands of the NKVD when Nicolai was shot at the end of July, and the following month the NKVD decided to follow the recommendation of the doctors at the institute. As a result, along with her daughter Katerina and her sister Olga, and possibly one of Nicolai's children, Sofia was sent to Kazan.

If the Serbsky was, in the words of one scholar of Soviet psychiatry, "the gates of hell," Kazan was hell itself for someone in Sofia's predicament. Five hundred miles east of Moscow, the city housed what a later writer describes as "the oldest and most terrible" psychiatric prison hospital in the USSR. In 1935 a ward had been created there for convicted criminals and in 1939 the whole institution was taken over by the NKVD because Serbsky had become so crowded. This takeover marked the first step towards the much more extensive involvement of psychiatry in the Soviet police state after the war: The commandant and doctors were all NKVD employees, barbed wire and high brick walls surrounded the hospital, and all communication with the outside world was strictly censored. It was very different from the leafy Yakovenko estate and there were horrors inside; indeed according to one source, in the winter of 1941–1942 all the patients there died of hunger and cold. Sofia may have been among the victims—whether she was interned there or living with her sister and daughter, in any case she did not survive the war and she died in what her file describes as a prison hospital. Long after her death and after years of forced residence in Kazan, her daughter Katerina was eventually released and allowed to return to Moscow where much much later, when she was an old lady, she would finally meet the half brother she had never seen. The eldest daughter, Natalia, who had been born in Liège in 1912, was alive in the mid-1950s, but her subsequent fate is unknown.

As the Cold War ended, and an aging André learned more about his Russian connections, the putative Hapsburg officer father that he had tried out on Dad was jettisoned and replaced with a new version. André came to believe that his real father had actually been Sofia's husband, Konstantin von Meyer, and that he had been von Meyer and Sofia's first child so that their two daughters back in Russia were his full sisters. In the last few years of his life, he began using the von Meyer name and patronymic.

The idea that he was descended from Konstantin von Meyer, the son of Russian military nobility of distinguished lineage, and not Mordkhel Mazower, the typewriter-selling suburban ex-revolutionary of modest Russian Jewish stock from the Pale, would have seemed attractive to the elderly André, given what we know of his political opinions. It was also not impossible, especially as it turns out that Konstantin was indeed living in Paris in early 1908 and 1909 around the time that Sofia became pregnant with André, and in lodgings on the other side of the Jardin du Luxembourg, less than a mile away. Konstantin may even have known Sofia earlier, in Russia. Had he in fact followed her to Paris in the spring of 1908 after her flight from St. Petersburg?

Pater semper incertus est — the father is always uncertain — was a long-standing principle in Roman law, enduring for centuries into the era of DNA testing. If Max was not André's father, that might help explain André's sense of discomfort in Oakeshott Avenue. But if Konstantin was, some other questions remain to be answered. Although André was born in early 1909, Konstantin and Sofia only started living together in 1911. Why did they wait until André was nearly three — odd behavior on the face of it if he was their son, given that they were in the same country for much of that time and not living far apart. And even more oddly, why did they send him to England in December 1912 rather than bringing him back to Russia with them and their daughter? The family story that it was too difficult to smuggle him in does not hold water: André had Russian papers when he was sent to England, so his status was regular, and even if getting him back across the imperial border would have been awkward for Sofia, who may have left Russia illegally, Konstantin's papers were in order and he could have traveled back with his son without hindrance. So could André's grandmother. Or was André sent to London because Konstantin felt embarrassed about fathering a son out of wedlock? But he did not feel embarrassment about Natalia, his daughter, who was also born before her parents got married. Indeed he and Sofia did not marry until some time after the birth of their *second* daughter. The inescapable conclusion is that neither Konstantin nor Sofia wanted to keep André with them.

Equally puzzling is why Max—who had a widowed mother and two younger brothers in Vilna to worry about, none of them well-off—would have agreed to bring André up if he wasn't his son. Max comes across as a man who took his responsibilities very seriously, but he was not, I think, someone to incur unnecessary burdens voluntarily—he had enough of his own, especially knowing he would be traveling abroad on business for many months of the year. So while the idea was not impossible, it did not seem to make much more sense than the alternative, especially since Max and Konstantin would seem to have had next to nothing in common.

Except, maybe, affection for André's mother. Sofia had left Russia in a hurry in 1907 because of her revolutionary activities, and she and Max met when they were both in exile. There is a story that Max was in love with Sofia, even that he may have proposed to her. It is impossible to say how true that was but what is certain is that on the 1911 census form he says he was married, which would seem to refer to Sofia. They were not married, but perhaps Max at one time wished they were. Had they, perhaps informally, become engaged? Could it be that after Sofia had André in the spring of 1909, Max believed the baby to be his? Or even if he did not, did he feel, at any rate, that he owed her and her baby — whomever the father was — some kind of care, especially as both his life and hers had been so fraught with flight and unpredictability? Later that year he went to London and found a job, perhaps anticipating that mother and son would join him only to find that in fact Sofia had no such intention. While he was giving up his life as an activist, she was intensifying hers. A few months later she began living with Konstantin in Liège — which may or may not have been their first encounter. Then she became pregnant and had his daughter.

The scenario I find most plausible is that several months after the birth of Natalia in Liège, with Sofia under the stress of trying to care for her baby daughter, and with no obvious means of support, either Sofia's mother brought André to London for Max to care for or Max collected André himself on his way back from one of his business trips to Russia. At this point, it seems hard to believe he did not think the boy was his and that André needed him. Konstantin evidently raised no objection, and neither did Sofia. Perhaps she was ill, after giving birth, and her mother felt it was best for Sofia to focus on herself and her daughter. The fact that Olga had made the long journey from Russia to Belgium suggests to me that she thought her daughter was in danger of being overwhelmed. Perhaps they all felt André would have been in the way in the new setup back in St. Petersburg. By 1914, at the very latest, when Sofia married Konstantin, Max would have definitively realized that she had made other choices. The simple story that Dad knew, the family version as it were—that Sofia had gone mad and died before the First World War—perhaps thus embodied symbolically the emotional core of the truth of the situation as it seemed to Max. When the war broke out that summer, André was in England and after that it was too late for second thoughts.[7]

Is it possible that, despite recognizing André officially, Max harbored doubts about his paternity? André once explained why he had stormed out into the garden in Oakeshott Avenue and chopped down that chestnut tree. He said that it was because he had been overwhelmed by the impact of the news when Max, ailing and feeling he was near death, had confided to him that he was not really his father. It is a powerful and dramatic image, a moment of revelation and clarity—an assertion of separation, a symbol of deliberate emasculation, a literal uprooting. And it would seem to strengthen the idea that Max had let André know he was not his father after all. The tree was chopped down; that is sure: Dad remembered the episode too. But as for the reason, it would be a lot easier to be confident it all actually happened as André said if we did not have that other example of his hyperactive imagination where his genealogy is concerned, the story of the bogus military officer, von Hörnigk, casting its shadow. Because that felled tree too clears the way for André to join the ranks of the aristocracy and to escape the shadow of his Jewish forebears.

It is hard to know for sure what and whom to believe: Those who knew the truth are long dead and we shall never be able to dispel the silence that enshrouded Sofia and enveloped André his entire life. If Sofia knew who his father was, she seems to have taken her secrets to the grave. A broken childhood and an uncertain parentage left what he once described as "a formidable void...an uncomfortable emptiness" that nothing ever quite filled, neither Cambridge, nor the myths of nobility that came and went, and certainly not the charged ruminations on world historical conspiracy that posited a logic where none exists.

In *The Red Thread*, André sheltered behind his mother's name. Yet his mother had spent her entire life on the fringe of the revolutionary Left and what united them was certainly not politics. By 1922, she was so far to the left of Lenin that she saw Bolshevism itself as an instrument of capitalism; her son in contrast espoused the most extreme form of anti-Semitic Catholicism, settled in Franco's Spain, and ended up intellectually on the far right. What they shared was a propensity for ideological extremism, an attraction to secrecy and the conspiratorial worldview, and perhaps too the combination of self-pity, stubbornness, and self-romanticization that often accompanied them. For both, the seeming polarization of the struggle for world power between communism and capitalism was an illusion; both believed that it fell to a penetrating and courageous few to see through the conventional hypocrisies of bourgeois life to the horrible underlying realities. Clutching at these esoteric certainties perhaps became for André a way of dealing with the sense he had of being unmoored by the storms of history, his form of reaction to living the aftermath of revolution. In an autobiographical essay, written a couple of years before his death, he described himself as "a piece of flotsam from the remote shipwreck of imperial Russia." He died, aged ninety-five, in 2005 and lies today in the Zentralfriedhof in

Vienna. But his uneasy, ambivalent relationship to Max is preserved in his writings: the typescript of *The Red Thread* includes among its dedicatees "my Jewish foster-father, M.M.," and as I feel I still have only the very haziest sense of André's character, I find it impossible to tell whether he intended this to be a genuine tribute or a last grim joke of revenge — or most likely something of both.

CHAPTER TWELVE

Frouma

It is a summer morning. The bedroom doors are open to the garden but the curtains are partially drawn and the room seems dark. I have stepped inside — outside it is warm and sunny — and I come to the large, high bed with its pale coverlet and open my cupped hands to free a red admiral that I have caught, and it flutters around looking for plants. This is my treat for Frouma, and because she is old and lying in bed, I probably thought she was ill and felt sorry that she could not enjoy the glorious weather, and I remember she laughed and clapped her hands. I am five or six years old and this is my sole memory of Dad's mother.

This little scene must have taken place in 1963 or 1964 in the apartment in West Hill Court that was her home for the last decade of her life. Gardens with their well-watered lawns smelling of mown grass descended to shady flower beds at the bottom of the property where it abutted the Heath; sedums and buddleia flowered below her windows and the warm flagstones attracted the butterflies. Hidden away round the side were secret paths and abandoned tennis courts behind the garages that had survived the disappearance of the old mansion that once stood on the site. It was always very quiet outside, as if no one else was around, although voices carried across the ponds from the Heath on the other side.

There is no question that Frouma was the one who turned 20 Oakeshott Avenue into a home, and the warmth she generated around her lasted long after her death. An old Bundist, a former comrade of Max's, wrote to Dad later that she was "the most gentle and affectionate person we met in our wanderings." My cousin Patrick remembered her as *une vieille dame adorable*, deeply intuitive and understanding, one of the two key figures in his life — *une femme de tête* (which is an untranslatable expression conveying independence, wisdom, and strength of mind all in one). And one spring afternoon just a year or so ago, my friend Paul, with whom I was sitting outside Le Monde on Broadway and 112th, introduced me to Anna Kisselgoff, a redoubtable elderly Upper West Side lady who passed by our table and whose eyes lit up when she heard my name because, it turned out, Frouma had let her stay on her couch on a brief teenage visit to London in the spring of 1955. That was sixty years in the past, but a smile spread across Anna's face as she recalled Frouma's hospitality and charm. She could still faintly remember the house, the staircase in the hall, the simple small dark living room, not lavish but comfortable and welcoming. Later we met again to trace the surprisingly durable web of émigré solidarities dating back decades that helped us understand how she had ended up there, a web linking Bundists and Mensheviks across borders and time that had connected her family and mine since before the revolution. Max was not a cold man, but he was bowed down by misfortune and illness and dashed hopes, and given increasingly to depression and melancholy. It was Frouma whose vitality invigorated the home of the Mazowers and whose energy kept the family together and passed on a lesson about the importance of this that Dad never forgot.

Frouma Toumarkine was one of eight siblings, five girls and three boys, members of a close-knit clan of moderately prosperous Russian Jews. Her parents both lived long lives—long enough to see the total transformation of their country. Moise Toumarkine, her father, had been born in the year the Crimean War broke out in an empire where the fields were still tilled by serfs; he died in Moscow in 1941, months before the German invasion. Her mother, Maria Berlinraut, who died at nearly eighty, came from a merchant family in Minsk that did well enough to obtain the coveted right to reside in Moscow. Their children were born from the mid-1880s on, and Frouma, who arrived in 1892, was the fourth of them, and the eldest of the three who eventually made their homes in the West. They were a physically impressive and attractive bunch: Visiting her brother Tsalya in Brezhnev's Moscow in the mid-1970s when he must have been around eighty years old, I still remember how the old Kremlin pediatrician stood out from the drabness of the apartment like an eagle, with his stern handsome face, piercing eyes, and aquiline nose.

Moise was a timber merchant who purchased concessions to tracts of the vast pine forests that covered much of western Russia, one of the few ways of making money that was open to enterprising Jews in the empire who did not wish to remain confined inside the life of the shtetl. He took leases on forests around Smolensk, and he would then build a temporary sawmill and arrange for the timber to be shipped downriver between April and November, the months in which the ice on the Dnieper thawed and traffic was possible. According to John Croumbie Brown's 1885 *Forests and Forestry in Poland, Lithuania,*

the Ukraine, and the Baltic Provinces of Russia, the Smolensk forests were the least accessible of all those around the Dnieper
and the real expense came in getting the logs from the woods to
the riverside. Tough and resourceful outdoorsmen like Moise
played an important role in the Russian economy in clearing
lands onto which farmers could move.

It was grueling work, and Toumarkine père, a short athletic
man with great physical energy and a love for the forests, did
not come by his money easily. One estate alone could take a
week to ride around to survey, and once work began, the first
thing he needed to do was to construct a small settlement for
the workers to live in, surrounded by a stockade. Each time
they moved, another timber house had to be built for his family and their servants. For small children it was an exciting,
transient, and remote life that brought them into contact with
nature at its wildest. It must have been from the Toumarkines,

and from his grandfather in particular—the grandfather that he never met nor even I think ever spoke with—that Dad inherited a love of the countryside that was one of his greatest pleasures, and the love of gardening too. Moise did not write much to his daughter after she settled in London—that he left to his wife—but when he did, it was about the vegetables in the dacha where they spent the summers, and the importance of exercise, and the unhealthiness of urban life.

Forestry had its dangers: Houses sometimes caught fire, not always by accident, and on at least one occasion, robbers came and they had to hand over the silverware knowing that there were no police for miles. Moise was not easily cowed—at various points in his long life he stared down anti-Semitic officials and Bolshevik commissars—but for child-rearing the town had obvious advantages, and Frouma and her siblings were sent off to the nearest city, Smolensk, where their father rented an apartment, and maids and a Swiss governess looked after them.

There Frouma received a middle-class Russian education to complement the domestic skills in sewing, dressmaking, and household management that her immensely competent and affectionate mother passed on. The children went to the local gymnasium rather than to one of the Jewish private schools that had sprung up to cater to new immigrants and this gave Frouma a formal education of the kind Max never enjoyed. Smolensk was different from Grodno or Vilna. It lay outside the Pale of Settlement and had a fairly small Jewish population. Russian was the main language of the town and the language of Frouma's education, and in this she was typical of her generation and class of Russian Jews, those born outside the Pale with some money, who generally grew up more shaped by Russian traditions than their parents. She entered Kiev University shortly before the war and marriage interrupted her studies, and unlike her mother's writing style, hers was that of an educated woman. The family was Leftist in its sympathies: Her brother Lev was a Bolshevik known to the police, and so were her older sisters Fenya and Ida. Her mother initially greeted the fall of the Romanovs with rejoicing. During the First World War, her siblings left the Bolsheviks and joined the Mensheviks, and later on the Soviet authorities regarded them all with mistrust for that reason.

In 1914, at twenty-two, Frouma signed up as an auxiliary nurse to help the war effort, and thus met her first husband. Alexander Baltermants, a much older man, was a medical officer in the Tsarist army. He had seen the world—he had formerly been posted in Cairo—and he too had Jewish origins. But his family was wealthier than hers—his father was a prominent banker from Vilna—and unlike hers it downplayed its faith and played up its money. Baltermants liked to gamble—the characteristic vice of the Russian upper classes and a means for him of emulating them perhaps. If one is to judge from the little leather album in which Frouma kept her most precious pictures, she does not appear to have remembered him with affection for he does not appear in it at all, and the first page, marked "1920," starts off with photos of Max as a young man. There is, however, a studio portrait of Baltermants that she must have kept for their daughter, Ira, and it is enough to convey his spirit and dash in happier times. It shows him as a still youthful army officer in 1894 in Kharkov, handsome in his uniform, the embodiment of an ambitious young man of means, bearing, and social polish rising through the ranks of the Russian ancien régime despite his Jewish origins. Not even his daughter tried to disguise his self-centeredness, his suspect charm, and his complete lack of dependability. "My father was the second of four brothers," wrote Ira, "all rather alike; cold-eyed, blond, handsome, with something feline about the high cheekbones and slanted eyes; undeniably attractive, but not faces to meet with comfort in a dark alley or to turn to in trouble."

Revolution and parenthood highlighted the mismatch. An army doctor's wife in a small garrison town, Frouma was nine hundred kilometers from home when their daughter was born in September 1916 in the middle of the war. Although they called her Ira—Irina—which meant peace, the coming years brought everything but, and Ira was barely a year old when news of the revolution arrived and the troops mutinied. Baltermants was carried off, narrowly escaping being lynched by his own men. He reemerged in Moscow months later wearing the uniform of the Red Army—Frouma had taken Ira there for safety and to be near her relatives—and it quickly became clear that the chaos of the times suited him. He took over the grand apartment of a departing British diplomat for them, but his plans to resume his medical career were endlessly deferred for the gambling tables. Frouma's family openly disapproved of his behavior and politics: His political views appear to have been more ambiguous than theirs and altogether less serious. In early 1919 he left again—to fight against the Whites in the Ukraine, he told them, until alarming hints came from official quarters that he had disappeared en route to the front along with a consignment of medical supplies. It was at this point that someone the family knew in the Kremlin obtained travel permits for Frouma and her younger sister Natalie—Nata, never a person to be trifled with, was later to become a colonel in the Red Army—for seats on one of the first trains to leave Moscow for the south. Their mother was already in the Crimea, but I think probably their departure was hastened by the rumors that Baltermants had joined the White side, rumors that could have made remaining in Moscow hazardous.

They left quickly, not knowing when or if they would return, carrying little more than Ira, her doll, and some hidden valuables. It was an extremely perilous time to travel, and as the three of them journeyed down across Russia and the Ukraine they passed through countryside that was in a state of complete anarchy, and they were held up at checkpoints by armed men whose loyalty was often obscure: Bolsheviks, Whites, anarchists, and others scrutinized the papers of those wealthy or well-connected enough to be traveling by train and shot spies, black marketeers, escaping aristocrats, or simply people whose political sympathies they mistrusted. Young women traveling without a male escort were especially vulnerable, and on one occasion, a woman Frouma and Nata were traveling with was taken out of the carriage and shot next to the tracks.

By the time they reached the Crimea it was no less hazardous, with the area changing hands every few months amid the massacres and counter-massacres that marked the endgame of the Russian Civil War. They found their mother holed up in a seaside villa crowded with uprooted families in the spa town of Yevpatoria, a prewar resort. (Alisa Rosenbaum, better known later on as Ayn Rand, the high priestess of American anticommunism and the free market, remembered the experience of attending school there — she too had fled south with her family — as like "living on a battlefield.") Before long, the region was taken over by General Anton Denikin's desperate army of anti-Bolsheviks, making their last stand in southern Russia after a wildly fluctuating few months that had seen them push close to Moscow before being driven back by the Red Army. They were in a terrified, vengeful mood, looking to punish any Bolshevik sympathizers. Frouma had found work in the local council. Fortunately she was off sick on the day the Whites came in because when they entered the town hall, they lined up everyone working there and shot them.

And it was there that Baltermants turned up for the last time — the few family stories about him revolve around mysterious disappearances and reappearances — released from White Guard captivity on the point of death. His daughter, Ira, wrote many years later:

> Nothing of that hot, endless afternoon remains in my conscious memory, but burned deep into the core of my mind is the picture of two men carrying in the stretcher, and the dying man lying on it covered with an army greatcoat, for all the heat of the day. They carry him past a woman who stands silent and a child who wails for the pink silk dress

she has been promised to wear "when your father comes home"...He died that night. Of wounds and exhaustion, my grandmother gave out, of cholera, ran the horrified whisper round the villa. The two loyal orderlies who had brought him home to die through two embattled armies, stayed to help my mother bury him in the old Tartar cemetery outside the walls. But they would not even risk remaining at the villa for the rest of the night and she never learned their names.

The loyal orderlies, the Tartar cemetery — such touches give the scene its poignancy. But in the spring of 1920 Ira was three years old, so her memory would not have been much help and what she knew about the grim years of the civil war she had gotten thirdhand, told to her not by her mother, who spoke very little about that period in her life, nor by her aunt Nata, who had been there too, but by her youngest aunt, Niura, many years later in Paris. The pink silk dress has the ring of truth but the rest has, in Ira's fashion, been romanticized. I have a copy of Baltermants's death certificate — it was among the handful of papers Frouma made sure she took with her when she left the USSR a few years later — and it puts a slightly different complexion on things:

THE YEVPATORIAN JEWISH COMMUNAL AUTHORITY hereby certifies that, on April 28, 1920, in the city of Yevpatoria, the Red Army doctor Stepan Yakovlevich Baltermants (otherwise known as Shapsel Yakovlevich) died and was buried in a Jewish cemetery, after having been taken prisoner by the White Guards. According to documents formerly presented to the Communal Authority, Dr. Baltermants did not serve in the armies of Denikin and Vrangel but spent his time as a prisoner in a staging-point hospital, where he suffered from spotted, abdominal, and recurring typhus, while being subjected to disgraceful treatment. He was freed several days before his death. He died of exhaustion after contracting cholera.

One of the things this tells us that is unmentioned by Ira — who like her father found no pride in her ancestral faith — is that his death was registered with the Jewish communal authorities and he was buried in the Jewish cemetery. But it tells us other things too — or tries to. In fact, one can almost feel the extreme care with which the document has been worded. The dead man is said to have served in the Red Army and this is underlined by the explicit denial that he fought for the Whites. Was the denial necessary because back in Moscow in 1924, suspicions would have attached to any man who found himself in the Crimea once the Bolsheviks pulled out? Or because the suspicion was that Baltermants in particular had ended up with the Whites? Ira described him as a gambler, a man for whom the revolution itself was just another turn of the wheel, which is basically what survived of his reputation in the Toumarkine family after his death. When I asked one of my cousins in Paris about Baltermants, he knew virtually nothing about him except a label handed down through two generations — he was, said Patrick, "an adventurer."

I think of Baltermants dying there, watched over by his wife and daughter. At least he received a proper burial, which was something to be thankful for in those times. And perhaps this thought occurs to me because his name reminds me of the circumstances in which across the peninsula, near the town of Kerch, another Baltermants, a nephew of his, was to achieve renown in the midst of an even more brutal war two decades later.

This was Dmitri Baltermants, who became one of the most famous war photographers in the world for his work documenting the German invasion of the USSR. It was at the beginning of 1942 when he flew into the Crimea that the events occurred which made his reputation.[1] Kerch lay at the very southern tip of the eastern front and the Wehrmacht had just pulled back from it. They had held it for only six weeks, but that was all the time that Reinhard Heydrich's Einsatzgruppe D had needed to round up the town's several thousand Jews. They had been driven in trucks to a nearby village over several days and lined up in an antitank ditch several hundred meters long in front of submachine guns. Their corpses were still lying there in a frozen field only a little way from the airstrip when Baltermants touched down. He arrived on the scene to see grief-stricken townspeople, wrapped against the cold, trying to identify the bodies.

As he shot two rolls of film, he tried to make sense of what was in front of him. Nothing was clear: If they were captured Red Army soldiers, how was it that their relatives were there looking for them? Why were there so many children and women? Now we know that he had come upon the gruesome work of the German execution squads that had been systematically shooting Jews across the occupied Soviet Union, the murderous pioneers of what was to metamorphose over the coming year into a completely unprecedented policy of industrialized mass killing. But in that field on the Kerch peninsula there was nothing manmade except an antitank trench filled with dead bodies. Baltermants's now iconic images show mud, snow, water, and sky, a landscape polluted by man, and something of the horrified bafflement and slowly dawning comprehension that I imagine he and his comrades felt that day still emanates from them.

Widowed before she was thirty, and with nothing for her remaining in the Crimea, Frouma took her daughter back to Moscow where the city was slowly returning to life under its new rulers. With the help of one of her sisters, she managed to find a lowly position in a government ministry. Her family had never thought much of her first husband, but they gladly helped her now, and it was through another sister that she and Max met. This must have been in 1922, or thereabouts, the time of Lenin's New Economic Policy, and there was a British trade mission in Moscow, even though there were as yet no formal diplomatic relations between the two countries. "Citizen

Mazower" (according to his Soviet permit) had given up his association with the Yost Typewriter Company and was traveling on behalf of a Sheffield steel manufacturer that made equipment that they had been exporting to Russia for decades. He took a room at the old Hotel Europe in Petrograd, the grandest in the city, and looked up his brother and some of his old friends. One of them, a man he had known before the revolution, was the husband of Frouma's sister Ida. And so, on a visit to Moscow, he and Frouma were introduced.[2]

They did not have much time to get to know each other, but people made big decisions fast in those days and both of them were decisive. Frouma could see behind Max's taciturn exterior and she could tell that even though, like her first husband, he was nearly twenty years older than she was, that was about all the two men had in common: Max was not as dashing as Baltermants, and he did not have the monied background; far from aspiring to the romance of an army uniform he was an antimilitarist, much more dependable and no less courageous. His political views were in keeping with her family's. But his combination of loyalty, competence, and realism were probably more important than politics: He was not the type of man to leave her for the gambling tables or anything else. And underneath the reserve, there was a dry humor and warmth and a capacity for commitment. She knew next to nothing about England—her family's ties were with Germany and France—but by 1924 it did not take genius to see that life in Bolshevik Russia as the widow of a suspect former Tsarist officer was not going to be easy. Anyway, Frouma had always had an adventurous side.

For his part, Max must have suspected that the thaw in relations between the USSR and England would not last, and that conditions might soon become impossible for him in Russia. He had savings in London and in Frouma he knew he had found the person to help him make a real home. He was approaching fifty, and both of his brothers had long been married. He began planning for their life together, in his usual efficient and understated way. He came to Russia for a few weeks in December 1923, and when he returned to England, he had a wedding ring made for her. He evidently intended to go back to Moscow to help her leave, but when he applied for a visa in the spring of 1924 he was unexpectedly turned down by the consulate in London—only now, as the different pieces of this story come together, does it occur to me to wonder whether the OGPU knew about his prewar relationship with Sofia Krylenko and whether his association with her played any part in the rejection—and Frouma and Ira were left to get out of the USSR by themselves. Max was never to set foot in Russia again; Frouma had to wait more than thirty years before she could return.

Frouma's family was close-knit but because of their nomadic upbringing, the Toumarkine children were used to uprooting themselves and making a home somewhere new. *"Une valise dans la tête, une valise dans le couloir"* was a family maxim. Somehow Frouma managed to get a visa for Ira and herself for a weekend trip to the Baltic port of Riga. Max was waiting for them and they wasted no time, marrying in a civil ceremony in an office above the central post office. Although both had been born subjects of the tsars, Max entered his citizenship as Polish and Frouma as Soviet Russian, which is what it would remain on paper for the next decade—they only acquired British nationality in 1935. Two weeks later they were in London, and on December 4, by which time Frouma was pregnant, they had a religious wedding ceremony at which Max pledged to

"honor and cherish" his wife and to support her "as it becom-
eth a Jewish husband to do." It is the one distinctively religious
ceremony I can find to associate with either of them.

For a year or two, Max had been lodging in a double-fronted
house at the bottom of Hampstead Heath, and he now brought
Frouma and Ira there. It must have been a strange contrast to
what they had left behind. In Moscow, everything was shabby
from the years of war, run-down and in flux. The grand apartment they had been living in had been taken over by their servants and strangers, a turning upside down of the old order that
Ira, who was eight at the time, never forgot: Mother and daughter, both suffering from malaria, had had to share a single room
with Frouma's parents. The apartment where Frouma and Max
had been introduced, her sisters' place, was in a once grand
art nouveau block on Ulitsa Prechistenka, the road beloved by
Moscow's aristocracy that leads straight from the Kremlin to
the Novodevichy Convent. As if to demonstrate the death of
the old order, Prechistenka itself had just been renamed Kropot-
kinskaya, after the renowned anarchist. The continuities of life
in the English capital must have been a surprise, the rows of
Victorian villas testifying to the serene hegemony of the metropolitan middle classes. This house in South Hill Park was Max
and Frouma's first home in London and the place where Dad
was born the following summer, in June 1925. By a strange coincidence, I used to pass it on my way to see Dad when he was in
the Royal Free Hospital, a month or so before he died. Heading off Highgate Hill through Fitzroy Park, and cutting over the
Heath between the ponds, once you came down off Parliament
Hill and turned into the sliver of an alley that runs between the

houses into South Hill Park Gardens, number 19 was right in front of you.

As soon as I learned the address, I felt a strange, indefinable sensation: I realized it was in the middle of a web of other places with some powerful associations of their own for me. The little enclave of South Hill Park was, when I went to school across the Heath in the mid-1970s, a shabby residential backwater. The North London line trains ran behind the gardens on its southern perimeter, and the terraced streets had not yet been tarted up by global billions and retained the slightly dingy pride of a city living on its past. Just uphill from the station was a pub, the Magdala Arms, in whose garden my schoolmates and I celebrated our liberation from the sixth form over a pint. It was a place with a seedy kind of fame because outside it one Easter Sunday twenty years earlier a nightclub manageress called Ruth Ellis had fired a Smith and Wesson at her lover David Blakely, shooting him five times, and becoming the last woman in the United Kingdom to be hanged. The streets above the pub were mostly Victorian, but a girl I knew lived in an angular modern

house a little way up the road with huge windows in the living
room that had a view over the ponds. Nearby was Nassington
Road where, a decade later, my first girlfriend had her top-floor
digs when she left university; it was the early Thatcher years,
and the electricity meter was insatiable, and mattresses were
strewn on the floor. The attic rooms were dark and cramped,
and we were thankful for the Heath on our doorstep: Marriage
and divorce lay ahead. Only fifty yards up the street, though I
did not get to know him until later, one of England's most eminent historians, Eric Hobsbawm, was living in a large hospita-
ble home filled with books and sofas and drinks. He befriended
me, as he did many other young scholars, and when he died at a
great age, I went back to the house and had tea with his widow
and looked at the shelves on which the fundamental texts of
Marxism-Leninism shared space with Sir Thomas Browne's
Religio Medici and worn Everyman Classics. The fusion seemed
characteristic of that part of North London on whose slopes
two or three generations of bookish émigrés from the Continent had raised their children and made bonfires and raked
leaves. The pull of local associations and memories, which I
thought had mostly grown out of the circumstances of my life

and my own choices and affections, it turned out had originated before I had been born.

And not only before my birth but before Dad's as well. The one thing Dad knew about the house in South Hill Park was that it had been known to his parents as "the Engineer's Delight." He had no idea why. What he did not know was that the house's owner had been another Russian Jewish immigrant to England, an engineer named Maxim Kogan, whose life, like Max's, had been shaped by the travails of the Jews in the Tsarist empire.

The mass emigration that followed the assassination of Alexander II in 1881 and the first wave of anti-Jewish riots in the empire had attracted enormous attention worldwide and led to around 1.5 million Jews migrating to the United States alone. A decade later, after new police raids were launched in Moscow to expel Jews illegally resident there, the star *New York Times* reporter Harold Frederic published a detailed indictment of Tsarist despotism. Knowing no Russian, Frederic had relied for details on a Moscow informant, Maxim Kogan, by then nearly fifty and already secretly passing damning material on the anti-Semitic outrages of the Tsarist authorities to the London-based newspaper *Darkest Russia*. It is the first mention of him I have been able to find.

It was probably as a result of his contacts in the international press that the following autumn Kogan was invited by one of the wealthiest men in Europe, Baron Maurice de Hirsch, to help sort out a philanthropic initiative. Hirsch had founded an organization called the Jewish Colonization Association because he was keen to find ways to solve the problem of Russian anti-Semitism. Like many at that time he believed colonial settlement was the answer. Ottoman Palestine was one option, but it was complicated by Sultan Abdul Hamid's lack of enthusiasm for stirring up trouble in his Arab provinces. And in that epoch when it seemed a simple matter to dispossess the world's primitive peoples and rational to resettle the empty lands of the earth with civilizing emigrants, plenty of other potential venues for a Jewish homeland presented themselves—Uganda, Cyrenaica, South America, New Jersey, even the western United States and Manitoba were all seriously considered for mass colonization at one time or another. Baron Hirsch's scheme involved Argentina—he dreamed of settling millions of Jews from the Pale there eventually—and after meeting Kogan, he hired him to sort out the scheme's teething troubles and make it work.

Kogan was no fool and quickly saw that what Hirsch regarded as teething troubles were in fact fundamental problems with the whole idea. He lasted barely six months before quarreling both with the colonists and with his megalomaniac backer and heading back across the Atlantic. As he understood, the costs were too high, and the odds of climate, terrain, and morale were stacked against success. Eventually several thousand Jewish settlers (many of them coincidentally from Max's hometown of Grodno) were housed in two hamlets called Moisesville and Mauriceville in honor of their benefactor. Today a few Jewish gauchos still roam the Argentinian pampas and what is left of Moisesville remains a fading testimony to the limits of extreme wealth to solve the world's problems. After Hirsch's death, the Jewish Colonization Association decided that if it wanted to help Russian Jewry, it needed to support them elsewhere—in Brazil, Cyprus, Romania, Turkey, Palestine, and above all Russia itself.[3]

With his Argentinian adventure behind him, Kogan did exactly what Max would do later: He made his way to London and acquired British citizenship. He became a consultant to the new automotive industry before the First World War and a fixer for British business in Russia, and eventually he and his wife bought the house in South Hill Park. Max moved in as a boarder around 1921 or 1922. But in the summer of 1924, shortly before Max returned from Riga with Frouma and Ira, Kogan died at nearly eighty. Did his widow perhaps harbor hopes her lodger Max might find more than mere lodgings in the Engineer's Delight? Had she been jealous when Frouma turned up on the doorstep? That, I think, was the hidden meaning in the phrase Dad had remembered from childhood.

An unwelcoming landlady was only part of a difficult start for Frouma in London. She spoke little or no English and missed her family in Moscow acutely. She was pregnant and unwell and having to cope with the demands of two difficult children. André was about to start at university. Eight-year-old Ira was struggling — the German her nanny had taught her was of no use now — and she and her stepfather were temperamentally very different. Then Dad was born, leaving Frouma seriously ill with peritonitis for several weeks. Max, upon whom domesticity had abruptly descended in force, dived into his wartime savings and commissioned a large house to be built on the new Holly Lodge Estate at the corner of Makepeace Avenue and West Hill. As soon as it was ready, the family left South Hill Park and made the move across the Heath to Highgate. Dad, the youngest member of the household, and the only one — apart from Alice the maid — to be born in England, was not yet a year old. Many years later, after his mother's death, his aunt Niura told him that Frouma had been so homesick that if it had not been for him, she would have gone back to Russia. In a new country, her baby was her anchor. It was a responsibility hardwired into him from a time before consciousness.

High Street, Highgate.

CHAPTER THIRTEEN

Highgate

A strong Russian connection has attached itself to Highgate over the years. Guryev, a phosphates magnate, is reportedly the current owner of the mansion that stands at the top of West Hill—a dour monstrosity called Witanhurst whose twenty-five or more bedrooms make it, one is told, the largest private house in London after the queen's. Lower down, the perimeter of Beechwood House is patrolled by the billionaire Alisher Usmanov's security guards. Decades before the neighborhood turned into what sociologists of global real estate refer to as Alpha Territory, the Soviet trade delegation down the road was lodging its employees in houses on the Holly Lodge Estate, some fifty families at least by 1971 when many of them were fingered for expulsion by the British government. Unlike the billionaires they did not hide away. They swam in the Men's Bathing Pond on Hampstead Heath along with the Hasids, the ex-NCOs, and the sun worshippers, and they were a familiar presence at the Duke of St. Albans at the bottom of West Hill where locals complained that they did not drink much and spoke Russian all the time. Many of them were KGB, and it was common knowledge locally that MI5 ran a safe house across the way to keep an eye on them.

Yet when Dad's parents moved there, all this was in the future and such Russian connections as Highgate possessed were fading. They were mostly Leftist, drawn by the proximity to Karl Marx's tomb, which was still on the original shabby family plot in Highgate Cemetery, watched over by an old gravedigger who could remember the day the great man had been buried. Before the First World War a few elderly survivors of that era were still around, like the eighty-year-old revolutionary Karl Blind, and Fanny Stepniak, the widow of a Russian friend of Friedrich Engels. Another Russian, Old Zund—Aaron Zundelevich, a living link to the Vilna socialists of the 1870s—spent his final years near the Heath in a tiny flat overflowing with rare revolutionary pamphlets. And the great anarchist Prince Peter Kropotkin, who had first settled in London in 1876, lived for a time with his family in a neat Edwardian terraced house on Muswell Hill Road.

By the early 1920s, they were all gone. Old Zund had died and so had Blind. Kropotkin had returned to Russia where he died in poverty. Bolsheviks like Maxim Litvinov and Samuel Rothstein had gone back to serve the revolution. The flotsam of the Romanov ancien régime mostly preferred other parts of London. The Grand Duke Michael Alexandrovich, a notoriously stupid grandson of Tsar Nicholas I, had rented Kenwood in the last years before it was opened to the public, but by the end of the First World War he had left too and in the 1920s Kenwood opened its grounds to the hoi polloi.

Thus when they moved across the Heath from South Hill Park to the Holly Lodge Estate, a new development on Highgate West Hill, Max and Frouma saw around them not Little Moscow but a London developer's dream of an English garden village. In 1925, the estate was still being built street by street and nothing could have seemed further from the Bolshevik revolution than the mock-Tudor half-timber houses, epitomes of affordable bourgeois comfort, which were slowly spreading across the hilly flanks of what had only a few years earlier been the Burdett-Coutts estate, attracting doctors, newspapermen, and theater impresarios who were drawn by the views, the quiet of the Heath, the old trees, and easy access to work. Its lime-shaded verges suggest suburbia, but the estate forms part of the city that surrounds it, and residents with their panoramic vista of the West End beneath them have only a brief stroll down to the grime and bustle of Gospel Oak. As the London property market was sluggish after the First World War, a resourceful immigrant from Russia with a little capital could even afford to commission a new building off-plan, which was what Max did. Number 1 Makepeace Avenue was the address, its very name a declaration of hope after years of bloodletting, a benediction for a newborn son in a new country.

It was one August evening, in the warm, rainy summer of 1925, on the eve of their life together in Highgate, that Max wrote a few lines in Russian to his new wife. Frouma had left him to go for some days of rest—to the coast, I expect—with Ira and Dad, then barely two months old. André was on holiday in Paris, bathing in the Seine: In those days, he was still sending news back to his father. Max was alone, shuttling between their South Hill Park lodgings and the builders on West Hill. It is the only letter of his that has survived, the only time we catch the sound of his voice in an intimate moment. So all-embracing is the silence that surrounds him across most of his life that it comes as a shock to see this resourceful, cautious man throwing himself without reserve into the fitting out of their home, the warmth of his embrace of a new familial domesticity, and its trivia.

> My dear Frumochka
>
> Today, I've spent almost the entire day dealing with fireplaces. I looked at some additional ones and came to the conclusion that those I had previously chosen were the most suitable. I eliminated the mahogany one you had doubts about. It is very difficult to judge them by looking at drawings. The *drawing-room* [in English in the original] fireplace is not flat but concave, which also corresponds to your wishes. I think you will be pleased with them when you see them.

As for Frouma, he leaves her—and us—in no doubt about the strength of his affections:

> Somehow, I don't want to see anyone and keep thinking about how you are spending your time without me. My room is absolutely silent; I feel sad and lonely. However, I do

not have to wait long. I'll soon embrace you and look with love into your sweet eyes. How is Bill? How are you managing Ira? I kiss you all warmly and with love, Your Max.

These lines, the first time I read them, seemed almost shocking, so firmly had I come to see in Max the epitome of a kind of political commitment and of masculinity that consigned personal feelings to silence. The man speaking here is a romantic. He will put the solitary life of the revolutionary behind him; he is done with lodgings and landladies and the provisionality of all that; Max cherishes his wife and now devotes himself to making in Highgate for her and the children the kind of home that he had lacked when he was a boy. His love: it is real, something to offset the anguish that beset her in those first months in a new country.

CHAPTER FOURTEEN

The Sheltering Word

"She was a very loving mother." I was asking Dad about Frouma. "She was a very gregarious and friendly woman. She had lots of friends among the Russian Jewish diaspora, as it were. There were an awful lot of people who managed to get out of Russia after the revolution. Most of our circle of friends were people like my mother. They mostly settled in Highgate, Golders Green, Willesden, and that sort of thing." As anyone who knew Dad well could testify, he could shift from the personal to the sociological at the speed of light; it was getting him back that was the hard part.

"She had a very rich Russian accent," he continued. "She never really mastered English as my father had done. My father was the opposite. He could pass for an Englishman."

"He had no accent?"

"He had no accent. Unfortunately we have no recordings of him. My mother wasn't what you'd call a well-educated woman. Her education had been rather interrupted…We shared much the same tastes in reading. We'd go to the public library together and often would read the same books."

"So she would read in English?"

"Yes."

"In Russian as well?"

"Yes. In those days, you could—in the early years after the

Soviet regime, they didn't export a lot of books. Later, they saw this as a way of earning foreign currency and you could buy Soviet editions of Russian classics and so on. When I was a child, as far as I know, in the West, you had to rely on stuff that had been published before the first war or they were émigré publishers who printed. But those were mainly political works or works by anti-Soviet authors. For a long time all the stuff printed in the West was in the old spelling, which was a bit tedious. There were newspapers published in the West, especially in Paris."

"I am interested in your mother, Dad, rather than publishing."

He laughed. "Right."

Deracination: The word scarcely begins to convey the psychological and emotional strains that exile and emigration impose on those who have undergone it. In Max's case, he responded with businesslike activity on the one hand and silence on the other, a silence so pervasive that even his wife, to whom he was close, knew next to nothing about his past. For Frouma, who toyed with the idea of returning to Moscow, making England her home depended upon preserving and nurturing her ties with her homeland and her loved ones rather than allowing them to dwindle. Two of her younger siblings also left the USSR and settled in France, but her yearning for the country she had grown up in remained powerful for years. Her strong Russian accent, which never left her, was thus a clue, a significant contrast to her husband's impeccably accented English.

We used to pride ourselves on the fact that we were the only Mazowers, that there were no others in the London phone book, or anywhere in England, we supposed. When odd bearers of the name cropped up in Israel or Argentina they were treated as a curiosity, as likely to prove an annoyance as anything else. Because of the iron wall of Max's silence, his brothers and their families did not seem real to us. But it was different with Frouma's brothers and sisters, the Toumarkines: Although we did not know the ones who had stayed in Moscow, Frouma made sure her children got to know their uncle and aunt, Niura and Vitalie, the siblings who had settled in Paris, and as a result we did too. France became more than another country for us; it became almost part of home and a way station to a certain inchoate sense of attachment to Russia itself.

What I did not discover until very much later was why we felt this way: The very fact that Niura and Vitalie had managed to follow Frouma out of Russia was thanks to her. Any enthusiasm the Toumarkine family had felt after the February revolution had worn off once the Bolsheviks came to power, and when Frouma and Max, now safely in England, offered to support the two youngest of her siblings abroad, her parents were glad. Over the decades that followed, she became a kind of surrogate mother for them, their adviser, consoler, sanctuary.

From the mid-1920s, travel to and from Russia was first hard and then more or less impossible. Occasionally a business friend would go to Moscow, or a student whose parents Frouma and Max knew from Tsarist days would come over to study—such things were still possible before the war—but there were no visits within the family between the one brief trip Frouma's mother somehow managed to make to London in 1929 and Frouma's own visit to Moscow thirty years later. In the interim the way she nurtured a sense of closeness to her family was principally through writing letters.

What a burden those dozens if not hundreds of tiny, fragile sheets carried over the years. The Soviet Union seemed to most people in Western Europe like a world apart, and it was for long stretches of time. Nevertheless when I look at the fading blue ink on the frail envelopes that crisscrossed Europe from the early 1930s onwards, each carefully written in the educated hand the Toumarkine children had learned in Smolensk before the revolution, what strikes me now is how much they were able to communicate to one another and how vital this communication was to their happiness. There were silences of course and sometimes entire sections of family remained invisible or unmentioned, but more important were the things that kept the siblings together—accounts of illnesses and recoveries, deaths or disappearances in Moscow mourned in London, a wedding into the haute bourgeoisie of the Third Republic celebrated in a telegram from Russia. Between Paris, Moscow, and London flowed a stream of news, endearments, condolences, and questions and at the heart of this was Frouma, passing things on, asking for more, sending letter after letter for decades.

Technological progress can also bring emotional impoverishment. What is certain is that no other technology in those days was felt to offer the same register of communication as the letter. Telegrams were reserved for only the most important of occasions. A telephone was installed in the Oakeshott Avenue house from the time they moved in, and very occasionally a call came through the exchange from abroad. But the difficulties with long-distance conversations were more than just logistical; the phone brought one too close, and the sound of the voice was too immediate, and conversations were over so abruptly that Frouma found them distressing. The first calls she received from France and Moscow after the war had her in tears for hours afterwards. "I am so sorry for my silliness," she wrote Vitalie. "Normally I don't break into tears easily at all, but only when I will finally see you and really feel you are alive will I be able to speak calmly to you all."

Letters were different. They were heaven-sent, the lifeblood of the family's continued existence after it had been sundered, and to write was, in the first place, an obligation. The sound of the letterbox was always a cause for celebration and letters were copied and circulated. Frouma would sometimes write two or three times a day to keep the news flowing to and from her mother in Moscow and then on to her brother and sister in Paris. Her mother wrote her in December 1936, "your letter, Frumushenka, I read with joy." When Frouma received this, she sent it on to Niura in Paris "to reassure you about Mum" even though she wanted to keep it a little longer to reread it. Her mother would pass on the latest about illnesses, summer travels, children's examinations, and chance meetings with old friends, and each time the news brought a sense of relief. "Vita dear," she wrote her brother in Paris, "today I got a letter from Mum and Dad. Thank God they are alive and well." Her sister Nata, who was studying to be a doctor in Moscow, told Frouma that she should not try to send them clothes in the post but rather "write more frequently, and tell this to Niura and Vita as well, because Mum can't sleep for several nights in a row for lack of letters." Their father, Moise, now retired, reminded his daughters "to write us more often because this is our only pleasure: your every letter is an event, not only for us but also for the whole family." Dad, then eleven, was now old enough, her father reminded Frouma in 1936, to write to them too, but like most of the other men in the family, Dad was not much of a letter writer. "Don't be worried if I do not write to you," ran a youthful postcard he sent Frouma from the Norfolk Broads.

In fact, as he knew well, in Oakeshott Avenue lack of letters always made her anxious. "Not a word from Moscow," she wrote in early 1939 around the time of her mother's last illness. "I asked my acquaintance to find out from her sister, who lives in Moscow, whether our mum and dad are still alive...My God, what hard times we are living in!" She got similarly worried when she had not heard anything out of France and the lack of letters from Niura in particular was often taken as a sign of unhappiness. The war years were an agony of suspense, although the resourceful Vitalie did manage to send a couple of precious postcards from Vichy France. After liberation, the letters could begin again. The first from France arrived in Highgate in October 1944. "It was," Frouma wrote, "the happiest moment for me since the beginning of the war." "Mummy went around holding [your letter] for days," Ira wrote to her aunt in Paris. A year later came a brief telegram from Russia saying everyone was well, which was not entirely true. In fact, after the war communication with Moscow was much harder and more dangerous than it had been before, and the letters dwindled, although they never dried up completely.

The biggest source of anxiety was the well-being of relatives, especially Frouma's parents, and the missives coming out of Moscow in the 1930s were often health bulletins, more or less reassuring. After a bad fall, her mother provided long self-deprecating descriptions of the luxurious linen and nickel-plated furniture in the hospital ("there were desk lamps by each bed, nurses in white aprons and caps, and it looked like a health resort") and plentiful food, including apples, tangerines, candy

("I would eat five oranges at a time"). There were trips to their country dacha and "thank God, every one is alive and well fed." She reported on her husband, still taking the stairs at the age of eighty-three, making himself pancakes for breakfast, and playing chess, while she tries to screen out the noise of radios in their apartment on downtown Myasnitskaya Street by knitting scarves and reading. "For me there is no greater pleasure than books." Both parents made light of their infirmities and their minds were clear and playful to the end. They dreamed of having their children come to visit, and every so often they walked with their youngest daughter, Nata, to the post office to book time for a brief call to France, reassuring their children that "you can't imagine how little it costs; it is not like your country at all. Thank God, everything here is cheap and available. God willing, we shall live the rest of our days like this; we have no debts and will not have any, thank God."

Frouma was equally self-deprecating, although she was less concerned to reassure or to hide her anxieties. But the intensity of her letter-writing evidently derived from the example set by her mother, who continued to write right up to the very end of her life. In February 1939, when news of Maria Toumarkine's death arrived at Oakeshott Avenue, the envelope that brought the letter with the details also contained her last letter, her farewell blessing to her children abroad:

My dear children,

I bless you all, my children, to live to a ripe old age in full health and happiness, to live in friendship and love. My health is deteriorating, but I am surrounded by much love and care from my children and family. I have lived for long enough, so now I am fine with whatever length of time God has in store for me. My dear children, be healthy and happy, my kisses to all of you.

Your mother and grandmother

She had signed off in Yiddish, one of the few times in the entire correspondence that she did not use Russian. Frouma lit a candle every year to commemorate the day of her mother's passing. And she always kept the picture of her mother surrounded by her husband and children, laid out on her bier.

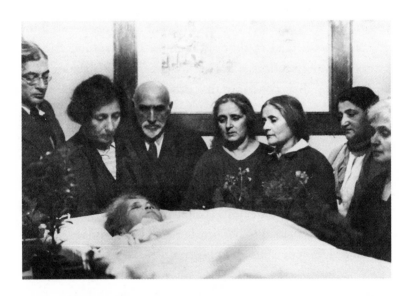

Frouma's father, who was to die at nearly ninety on the eve of the German invasion, kept up the tradition. He felt he needed to tell the children where his wife's grave was—a vital piece of information—and he also, as always, dispensed advice: eat healthily, try to move to the countryside. "Tell Ira it is time for her to get married," he advised Frouma about the granddaughter he had not seen for fifteen years.

The penultimate letter that has survived from him contained counsels of this kind as well as demands for photos of his grandchildren. But it also dealt with something else, something less happy. Frouma must have asked him for news of her older brother, Lev (Alunya). A lawyer and the eldest of the Toumarkine boys, Lev was not only a holder of the St. George Cross from his time in the imperial army, he had also been a longtime member of the Bolshevik Party *before* the First World War who had quit in 1914 and never rejoined. In the 1930s, this was not the kind of past that easily escaped the notice of his former comrades. Why had her parents not said anything about him? What she suspected could only be hinted at, and her father's response was circuitous. "I cannot answer your question," he wrote back to her, conscious that other eyes might be scanning his letter. "He doesn't write us. I don't know if he is angry or if something else is the matter. Let us hope he writes soon and then I will write you right away." When Frouma sent this letter on to her Paris siblings, she added: "Dad is answering the question about Alunya—and we don't know any more than we did, but I still have some hope that he is, maybe, alive." Lev was not the only one. One of her brothers-in-law, her sister Fenya's husband, Herman Shub, had been in prison for years and his fate was similarly uncertain. "Mum wrote to me," she confided to Vitalie, "that a parcel sent him was returned to Fenya. I am afraid something happened." Something had indeed happened: The Terror had come to Russia and to the family, and their letters traveling to and fro across Europe convey the slowly dawning and agonizing realization of a new kind of absence and what it might mean.

In 1959, when Frouma was finally able to return to Moscow, a visit she had been cogitating for several years, it was a new era: Stalin had died, Nikita Khrushchev was in power, and Russia was opening up to the West. Frouma wanted to visit her parents' graves and see her surviving siblings. She managed to do both and photographs from that trip show three of the sisters—Fenya, Frouma, and Nata—in Nata's apartment on Petrovsky Boulevard, seated around a large dining table spread with a white tablecloth to mark the occasion. There are grandchildren, nephews, nieces, scattered papers, an unwrapped box of chocolates, flowers, and tea. It should have been a happy time—the long-awaited return to Russia, the family reunited after thirty-five years—but as they stare into the camera the faces are somber and one can feel the ghosts in the room. It was not only their parents who were gone. Ida, whose husband had known Max and brought him and Frouma together, had died in

1942, during the wartime evacuation to Novosibirsk. And neither Herman Shub nor Lev Toumarkine had ever returned.

In 1959 Fenya Shub—on the far left in the photograph—still did not know what had happened to her husband. The two of them had started their life together half a century earlier, in another world, when Shub had landed his first job in 1909 in the municipal statistical office in the provincial backwater of Penza. This posting had been the unlikely launchpad not only for his career as an economist but for something much larger, something that was to transform both communism and capitalism in the twentieth century—the modern conception of the planned economy.

Shub had been part of a team of statisticians and economists that won such a reputation for their technical skills during the First World War that at the request of the Tsarist government they were brought back to Petrograd and assigned a task of overriding national importance—to help secure the supply of food for the Russian army and the capital. Politically, Shub had started out in the Bund as a schoolboy in Minsk, and then joined the Mensheviks, as many Bundists did, so he was over-joyed when the revolution broke out in February; in later life he always celebrated the anniversary. He was elected to the city soviet—in effect for a time the country's administration—by a regiment in the Petrograd garrison, and he began working as its economic adviser. He was close to the Mensheviks in the Provi-sional Government, but once the Bolsheviks seized power, they found they needed him too, especially after the civil war was over and the politburo could turn to figuring out what a peace-time communist economy should look like. Shub's skills and experience were more relevant to that question than any of the theories to be found in *Das Kapital*, and by the mid-1920s, in an environment that seemed much more favorable to their ideas about holistic strategic state planning than what had existed before the war, he and other members of the old Penza team were staffing Gosplan, the central planning agency that lay at the heart of the communist economic experiment.

But the result was that when bitter disputes began over the pace of industrialization—the very debates that fueled Stalin's rise to sole power—Gosplan, with its large number of former Mensheviks, was at the eye of the storm and an easy target. Shub and others questioned the planning targets the regime wanted to set, but to Stalin there was no such thing as disin-terested technical expertise: Disagreement implied opposition and conspiracy, especially when it emanated from a group whose long-standing reservations about Bolshevism were com-mon knowledge. In 1929 Shub had just left for a new job in the Moscow regional statistics office when he was arrested by the OGPU, imprisoned in the Lubyanka prison, and then exiled to Kazakhstan. Eventually Fenya managed to get permission to go with the children to visit him; the local planning boss valued Shub's skills and allowed them to live together in a dacha near Almaty. She always remembered how on her birthday she and the children had been serenaded by her husband and some old friends of his, former Bundists, Mensheviks, and other fellow exiles, singing revolutionary songs from the Tsarist days.

Worse was to come, much worse. In 1931, with Nicolai Krylenko prosecuting, there was a trial of the so-called Bureau of the Union of the Organization of the Mensheviks, and Shub was brought back to the Lubyanka to testify against his old chief who was one of the defendants. It was an important stage in the development of the public show trials that were to flourish later in the decade, and there was enormous pressure on the prosecutors to conjure up a plausible target. Shub was supposed to be a star witness.

Years earlier, Shub and Krylenko had been comrades within the Social Democratic Workers' Party; indeed Shub had once hidden Krylenko at his father's house in Moscow to protect him. In 1931 this counted for nothing. He was accused of working for "the counterrevolutionary Menshevik organization" from within Gosplan, of wanting to reestablish capitalism, and of sabotaging Soviet economic development through incorrect planning estimates and prognoses. Despite torture, sleep deprivation, and all the other tools used by the Soviet secret police, he refused to cooperate in what he called their "comedy." There were a few hurried, whispered meetings with his wife, who managed to visit him in jail in Moscow. But after his former boss at Gosplan, Vladimir Groman, and others succumbed to the pressure, Shub received a new sentence and spent the last few years of his life being transferred between the secret police prison in Yaroslavl north of Moscow and the special isolator unit reserved for hard-core political prisoners at Verkhneuralsk. Even there, more than one thousand miles from Moscow, two hundred miles by sledge from the nearest railway, Fenya fought her way to see him. Only when he was moved to the NKVD prison in Chelyabinsk did visits of any kind become impossible. On October 2, 1937, the local NKVD reviewed his case and described him as an implacable opponent of the Soviet Union, disobedient even inside prison. He was obviously a man of enormous courage. He was ordered to be shot and the sentence was carried out three days later at seven in the evening. Fenya never gave up hope that he was alive. In 1962 a letter came with the official notification of his death although the certificate falsely claimed he had died of heart failure; she died shortly afterwards and the full truth did not emerge until 1991.[1]

Frouma's brother Lev, the eldest of the Toumarkine boys, had vanished too; he had been arrested by the NKVD on February 7, 1938, after being denounced. He was not as high profile a figure as Shub but, as someone who had left the party out of disgust at their methods in power, he too had been vulnerable. His fate also suggested some of the other, more intimate ways in which the Terror could wreak its havoc. In the family, the story was that the person who had denounced him was his wife, Vera, which was possible because of an earlier tragedy that had fatally compromised relations between the couple. In August 1936, their fourteen-year-old daughter, Nina, had suddenly and unexpectedly died of dysentery. She had been at a summer camp and a harrowing letter from Moscow to Frouma describes the entire episode: the sudden onset of the illness while her friends are playing, her rapid weakening and last painful agonies, her unexpected death at home. Nata, who had been studying for her medical exams, only arrived in time to prepare Nina's corpse for the funeral so that she could lie in her favorite dress and her Young Pioneer tie with a bouquet of flowers in her hand. It was the worst thing to have happened in the family for a very long time. Lev's heart was broken and in his grief he told his mother that he felt he had no reason to go on living. He spent most evenings at the cemetery after that, summer and winter, for hours at a time, even when the temperature plummeted. Relations between him and his wife became poisonous because he blamed her for having been drunk and not having noticed how sick Nina was. Did she really denounce him, as Frouma and the others believed? In any event, he had all but lost the will to live when on April 27, 1938, he was sentenced to death—the charge sheet comprised espionage, terrorism, and counterrevolutionary activity; one wonders if those letters to and from London and Paris played any part in his conviction—and he was shot at the Kommunarka execution ground the same day.

As in the case of Fenya's husband, the family was not informed what had happened to him, and his father, well over eighty, traveled east to try to find out. The letters between him and Frouma about Alunya had thus been in a kind of code, conveying only this: that they had no idea what had become of him.

There was a third Terror victim in the family — Frouma's cousin Lev Berlinraut. The mug shot that the NKVD took of him after his arrest is a striking contrast with that of his cousin and namesake, Lev Toumarkine. The latter looks haunted, resigned, already half dead after his daughter's death the previous year. Berlinraut's face is gaunt but there is a spark of defiance and energy in the eyes, an alertness. It is as though he had been expecting this day of reckoning and was ready for it. And it would not be surprising if he had, for Berlinraut was an intellectual and an activist who had been intimately involved in some of the key moments of the Russian Revolution of 1917. Like Herman Shub and Lev Toumarkine, Berlinraut had walked the revolutionary tightrope—Marxist but non-Bolshevik—after 1917, but in his case a passion for politics had tested the limits of the possible. He had been that rarest of creatures, a non-Bolshevik political activist in the Soviet Union.

Berlinraut had been a leading member of a left-wing party called Poale Zion whose origins went back to the turn of the century. Fusing Zionism and Marxian socialism, its leading thinker, Ber Borochov, had argued that assimilation was a dead end. The Bund, with its stress on the here and now, had it wrong, he said. Jews would be limited in opportunity any-where that they lacked political power, and their minority status would always prevent them from becoming a properly organized working class. It was only in a Jewish-run Palestine that a genuine Jewish proletariat could come into being and hasten a socialist revolution. This new vision of proletarian Jewish nationalism spread rapidly. By 1905, at the age of nine-teen, Berlinraut was a member of Poale Zion's central commit-tee and a trusted confidante of Borochov, whose writings he would later edit. When the bespectacled, well-educated, clean-shaven young Muscovite attended a regional party meeting in Minsk, he seemed to the local activists to have come from a different world: At home in Russian (thereby impressing most of his audience, who were much more at ease in Yiddish), he struck one of them as resembling "the son of a good family who had fallen into a gang of thieves."[2] By the time the First World War broke out, he was a prominent figure on the left wing of the party. In early 1918 he negotiated with the Germans over national rights for the Jews of Russia, and at the same time he was elected to the central committee of the Soviet preparlia-ment—at that time effectively the country's executive—which put him, for a brief period, at the very apex of power in the revolutionary state. The following year, as the party spokesman on nationality matters, he pushed for Poale Zion's adherence to the Comintern, and when the party split on this issue, he did not leave for Palestine as many others did but stayed with the small Leftist fraction that remained in Russia, independent but tolerated. In effect, although he surely would not have put it so starkly, he had opted for Marxism over Zionism. One of his comrades, a Russian Jew from Plonsk named David Gruen, had already made the opposite choice, emigrating to Ottoman Palestine where he was active in the local Poale Zion branch in Jaffa. Much later, known by his Hebrew name as David Ben Gurion, he would become Israel's first prime minister. In the guise of its pro-communist faction, Poale Zion was one of the very few political parties permitted an autonomous existence inside the Soviet Union, and until 1928 Berlinraut was listed in the Moscow phone book as one of the party's designated representatives. It was only when the Kremlin decided to create a homeland for the Jews in Siberia on the Chinese border at Birobidzhan, its own contribution to the long history of Jewish settlement schemes, that the OGPU closed Poale Zion down.

Berlinraut was not only a party activist; he was also a scholar, a trained economist, and a writer. In 1912 he wrote a study of the sociology of a Russian Jewish community that remains a classic. But his interests and commentary extended far beyond purely Jewish matters. Under the pseudonym R. Arski, he published a stream of articles and books, including an instant study of the crisis of 1917. These revealed an impressive intelligence that combined commitment to the proletarian cause with a critical realism all his own. And courage too: He was not afraid, for instance, to warn Lenin in print that rushing into a total nationalization of the economy was premature. Leo Pasvolsky's 1921 *The Economics of Communism*, the first serious Western study of the subject, describes him as "one of the best of the Soviet economists."

We do not know why Berlinraut was arrested. But with his political background, his independence of mind, a sister living in Germany, and his own range of foreign contacts—he had spent time in Berlin in the early 1920s, and his daughter was a German literary expert who found a niche as a librarian at the Marx-Engels Institute in Moscow, the body entrusted with the definitive publication of the works of the founders—he was clearly vulnerable. Berlinraut was working at a state mining company's Moscow office when he was arrested in late March 1938 and charged with membership in a counterrevolutionary terrorist organization. He was sentenced to death on June 14 and shot the same day on the Kommunarka execution site, where by late 1941 at least 4,700 people had been killed by "special duties officers" of the NKVD. It was only after the Second World War that the family learned he had been killed.

That family gathering in Moscow in 1959 was the beginning of renewed communication among the Toumarkine children. Tsalya was by then an eminent pediatrician with solid Kremlin connections. Herman and Fenya's children included a son who was on the way to becoming one of the Soviet Union's most eminent theater critics; Ida's daughter was an aircraft engineer in the space program, who lived in the closed city of Zhukovsky. The Terror had struck the family, but the Toumarkines had risen in Soviet society nonetheless.

Long after Frouma's death, it was Dad's turn to make his first visit to Russia and he took me with him. The Brezhnev years were a time in which all revolutionary energy had long since ebbed away from communism. In those days I was going to school in Burnt Oak, a working-class North London suburb with its own kind of dystopic grimness and random aggression. *A Clockwork Orange* was no fantasy. I remember the gaggles of skinheads lurking under the bridge by the station in the mornings, the scent of class hatred and violent distraction in the air. I used to make my way off the train past the cottages that lined the streets of the Watling Estate, an interwar planners' dream of socialized capitalism, which had worn worse than most and which already seemed to have its best days behind it. The estate had been dubbed "Little Moscow" by nervous middle-class North Londoners between the wars, but a week in the real thing was enough to provide a sobering perspective. Our Russian relatives made a loving fuss of Dad and me, and the feasting seemed endless, but in my mind I associate our trip with the emptiness of the dark Moscow boulevards and the snowdrifts piled up around the entrances to the drab apartment blocks on the city's outskirts. It felt more like an expedition than any kind of return and I was happy when we got home. In London I sat in the warmth of our living room. We played the somber opening of Tchaikovsky's Fifth Symphony on the gramophone, Mravinsky's Melodiya recording, its quality traduced by the rough paper cover, about the only thing we had found in the shops that we wanted to bring back with us.

Nata, the last surviving Moscow sister, was familiar to us because she had been able to get to Paris more than once. Natalia Magnitova, to give her married name, was by this time retired as a military doctor, and army life and three husbands and years of caring for their parents and hers had exhausted her. But that was not the half of it: Hers was a story that embodied so many of the incredible paradoxes of existence in the Soviet Union, I could scarcely believe it when, years after her death, I learned that although she had been a doctor, she had been working not in the Red Army, but in the NKVD; indeed, it was more or less in the years when first Shub and then her brother Alunya disappeared into its clutches, that she was supervising Gulag prisoners building the Volga-Don canal. And there was more: it was in those harrowing conditions that she met one of the convicts, a *zek*, and married him—this was her third husband, an engineer called Magnitov, who had spent years in the camps before his release.

In the war both of them saw frontline service against the Germans, and after suffering shell shock, Nata's hearing and balance were never the same and her hair turned white. But the most extraordinary chapter in her life was yet to come because she was reassigned by the NKVD and put in charge of medical services in the POW camp in Krasnogorsk, just outside Moscow. In January 1948 she sent Frouma a letter about her life: Written nine years to the day after the death of their mother, it was the first she had been able to send since the fighting had stopped. Nata mentioned her four-hour commute and her pride in her work. But she said nothing at all about what she was doing. With good reason: Krasnogorsk, which housed some of the most prominent German prisoners in Soviet hands, was an Anti-Fascist School, which aimed to convert erstwhile Nazis into pro-Russian "fighters for peace." This was where the National Committee for a Free Germany was formed during the Second World War, followed by the League of German Officers. The most prominent of the inmates was Field Marshal Paulus, the most senior general in Russian hands, who had surrendered to the Red Army at Stalingrad: Nata was his personal physician. Paulus's adjutant, who later rose to prominence in East Germany, mentions "Dr. Magnitova" in his memoirs in terms of some affection: She was known as "the angel of Krasnogorsk" among the prisoners not only for her medical skill but because she did her best to keep their spirits up as they waited to return home. Paulus himself, at one stage quite ill, became fond of her, and at the time she wrote to Frouma, he was still in her care. Within the family in Moscow it was a standing joke that the famously gruff and irascible Nata had finally found a kindred spirit in the Wehrmacht field marshal.

A few years later came the anti-Jewish purges, and Nata retired. It had been a hard life, and she had never really gotten over the death of her mother and her own lack of children. After her husband's death, she moved into one room of a *kommunalka* in the same block as Tsalya and his family. Feeling unloved and lonely, she would return again and again to her childhood, regaling visitors with stories of growing up outside Smolensk, the family's prosperity before the revolution, the good fortune and wisdom of her parents in educating their daughters as well as their sons—all delivered in a tone that condemned the Soviet present as it mourned the lost past. In 1985 the Krasnogorsk site opened as a museum, and Nata must have bequeathed her medical tools and other objects that she had kept from those years, for among the exhibits, along with Paulus's fur cap and leather gloves, one can today find her official stamp as head of the medical staff, her bifocals, and a radio that some of the prisoners had made for her. A black-and-white photo of her in her prime shows her staring wistfully off in profile, her white hair defiantly wavy. She has an unmistakable air of command. But there, in the camp, she seems also gentler, less recriminatory than we ever saw her later on.[3]

I was too young to know any of this then; all I remember is a tougher and less smiling version of her younger sister Niura. *"Elle n'était pas drôle, pas du tout,"* was my cousin Patrick's verdict. Not much fun: I can see why he might have thought that. In Paris what Nata most liked was to visit the cemeteries, especially Père Lachaise, where she paid homage to the martyrs of the Commune and came back singing revolutionary songs. She and Tsalya were now the last of the siblings left alive in Russia, and the gap in living standards between the USSR and the West, which had not been pronounced in the 1930s, had widened mercilessly.

For Frouma, living next to her daughter in a tranquil apartment overlooking the Heath, the visits to Moscow were revelatory. When she returned to London she told Dad that she realized she felt much more at home in England than in the country of her birth. The ailing Max had come to depend on her more than ever in his final years: Each afternoon he used to wait for her trolleybus as she returned from the shops and his need for her companionship was palpable. By the time he died, not only had she been running the household for years and caring for him but she had also been the main breadwinner, looking after a stream of tenants. Once she was on her own, there must have been a sense of relief. Life was finally getting easier. The Oakeshott Avenue house was rented out, and Ira found her a flat in the apartment block where she lived, on the edge of Hampstead Heath. Old friends lived in the building; her grandchildren were not far away. One Christmas Eve, thinking about her old friend Mrs. S., who was separated from her husband and had ended up living alone, Frouma wrote to her brother in Paris that she felt grateful for how things had worked out. "The kids are more than attentive…As for love surrounding me, I sometimes feel that I have more of it than necessary."

CHAPTER FIFTEEN

Ira

Each year on Christmas Day, Dad's half sister, Ira, and her husband, Jeff, would drive over in their Jaguar, a car that marked them in our eyes even before they entered the house. Jeff, bespectacled in his sports jacket like a taller and less prickly Evelyn Waugh, would take up the rear while Ira would enter Wessex Gardens like some exotic bird—slim, tanned, dark makeup round the eyes, lipstick that took no prisoners, and an emphatic wasp-waist belt that made a statement of her figure into her sixties.

Unlike the absent André, Ira was a definite if intermittent presence in our childhood. Yet she and Dad were so dissimilar that sometimes it seemed unlikely that they could have shared even the one parent. It is not as though we were entirely foreign to elegance, but this was higher wattage than we were used to, as if an alien force that claimed kinship with us was electrifying the backwater of our home. And yet there was a tenacity to the relationship between Ira and her younger half brother, powerful enough to override the differences in their temperaments and taste: Memories of their shared years growing up on Oakeshott Avenue, the great care they both showed to their mother and aunt as they aged, and in the distance, behind this, as much an idea as any kind of reality, the Russia they both felt so attached to. The infrequency of our meetings, however, and perhaps also our disdain, made it impossible to get to know her before her death. It did not help that Ira had become quite reactionary and was given to making outrageous statements about peasants and workers. Nor did the fact that she was a published author with novels to her name raise her stock in our eyes because her genre was swashbuckling romantic fiction, and she seemed to us to be purveying little more than fantasy and wish fulfillment. Who cared about aristos and ballerinas at the court of the tsars, about devil-may-care Burgundian knights and Regency rakes? The books turned into paperbacks with lurid covers. It felt more like a literary embarrassment than a source of pride. We were very high-minded.

And then it was too late. On July 2, 1985, Jeff had a heart attack while driving; his car crashed and he was killed. Three days after his funeral service, Ira was dead too. An announcement was placed in *The Times* by Dad—she had no other relatives—and it was brief:

> JEFFERIES—On July 11th, 1985, suddenly, Ira Jefferies, loving wife of Jeff. Funeral Service strictly private at her own wish. Please no flowers but donations to Cancer Research would be appreciated.

She had taken an overdose.

At the time of her death I was abroad, and the news barely registered: I never asked Dad about it because it did not cross my mind. Our loving family, I start now to think, had erected its own invisible frontiers and boundaries, and Ira had been rather definitely on the other side. It is not just the loneliness of Ira's ending that now strikes me. It is also what it says about her sense of herself in the world. When her husband died, she seems to have felt it was no longer worth going on. She was not yet seventy. Dad, who had worried about her in the days after Jeff's death, and rushed her to hospital too late, thought she was living out one of her novels. Maybe she was—fiction and fact kept colliding throughout her life—but there was steel in the way she ended it too, and it suggested that we had not seen all there was to see in Ira, nor even come close. Afterwards we learned she had left each of us, her four nephews, three gold imperial rubles, reminders of the glittering world whose vanishing haunted her every bit as much as it did André. For unlike Dad, Ira had not been born in England, and in fact it was only in July 1935 that Ira Baltermanz—spelled thus in an entry in *The London Gazette*, she is listed as an art student "also known as Ira Mazower"—had become a British citizen.

Born in Russia in 1916, by the time she was five Ira Baltermants had lived through a world war, a revolution, and a civil war, mass epidemic and famine, and she had seen her father die in front of her eyes and witnessed people being arrested and possibly shot around her. To the sardonic, self-absorbed, willful English-speaking teenager with an artistic temperament that she became, the North London suburbs must have been insufferably tranquil.

Her earliest memories dated from the summer of 1920 when she and her widowed young mother were still living in Moscow. Lenin was in command, the grimy city had become an endless theater of speeches and parades, and they were reduced to one room of their formerly spacious flat. Her German governess read romantic literature with her, but former servants and complete unknowns shared the apartment with them, much to her disgust. In Oakeshott Avenue later she would

spend hours in the small bathroom—we heard much about this
long-standing grievance of Dad's, a younger brother's oft-told
testimony to her juvenile narcissism, and thus we forged our
own association between beautification and self-indulgence.
Now I am inclined to see Ira's originary sin as her effort to ban-
ish the memory of revolutionary deprivation, re-creating in the
safety of an English suburb something of the comfort that had
been snatched from her in childhood.

Few remnants of Ira's Russian life made it to England, but in
Dad's shed, his sanctuary, he used to keep tools in an ancient
but well-made plywood box that fastened with a leather strap.
This box was the one thing Ira had carried with her out of the
USSR in 1924, because it had housed her favorite teddy bear. It

was for this reason that it remained precious to her, and after her death it was to him too so he kept it in the most reliable way he knew, by turning it into something useful with the same lack of sentimentalism that he showed to the gold rubles she bequeathed us in her will, each of them converted by him on our behalf into a small but tidy sum and put in the bank.

Ira had been eight when she and Frouma waved good-bye to the rest of the family, and when I try to imagine the parting at the crowded railway station, I think of the grandparents, uncles, and aunts, the entire Toumarkine clan coming to see them off in tearful farewells that for many of them would turn out to be forever. Ira herself liked to tell it differently. In a memoir designed to turn childhood pain into 1950s cocktail entertainment, she composes a kind of imaginative soufflé of a scene in which all the women of the family are "Slavic beauties," their maids are "wenches," and pearls and sables are plentifully scattered throughout for Russian color. The fact that the family was Jewish is not mentioned, the revolution intrudes primarily to be defeated by style and flair, and there is "the usual squat, bullet-headed Cheka type" whom her mother naturally twists around her little finger. The men are debonair, the women are adept in using their charms. The whole thing is a kind of Ballets Russes fantasy, and when the family comes to see them off it is "Russian-fashion, with enough food, flowers and last-minute gifts to fill the whole carriage, let alone our compartment." Did she really fall asleep on a bed of roses? I find it more likely that she was, as she says, excited at the journey ahead, the prospect of "yellow motorcars, flats, ice-cream and other capitalist glories."

This lighthearted style was very important to her and something that she worked on assiduously. It became a passport to professional success and the way she kept at bay fears, knowledge, and memories that lay close beneath the surface even much later on after her life had become settled and prosperous. Troubling recollections could return at the most unpredictable times and retained the power to transport her back instantly to the terrors of her childhood.

In 1955, for example, more than three decades had elapsed since she said had good-bye to Moscow. Lenin was long dead, Stalin had passed away a couple of years earlier and his successors were keen to spread Russia's prestige into the Third World. The Soviet leaders Nikita Khrushchev and Nikolai Bulganin made a state visit that year to independent Burma. On the second day of their trip they were escorted out of Rangoon to a new Peace Pagoda that recently had been built by Premier U Nu. Their motorcade swept out of the city and came to a halt in front of a red carpet that had been laid across the field to the temple. The two Soviet VIPs, sweating in their crumpled tropical suits, emerged and began to ascend the temple steps. Momentarily they came to an unscheduled halt and the security men looked around nervously. Khrushchev, quicker on the uptake, whispered in Russian to Bulganin that they were expected to take off their shoes. A well-dressed English brunette who happened to be visiting with a group of foreign businessmen began to giggle. Face-to-face with the most powerful man in the USSR she suddenly said to him in fluent Russian: "Take yours off right here." It was Ira.

Bulganin bent down with difficulty, she wrote later, and did as she told him, and as he did so: "Over his bent back I found myself looking straight into the eyes of one of the Security men. My heart jumped like a rabbit and for one suffocating moment I was in the skin of the woman I would have been had I lived out my life in Russia—looking into the eyes of a Security man who could kill or torture or imprison me at will for my nonsense..." What had begun as an entertaining tour of the region with her husband had suddenly become a reminder of what she had escaped.

Throughout her life Ira pursued an ideal of beauty and glamour as if seeking to wipe out her earliest memories and revive what they had effaced, but perhaps as a result her first years in London were not happy ones for her, or for those around her. Always close to her mother—though she often drove Frouma mad with her self-centeredness—she did not find Max easy, nor he her. Moody and frustrated in her ambitions, obsessed for a long time with keeping her weight down—by 1946 she was so skeletal that doctors put her on the diet they had developed for the surviving inmates of Bergen-Belsen—she left school as soon as she could, ignoring her mother's desire for her to go to college in order to earn a living as a commercial artist. She had many talents and when she was still young, she won a competition to design a poster for the League of Nations and saw her work featured at Radiolympia, the national radio exhibition that enjoyed immense popularity in the late 1920s and early 1930s. Gifted with the pen, she freelanced for an advertising agency in the West End because, for all its sleazy associations, advertising provided one of the very few avenues of professional employment open to single women between the wars. It was also of course a line of work which injected romance into capitalism.

Real romance was something else. She met Morris, an easygoing man—a tailor's cutter, glamorous enough for a teenager in a hurry, a nonentity her mother thought—and in the summer of 1935, about the same time that her naturalization papers came through, she married him. It was a spur-of-the-moment decision. He had a car and earned well and in those days the tailor's cutter was a respected figure. Her mother's disapproval bounced off her. Her best friend Mari Stevenson had already gotten married and Ira was determined to do the same thing. It was a mess, as it was bound to be. Mari died in childbirth and Ira was so unhappy with the reality of intimacy with Morrie that she returned home within weeks, although he continued to hang hopefully around her for years. There is a photograph of her in the garden of Oakeshott Avenue in which she and Dad are sitting next to each other on the grass with their parents. He is an eleven-year-old schoolboy in shorts. Ira's impossibly long legs are stretched out, and she has certainly not given up her dreams of a life more exciting, romantic, and freer than that available inside the dark and cramped quarters of Oakeshott Avenue, where her aging stepfather sits morosely in the corner worried about business, and her mother's devotion is increasingly lavished on the little brother who has not yet disappointed her.

In the male world of interwar London marketing, Ira must have been an exotic element. But without a steady income she lived at home, and the tensions accumulated. While her mother scrubbed, mended, sewed, shopped, and cooked, Ira spent the days curled up in her bedroom with a book, subsisting on a diet of apples. Frouma wrote to her sister in Paris at this time that her daughter was "her normal self, messy, always living in an unreal world and 100% selfish." Only once the war broke out did life become more exciting for Ira—as it did for many young women—and she would head out in the early morning in high heels and stockings to work on government campaigns to safeguard the nation's health, which was ironic, given her own difficulties with food. "Those who have the will to win / Cook potatoes in their skin / Knowing that the sight of peelings / deeply hurts Lord Woolton's feelings." It was the time of the Dig for Victory campaign, and Ira's drawing of Potato Pete played a small but iconic role. Each evening, Ira changed into what she described as a "smart blue uniform" and headed up West Hill to do her bit at the local fire service headquarters.

The move into fashion that followed was a good example
of her talent for turning life at home into something stylish and
stylized. Her mother and her aunts were handy dressmakers and
cared about what they wore. Frouma made dresses for friends,
and would take Ira to be fitted out in London and occasionally
to Paris. But Frouma's ceaseless round of domestic duties left
her little time: The clothes one wore were a practical matter
and making them saved money and sometimes brought some
in—that was her approach. Her daughter shared her attentive-
ness to dress but converted it into a source of fantasy and then,
against the odds, into a living because as the war wound down,
she was offered the position of art editor of *Everywoman*, a popular fashion magazine. It was her big break.

Like André, but with more success, Ira was consciously rein-
venting herself and devising her own riposte to revolutionary
self-righteousness. She had arrived at the age of eight at Har-

wich docks knowing no English at all. By the time she was in her twenties, she refused to speak Russian at home or to attend her mother's endless round of émigré teas and dinners, and she did her best to forget what traces of her family's ancestral faith remained. One reason for her rise in the fashion business was surely its attractiveness as a form of everyday mythmaking, a promise of transformation. She understood the importance of this, and she understood too why it appealed to many other women of very different backgrounds from her own, especially once the war was over and rationing persisted and drabness reigned. She got the idea of writing a book on "the best-dressed woman in the room," and in 1946, tapping away night after night in her small upstairs bedroom on Oakeshott Avenue, she wrote *The Glass of Fashion*. It is a product of the era of austerity, but it is also testimony to her drive, a paean to glamour in hard times. Her stepfather complained about the noise of her typewriter, but to her parents' surprise and pleasure the book got good reviews. In fact its flimsy paper and plain covers belie a work of smooth style. Ira reassures British women that they can take grooming seriously, and achieve poise and elegance despite the many obstacles that lay in their path in the late 1940s. She looks ahead to the future, addressing her advice to teenage girls, to working women, and to older women too. She has an easy way with words and does not take herself too seriously.

A few years later, having left the world of fashion publishing, she would describe its ethos with clear-eyed sympathy:

[Women's magazines] reflect the real world all right, up-to-date as a newspaper, but its image in our pages is romantically distorted as in water, and in that distortion are reflected the daydreams of millions of women.

In it, all girls are pretty, all babies healthy and smiling, all
husbands handsome and all the recipes produce Cordon Bleu
banquets for half-a-crown. Love always finds a way; sin is
punished; a new hairdo brings scads of admiring young men;
and no human problem from acne to xenophobia is beyond a
happy solution.

It all does some good and little harm to women whose
lifelong grip on the naked realities of love, money, birth and
death makes them seek our gay dream-world for their relax-
ation. They remain realists at heart; and even the realist in
them is catered for in our pages by stacks of information, especially on anything you can conceivably Do Yourself—gener-
ically known as Knit Your Own Man to the office. Levity is
our professional defence against admitting that we are caught
and held by the fascination of producing the dream-world.
But caught and held we are.

Without leaving home, Ira had found her dream world. And
she was evidently not only talented but recognized because a
few years later, she landed a bigger job and became the art editor of *Woman's Own*, where she worked for the best part of a
decade.

This kind of success—unusual and impressive in Britain at
that time—was only possible for a single woman but it was
not the destiny Ira imagined for herself. After the fiasco of her
brief marriage, she had been surrounded by the admirers and
hangers-on her mother dismissively called her "heroes"—a
term that suggests how far Ira projected a desire to be res-
cued for a more epic life, as well as what her mother, who had
endured an epic of her own, thought about this fantasizing.
Among the men there was still Morrie, available for evenings

at the cinema or occasional holidays abroad, and from whom she was not yet divorced. There were actors, dancers, and writers. And then she met Jeff, a businessman who worked in the City and lived down the road. He happened to be married and a father several times over, and neither Max nor Frouma was happy with a situation that dragged on for nearly a decade and which Frouma described in frustration as "a cross between Chekhov and a comic opera." Not one but two divorces were needed—to part Ira belatedly from Morrie and Jeff from his wife. Morrie was accommodating; Jeff was torn. But Ira was infatuated and after years of agonizing, Jeff left his wife and children and moved into a flat with her.

A photo from 1954 shows Ira approaching forty, having left Oakeshott Avenue only a few years earlier. Dressed in a dark knee-length dress, with one of the tight belts she liked, she is in heels and pearls, carrying a French straw country basket and posing, best foot forward, looking straight if unsmilingly at Dad's camera. The whole effect is a fashion-shoot version of suburban come-to-lunch simplicity. She was unquestionably the most elegant thing on the street that spring morning. Standing next to her, sporting a smile of contentment, is Jeff, and behind them is their pale-colored Morris Minor. Their cars would soon get a lot bigger.

Jeff's real name, unknown to us, was Richard Sellier Jefferies: Ira evidently liked calling her men by their surnames, a way of keeping her heroes at a distance. He was someone we would have described as "very English," which conjured up a set of associations we so rarely put into words it is hard to pin it down now. Let us say a certain manner, pleasant and crisp, a touch drier and more formal than we were used to — with the houndstooth sports jacket and tie and a pocket square in the breast pocket. There was the barked laugh, a hint of sherry and Home Counties clubbability, and, it was tempting to imagine, an ease with servants in the tropics. There was also his not being Jewish (so far as we knew), though that did not seem important and I don't remember it ever being discussed. Jeff's Englishness was surely no small part of his attraction for Ira. He now seems to me, who hardly knew him, to have embodied the Square Mile at its most self-assured, in the prosperous solid days that ran on, it felt like, for decades after the end of the war before the Big Bang of the 1980s helped turn everyone into a get-rich-quick banker on bonuses, by which point the City itself had ceased to be much connected to England at all. At the time we are talking about, in the afterlife of empire, when London firms controlled plantations and mines and the destiny of natural resources across the former colonial world, Jeff ran one of Britain's largest tropical timber traders. Denny Mott, his outfit, had become rich supplying wood for railroads and ships, and by the 1950s it had holdings everywhere from West Africa to Southeast Asia. It is characteristic of the era that this businessman, who liked the first-class cabin and enjoyed nothing so much as taking his wife to stay at the Paris Ritz, was also a lifelong Labour man, who had organized local party meetings. A tailor's cutter was a teenage fantasy; making a home with the chairman of Denny Mott, Ira could realize the capitalist idyll that had beckoned to her at the Petrograd station in the summer of 1924.

When the two of them settled into West Hill Court, round the corner from Oakeshott Avenue, that was it with local party meetings. And with fashion too: Ira left magazine publishing and turned to writing books. Her 1958 account of traveling with Jeff to Siam did well enough and was followed by her historical romances—*A Kingdom for a Song*, *The Witch's Son*, and *The Troika Belle*, ending up with *The Fortune Hunter*—fantasies packed with court intrigue, noble gamblers, dashing rakes, illegitimacy, mad passion, and fatal attractions. Georgette Heyer had paved the way for this kind of thing, and Ira trod a similar path and enjoyed a modest success. But although she was a writer with real talent, the books too stopped. Nothing, it seemed, with Ira was to be taken too far, and writing remained a divertissement.

After Max's death, Frouma moved into their block of flats and continued to cook for her daughter as she always had in Oakeshott Avenue. Her mother, her husband, and the Heath—these were Ira's devotions, hidden behind the fine clothes and careful elocution. She used to look out of their living-room window across the sunken lawns past the chestnut trees and the willows to the pond, listening to the geese in winter. In my small-boy's memory, drawn from no more than a few visits—we hardly ever went there—the most conspicuous feature of their apartment, which had surprisingly few books, was a gleaming and well-stocked drinks trolley. It was a comfortable life, one she had made and ultimately chosen for herself. But the wildness and the fantasy of her early years were now confined to her writing. The sarcasm had been reduced to formality. What remained were luxury cruises, company dinners at the Grosvenor or the Ritz, and drives in the Jag through France where they had some well-heeled friends in nice châteaus. Both of them liked a drink—another reason perhaps why our abstemious parents didn't look forward to their company—and I guess they were drinking more as time went on.

The surfeit of bodice-ripping romanticism in her prose hid an underlying astringency that had once been much closer to the surface. In the spring of 1943 she had written to Dad to congratulate him on his birthday: "My dear Bill," she had begun. "Please accept my felicitations on reaching (safely) the ripe old age of eighteen, with a small token of my esteem and astonishment at your having made it." Of course she was the one who had been lucky to make it and for it all to work out the way it had, which was what, in a way, she was saying. This kind of irony became, for a time, second nature. "I understand that we are soon to be blessed by your presence again for a considerable period so I shall keep my congratulations this side idolatry, many happy returns, Love Ira." These were years when she and Dad had been closer than we realized, despite all the differences in their upbringing and perhaps also despite jealousy at the attention his parents lavished on him. Yet life afterwards had not brought them together nor been able to preserve this intimacy. Ira's way of dealing with the violent changes of her childhood years had been to forge a persona—cigarette or drink in hand, studiously unserious and self-consciously romantic—that was too contrary to Dad's likes and taste to leave much room for enduring affection. She had tried to fix him up after the army with some of her fashionable friends, but neither they, nor she, were really his type. She became, in her egotism, her troubled and turbulent love life, her tendency to fantasy, her pursuit of looks and polish, another kind of anti-model for him, and it was difficult for us to see behind all that.

Many years after her death, the authorized version of our aunt's character, authorized that is to say within our immediate family, was challenged unexpectedly by a conversation that I had over lunch with my cousin Patrick in Paris. I remembered Patrick, my senior by a decade and more, from my visits to Paris as a twelve-year-old boy because I had gone once to his shop, an Aladdin's cave of African masks and textiles, which had made an impression on me chiefly because it was located on the Faubourg-Saint-Denis, in the heart of the old red-light district. Now in retirement in a quiet medieval backstreet near the Bastille, he and his companion, Françoise, shared a tiny flat filled with paintings, plants, and books. The gate from the street gave on to an ancient passage between two houses with carefully tended hydrangeas in large pots along its length. Inside their apartment, kilims covered the floor of their living room. It had not occurred to me to talk with Patrick about Ira, but when the conversation went that direction I was glad we did. The way he spoke about her was in such different tones to what I was used to and the warmth of his feeling was evident. She was "a woman of class," he declared with admiration, always happy to leave the Ritz and come to dinner with the family in their small

flat on rue Montparnasse. She would bring champagne and
wine — he tapped his elbow in respect to show she could handle
a glass or two — and she enjoyed a good time. Both of Patrick's
parents had liked her enormously and so had he. His father had
died before Ira took her own life, but Alice, his mother, was
alive, and when she heard the news, Patrick told me, "she collapsed in tears and wept." The contrast with the reaction, or the
lack of it, in our house made me aware of how powerfully one
can be shaped by the distribution of affections that one grows
up with, how specific and arbitrary these can be, their lack of
visibility allowing them to penetrate deep and take root until
one day something can come along and suggest an entirely different angle of vision and a new set of regrets.

CHAPTER SIXTEEN

Childhood

When I asked Dad what his first memory was, he said he remembered crawling into bed with his mother while his father was away on business. A large envelope had arrived for him and he had opened it in bed. "It turned out not to be a letter but a story by H. G. Wells. I think it was called something like 'Tommy and the Elephant.'" His mother's warmth, his father's absence. The start from which the rest will follow. He was three years old.

And the story?

"Tommy and the Elephant" tells of a rich man whose pride leads him off a cliff. Fearless Tommy, who is fishing for sharks, pulls him out of the sea and refuses to take any money. He is a resourceful boy and a virtuous one, who believes that "a good

deed is its own reward." But eventually he concedes, and asks
for a pet animal. The rich man visits a pet shop and rejects all
the obvious candidates: He is very proud and they seem too
ordinary. A tiger is ruled out because Tommy's mother might
object: "Mothers are sometimes so peculiar." So after spending
an entire day perusing the contents of all the shops in London,
he chooses an elephant and sends it by train, express delivery,
monogrammed. It arrives in less than a month, "so swift and
perfect has the railway traffic of our country districts become."
Tommy decides to call it Augustus after the Roman emperor.
He is not easily intimidated by sharks, money, or elephants. But
he likes boats, and the trains work.

"Another memory I had was of playing in the garden. We had
a garden on three sides. I think we might have been having tea
or something in the garden in the summer and the baker's boy

wandered into the garden—or the butcher's boy. This would have been 1929, something like that. He had wandered into the garden by mistake; he should have gone to the back door which was round the other side of the house. But he didn't know the geography. I remember how confused he was. It was an example to my mind of class consciousness. That was the worst thing you could do…to invade someone's garden like that."

It is hard to think of anything that played a more important role in defining Dad's sense of well-being than gardens. Growing up in suburban London, he flourished in spaces where one could build on a small and homely scale, a world of sheds and bonfires and compost, lawns, fences, and rockeries. Dad's connection to gardens was to give him lasting joy, and one of the most immediate memories I can conjure up if I want to think of him is the sight of him in a short-sleeved shirt and Wellington boots, his fork underfoot turning over the earth in the vegetable beds. A life to come: carrots and beans, rhubarb and gooseberries, London clay and the rich loam of west Oxfordshire, a home, and thoughts that remain close to the ground. The gardener is not a metaphysician; his is a different, less speculative, more active and experimental kind of knowledge, acquired by acting in and on the world. Dad hated to be idle, and one of the reasons he loathed his time in the army was that it stuck him behind a desk. "Lazy day," he would sometimes write in his diary; they were rare enough for him to note. "Dig, dig, dig": That one we find especially during the war when he was hard at work in the Oakeshott Avenue back garden under the gaze of the barrage balloons, putting up a chicken coop, setting up the Anderson shelter ahead of the expected bombers—the first of other future gardens, all made productive and useful by physical labor.

But what strikes me now equally about this image is not only the summer and the tea and the sense of a sanctuary momentarily violated, but also his sympathy for the intruder, a boy not much older than himself, and his wondering why his mistake mattered so much. It was an early experience of the significance and arbitrariness of the English middle-class social code. You have to know your place.

Dad had a feeling for place, and a capacity to recognize the places in which he could be himself and feel at home. And for him the soil that counted was always English. Eternally curious about the Russia his parents had left behind—the half a dozen volumes of *The Story of a Life*, the lyrical memoirs of the Soviet writer Konstantin Paustovsky, sat on the bookshelf in our living room as long as I can remember; and a tiny Kustodiev snow-scape on the wall was a reminder of the Russian winters of Max's and Frouma's childhood—he would have shared the very English sentiment expressed by the popular nineteenth-century author Charlotte Yonge that "the record of a thousand peaceful years is truly a cause of thankfulness." Tracking footpaths on family walks across the Downs, snagging blackberries with his walking stick, warding off inquisitive cows with a trusted Ordnance Survey map in his hand, he was in his element.

A quiet and nurturing childhood had been all but unknown in the Mazower family before Dad's birth. Max's father had died when he was fairly small, and the move to Vilna and the responsibilities on his shoulders had precluded much of a formal education. With his mother missing and his absent father, André's early years had been almost entirely deprived of parental affection or stability. Frouma's had been punctuated by the constant movement of her father's work, and Ira's first memories were of checkpoints, squalor, and fear. So Dad's settled upbringing was unprecedented and goes a long way to explaining, I think, the gratitude and respect he always felt to his parents and his sense of obligation towards them.

"The last memory I have is of a lorry running down West Hill out of control. The curb in those days was quite high. The pavement must have been a foot above the road. The lorry crashed into the curb and I think somebody was hurt or injured or killed. I remember my mother taking me indoors so I shouldn't see this because there was some sort of crash. It was just on the other side of this hedge and fence onto West Hill."

The Holly Lodge Estate was and is the most genteel of enclaves, its gates and fences allowing pedestrians in but otherwise keeping the world at bay. It is flanked on one side by the overgrown tangle of Highgate Cemetery and on the other, across West Hill, by Hampstead Heath, where under his mother's gaze Dad remembered making houses out of the giant plane leaves that fell in autumn.

This environment, which was rarely disrupted by anything noisier than prams and nannies and their charges, is where he roamed in boyhood with his best friend, a little daredevil from down the road. He was called David Stevenson, and if one asked Dad about his memories of childhood, that was the name that had stuck. In his child's view adults were mostly absent, but in fact the Stevensons were the first family the Mazowers got to know on the Estate, and it was, I think, no coincidence that they were Leftists. Good-looking, affable, and a marketing genius, David's father, W. H., was at that time the editor of the *Daily Herald*, a newspaper that he had turned into the world's top-selling daily. As a result, Bill Stevenson occupied a position of considerable influence in interwar Britain. The *Herald* was umbilically connected to the Labour Party and the trade union movement, and the newspaper's massive two million–plus circulation—unthinkable today when unions wield little clout and the press everywhere is in crisis—testified to the power of organized labor in Britain, an unexpected realization—in a different clime—of Max's youthful dreams. The newspaper used to bestow an annual Order of Industrial Heroism to celebrate the courage of ordinary workers, and as the national voice of Labour, it was deeply interested in Bolshevik Russia. The Holly Lodge Estate was thus more than a haven; it looked outwards too and gave Max and Frouma and their little boy access to the ideas and people who were steering the country towards a new kind of socialism. Through the Stevensons and others like them, welcoming and open, newcomers to the metropolis themselves, the world of the Bund encountered the very different yet oddly kindred ethos of the British labor movement.

But the Stevensons and the Mazowers were bound by things more consequential and enduring than world affairs. David's sister, Mari, was Ira's best friend, the role model for her first brief disastrous marriage. Mrs. Stevenson, Welsh-born, was a justice of the peace, and became something like the Mazowers' interpreter-guide to the invisible codes of the new society they had landed in: It was in her living room that Max and Frouma swore the oath for their naturalization in 1935, and she and Frouma remained close until their deaths. An aura of melancholy hung over her towards the end, at least in Dad's recollection. Into the 1950s he would cycle over at his mother's request to take provisions to Mrs. S., now living alone in a modest flat above the post office in South End Green, a far cry from the beautiful house they had occupied when her husband ran the paper known as "the Miracle of Fleet Street." Her daughter had died tragically, her husband had drifted away in the grip of drink, and they had separated. Her two sons had made new lives in America. Leaving your aging mother for a foreign land—it was not something Dad could have contemplated for himself. The memory of the Stevensons, I think, came to embody in his mind not only the exuberance of his boyhood but everything that could intervene over the years to tear a family apart.

The Estate had its place for the working classes of course: It relied on them. Dad never forgot Alice, the maid, and the sight of her combing her hair in the kitchen in Makepeace Avenue: She was gone by the time he was five. Trade came round the side: the grocers' boy, the butcher, and the coal merchant. Most excitingly, there was the milkman: At a time when there were still horses on the roads and few of their acquaintances had cars, his electric Express Dairies milk float was a portent. Dad's first job was to help him on his dawn round; his first pay, a tub of

ice cream. The milkman was not normally allowed to take him
outside the estate, however, and when he asked Dad's parents
for permission to take him to see Arsenal, then dominant in
English soccer, at Highbury Stadium, it was in tones of extreme
deference, for the Mazowers were, despite being "foreign,"
unassailably middle-class.

Even as a boy Dad knew that the impoverished elderly
"lady workers," who had fallen on hard times and lived in the
half-timber apartment buildings on the other side of Hillway,
must have come down in the world because they shared bath-
rooms and lavatories, a humbler station than that enjoyed by
the residents of semidetached homes on their section of Oakeshott Avenue. As for David, he disappeared into a posh school
and ended up in one of the most prestigious of regiments, the

Welsh Guards, and Dad lost touch with him. These were lessons in the mysteries of English class, lessons without which his generation's commitment to Labour's vision of a more egalitarian society would scarcely have been possible. Thanks to the dairyman, Dad was briefly a passionate Arsenal fan—it was the heyday of Ted Drake, a center forward described later as "strong, powerful, brave and almost entirely unthinking"—but only up to the war; after that, any real interest he had once had in sports vanished.

Max was fifty-one when Dad was born, and he remained reserved with his young son, never reading to him as Frouma did. He did not hug him and was sparing with praise. They went to the cinema together, but Max's pleasures were mostly solitary: an evening whisky, reading quietly in a deck chair in the garden. As time went on, he became more and more preoccupied with the state of his health. He told Dad next to nothing about his own youthful political exploits, and said equally little about his line of work. The first time Dad figured out the nature of his father's modest and mostly unsuccessful dabbles in property, conducted from a small office above a parade of shops in the nondescript suburb of Muswell Hill, was as they were being wound down after the Second World War. Dad found Max taciturn and undemonstrative; he thought he seemed to be a man to whom fatherhood had not come naturally. But Max was not entirely detached and he did keep an eye on Dad's progress. "You need to write more to the point of the subject," he and Frouma advised Dad while he was in school—to stick to the unshowy and direct approach to writing that Max had adopted since his days in the Bund, and that Dad was to take as his own.

In 1938, on Dad's thirteenth birthday, he got a missive from his parents jointly wishing him "many happy returns of the day" and reminding him — in a very rare reference to their all but nominal faith — that "according to Jewish Law you are already considered to be a responsible person...We hope you will grow up to be a joy to us and a success to yourself. We embrace and kiss you with all our love and expect you to enjoy your birthday as much as you can." And it was always "Dear Billy" and "Love Dad," a degree of affection that was by no means automatic in middle-class interwar England and, later on, during the war, when Dad was away from home, his father let him know, in his self-deprecating way, that he missed him.

For Frouma, it was the presence of her boisterous son that made the dull pain of emigration bearable and brightened days filled with material anxieties and hard manual work. Even with a maid's help, the business of keeping a household was arduous. Shopping often required a walk down the hill into Kentish Town, a distance of a mile or more. At home, there were generally six to eight people to be fed. There was no fridge until after the Second World War, no washing machine and no central heating. Clothes were washed in the sink in the poorly lit kitchen, scrubbed on a washboard, and wrung out by putting them through heavy wooden rollers that were turned by hand. Coal needed to be brought in daily, the fireplaces cleaned. There were the chickens to look after in the coop, and rabbits and the garden, none of which her husband was in a condition to help with. In addition, Frouma made clothes for herself and Ira. And there were, as time went on, more and more visits to the doctor and the hospital—for Max, who was often in ill health, for her children, and often too for her friends who came to depend on her for support. Frouma was very fond of her daughter but she was worn down by her flightiness, and so her son became her chief solace. For many years they went together to the local library and shared the books they brought back; and they went often to the cinema, usually with Max, sometimes without him. Tired by the daily grind, she delighted in and depended on the company of her "Billychik," and she missed him enormously whenever he was not at home. I don't expect it is a coincidence that unlike André and Ira, both of whom were initially dispatched to boarding schools, Dad was schooled nearby until the war intervened. Arguments over their son when he misbehaved were one of the few things that could lead to discord between his parents, but in this area, as in most things to do with the home, Max deferred to his wife, and Dad's upbringing was characterized by a high degree of tenderness and gentleness and the omnipresence of his mother's affection.

Thanks to the maid, and the milkman, and the Stevensons, and not least to his father, English was Dad's native tongue. But plenty of Russian was spoken in Oakeshott Avenue too—between his parents, or whenever his aunt or uncle came to stay, or when visitors came to tea—and this attuned his ear from an early age. Ira kept to English (she was, in Dad's words, the "most English" of the family), but by the time he was fourteen, he and his parents were habitually mixing Russian and English in the same sentence. He was also writing in Russian almost as early as in English, and although he needed it less and less as his older relatives died, he could slip effortlessly into it once or twice a year when he spoke by phone with his cousins in Moscow. In 1975, I think it must have been, he and I flew to Moscow from London and, shivering in the immigration hall at the airport, we waited in line. When one of our fellow passengers, a Spaniard, could not make himself understood to the official in the booth, Dad, who knew both languages, went up the line to offer to help out. Naturally, no sooner had he opened his mouth and uttered the first fluent words of his antiquated and mostly pre-revolutionary Russian than we were pulled aside for questioning. They let us go eventually, but by the time we emerged, everyone else had already left. I suppose this episode left its mark on me not only because it showed some of the more unexpected consequences of Dad's default helpfulness but because it seems to sum up the ambiguous value of his fluency. Even in the Cold War, it opened surprisingly few doors for him. Not that he ever pushed very hard. He never used it in his thirty years of service in the United Africa Company where his hours were passed in his office by the Thames, supervising the construction of breweries and devising marketing strategies for selling beer in West Africa. I think now he was probably content to keep it, like so many things, for the family.

Like André and Ira, Dad could also speak and write French with ease thanks to regular stays with his uncle and aunt in Paris, not to mention those August weeks with his parents on the coast of Normandy at the resorts they loved along the stretch from Franceville and Houlgate to Deauville. An army translator's course allowed him to add German to his quiver, though he never much used it afterwards, and later he learned to speak Dutch and Spanish fluently too. But the interesting thing is not that he could speak so many languages. His father could too, and so did many Jewish émigrés of that generation. What I find more remarkable is that while this marked him out from the average Englishman who could at best murder a few words of French and took pride in making no concessions to accent of any kind, Dad seems in most other respects to have been indistinguishable from any English boy of his age.

Assimilation, a term that has spawned dozens of social-science treatises, is both too grand and too crude a label to help us understand how this happened, not least because it suggests the Procrustean bed of a dominant culture, into which in some monstrous process the alien immigrant or immigrant child must fit, at greater or lesser cost to themselves. One thing wrong about this is that it implies a degree of cultural cohesion that did not exist: Neither England nor the world of North London Jewish émigré life represented anything as straightforward as a unitary culture. Also, none of the obvious academic categories—refugee, immigrant, minority—really gets at the specific social position of Dad's parents who were, if anything, émigrés by choice and design rather than refugees. Perhaps the

best description of their position and outlook can be found in
a memoir penned not long ago by a man who shared much of
Dad's background:

> We were not immigrants to Britain. We were not members
> of the Anglo-Jewish community, nor did either of my par-
> ents make the slightest effort to join it. So far as they could
> be defined socially, and so far as their interests, perspectives,
> and habits of conduct were concerned, it is almost enough
> to say that they were of that distinctive and remarkable
> class—essentially a cultural, not an economic or professional
> or even, properly speaking, a political class—known as the
> Russian-Jewish intelligentsia. They were never to leave it,
> and were never to be transformed into something else.
>
> Little enough has been written about these remarkable
> men and women of the turn-of-the-century Russian-Jewish
> intelligentsia, least of all in their exile: of their boundless
> energy, their intensity, their seriousness, the freedom with
> which they moved from one level of non-Jewish society to
> another, and the ease, betokening a kind of aristocracy, with
> which they were able to deal with whomever they encoun-
> tered on whatever terms immediate circumstances seemed to
> require. But their supreme characteristic was their undeviat-
> ing interest in public affairs, by and large to the detriment of all
> other concerns: income, literature, art, simple entertainment,
> or, not least, family. Virtually everything else came second to
> the common, consuming interest in public questions and pub-
> lic activities, or, not to put too fine a point on it, politics.[1]

In the case of Dad's parents the idea of family was much more
important than this suggests. But it otherwise illustrates very
well the importance of their background, and their detachment

from the existing gradations and hierarchies of Anglo-Jewish London. As it happens, the passage's author, David Vital, had been at school for a time with Dad in Highgate, although later they lost touch because the politics of their families were very different. In those days, he was not called David Vital but David Grossman; Meir Grossman, his father, was a leading Revisionist Zionist and a close associate of Vladimir Jabotinsky, the Jewish nationalist whose opposition to the Bund went back to the start of the century and who became the chief inspiration many years later for the Israeli Right. In 1934 the Grossmans left London and emigrated to Palestine, something Max, with his anti-Zionist background, would never have contemplated. After a gap of sixty years, and by now a well-known Israeli historian and former government policy adviser, Dad's childhood friend resurfaced and was invited to our home in Golders Green. The evening stands out in my mind. Dad was a courteous host and dinner was passing in a predictably low-key way. But an old family friend was also there, and at one point Deborah, who must have been in her mid-eighties, lovely and eccentric and nobody's fool, expressed surprise when Vital started explaining, in terms suggestive of approval and respect, his father's close ties with Jabotinsky. "Jabotinsky," she mused. "Wasn't he like Hitler?" It was the only time I can recollect something like a political explosion at my parents' table, and an outraged Vital got up to leave. "No, no," she went on quite unfazed. "I don't mean that Jabotinsky was like Hitler so much as that Hitler was like him." I still can't tell if she was really trying to calm the waters or the opposite. Dad, who usually liked the quiet life, did not strike me as very disturbed: Deborah had only slightly, I think, exaggerated his own views. As he knew, the polemic was almost a century old, and our dinner table was witnessing one of the last rounds in an argument between Jabotinsky and the Bund that had begun around 1900. David Grossman had emigrated with his father and became David Vital. Was there ever any question of Dad doing anything but staying in the country of his birth? None at all. In fact, when the army asked him, during the war, whether as the son of two foreign-born nationals, he was planning to settle elsewhere, he told them he was not, and off he went to Sandhurst and officer training.

Oakeshott Avenue, Highgate

The living room of 20 Oakeshott Avenue looked over the small front garden to a grassy curb, a tranquil road, and the flower beds of the house opposite. North-facing, the room was dark but homely; a thickly impastoed forest scene hung on one wall, and two Russian peasant women sitting under birch trees on another—somehow Max had spirited the canvases out. There was whisky on the heavy sideboard from Maples, a tree at Christmas, borscht in cold weather, and blinis for Easter.

Growing up in interpenetrating worlds, Dad never gave the impression later on that combining them had required great effort or that he had felt caught between them. There had certainly been moments, some of which he mentioned, when he had been forcibly and perhaps uncomfortably reminded of his parents' origins, when life had struck the occasional xenophobic note, but I do not believe that this apparent effortlessness was a façade. His parents had given him a lead by making their fundamental declaration of outlook in his very name: Joseph, after his paternal grandfather in accordance with tradition; Mazower, a family and a place of origin; and, first and foremost, and most unexpectedly, William, a name from the land that would henceforward and through him be home—a name that we can be sure had never before been found in the family. A homage to the Bard, it was supposedly the only English name his mother knew when he was born, a signal that both she and Max wished to look ahead and not back to the old country, a signal he always followed. It seemed so naturally a part of him, I never thought to ask him about it, although in his case it was further anglicized to Bill, which was how, never being one to stand on ceremony, he always liked to be known. So in those three names there was the Russian background, there was England, and in addition there was the being Jewish, the last being probably the least important within the family but certainly not negligible—neither something to be flaunted nor to be hidden but diluted and flanked by the double acculturation provided by the other two.

He knew of course that his parents stood out locally, with their unusual name, their stream of foreign visitors, and his mother's heavy Russian accent. In those years before the influx of refugees from Germany and Austria there were few other

foreign families in the neighborhood. *Westwood* is a wonderful
novel set in Highgate that was written by their neighbor Mrs.
Webb—better known as Stella Gibbons, the author of the best-
selling *Cold Comfort Farm*, she lived just across the road from
them at number 19—and in it one sees how rare it seemed to
encounter a "Jew" in middle-class life at that time even in London. "It was a very, very English atmosphere," Dad recalled.
None of his closest friends at school had come from farther
away than Wales, and when his parents bought their first radio
around 1933 so that they could anxiously follow the news coming out of Europe, what their eight-year-old son really wanted
was to get to the cricket scores at the end so that he could discuss
them in class the next day. The swapping of comics and collecting of stamps were his favorite pursuits. His parents would get
summertime postcards from excursions to Littlehampton and
Wroxham and Southbourne-on-Sea addressed to "Munch" (or

more rarely to "Punch," the English turned into an almost Russian diminutive) with requests for magazines (*Rover*, *Hotspur*, or *The Modern Boy*), batteries, and torches, filled with stories of kidnapping and signed "Your loving son Billy (ex-brainy boy)" or on one occasion "Sir William Mazower."

School, often traumatic for children, seems to have suited Dad, perhaps because it allowed him to escape the pressure of his mother's unceasing love. But it is also true that he liked facts and words and was always curious so he found the work easy, and he had a circle of friends and got the rudiments of a fine education early on. With his mother, he had begun reading even before he was six at which age he began making the half-mile walk to school alone. The Hudsons had retired many years earlier, and Ingleholme had closed, so he went to Mrs. Holcombe's grandly named Osborne House School, which was in fact a room or two in one of the larger terraced houses in nearby Dartmouth Park. Two years later, he started at Highgate Junior School, which meant a blazer, canes and detentions, Latin and French grammar with the rest of his form in IIIB, mental arithmetic, and cricket and spelling taught by men who had survived the trenches of the First World War. It was schooling of the most conventional kind, but declensions and conjugations and logarithmic tables suited Dad's orderly mind. Later on, in his desk in IVB, there was a copy of the sixth edition of Lister's *French Grammar: Simple and Complete* and the school's own *Outline of Latin Syntax*, with much the same sequence of participles, gerundives, and case endings that schoolboys had learned forty years earlier and that would be drummed into me in the 1970s, the disciplinary bedrock of a serious education that was taught to impart not so much sociability as some kind of almost sadomasochistic mental rigor.

By now Dad was wandering alone well beyond the Estate. The walk to school would take him up through Highgate village; the journey back brought him past the sweetshop for a two-ounce bar of Cadbury's. One day he was alarmed at the sight of a tramp resting outside the Flask pub—in the depths of the Depression tens of thousands of men were unemployed and homeless—and it so startled him that he ran down the hill and cut himself dashing through a hedge. This was not much to compare with the riots, pogroms, massacres, and anarchy his sister and parents had grown up with, and it was in a spirit of self-deprecation that he retold the story, a testimony to the sheltering environment of his early years. Sometimes he would walk down to Lissenden Gardens to spend the evening with his friend Sherwood (first names being verboten in those days); they would listen to a music-hall radio show along with the parents and then the boys would head to the balcony to drop paper bags filled with water on unwary pedestrians. Sherwood's folks were proper in their speech and formally dressed and there were no books, a contrast with Oakeshott Avenue where everyone was always reading. Mr. S., who worked in the Foreign Office and was, in Dad's recollection "very hidebound," was Leslie R. Sherwood of Accounts, who would later get the Order of the British Empire and rise to be the head of finance. Friendship with Sherwood junior thus offered an entry point into the life of the English mandarin class, early familiarity with its habits of speech and behavior. And also perhaps with the feeling that often lay concealed beneath the surface stiffness because the Sherwoods for all their correctness were evidently welcoming, and in the summers of 1935 and 1936 they took him with them sailing on the Norfolk Broads. Sixty years later, he still had a boy's memory of night fishing, the wonder of those evenings, like something out of *Swallows and Amazons*, his favorite book in those days, when they would moor the yacht at dusk, and he and Sherwood junior would push off in the dinghy and quietly sail through the flat landscape, listening to the birds calling in the darkness.

In Dad's mind, places remained long after the faces and names of former friends were forgotten. He lost touch with Sherwood but always remembered Norfolk, and he took us there to spend summers by the sea when we were the age he had discovered it. The intensity of his attachment to certain landscapes meant that he would return to them with us, often repeatedly, and sometimes many decades later—not only Norfolk but the Normandy beaches and the villages in Dorset and South Devon where he had spent some of his first holidays—so that my own earliest memory of the sea is of peering out of the car window as we drive up the high street in Seaton one summer morning in the early 1960s. I can still hear the seagulls and smell the salt and then, as we crest the rise, the brilliance of the sunlight on the water, a thin blue line suddenly stretched before us, unforgettable. It is a memory he must have wanted to share by bringing us there, one so similar to his own but with the difference that in mine he is present and so is Mum, and my brother Dave is on the backseat beside me, whereas when he first visited the seaside, in 1932, he had been sent to stay with the Stevensons for reasons I have not been able to find out—lack of money is the likeliest explanation—and he was on his own and everyone else was back in London and he was sending them postcards reassuring them he was all right and asking his parents when they were going to visit. And now that I think about it, it occurs to me that perhaps we were there not only because of the pleasures those places had brought him but to exorcise a kind of loneliness he had felt then too.

47613 SOUTHBOURNE: ON THE SANDS LOOKING WEST.

I don't think we ever fully grasped—and perhaps that was the whole point, that we were not meant to—how precarious that middle-class way of life in Oakeshott Avenue must have seemed at times in the mid-1930s and how much the memory of those years of making do contributed to Dad's later desire for security, his hatred of waste, and his hoarding of scraps of all kinds on the off chance they might come in useful. (This was the man who in Mum's recollection only lost his temper once—when she threatened to throw out an old kettle he wanted to mend.) The reality was that the family's savings were running low. Max had abandoned his life as a merchant—world trade had collapsed during the Depression—and begun investing in property. But converting cramped terraced houses in Friern Barnet, an outlying suburb, yielded nothing of substance and he began to worry that his business partner was cheating him. It was a struggle to sustain the life and comforts they had enjoyed earlier, and Max himself was in and out of hospital. It was now that Frouma took charge. She got rid of the maid and began making dresses for people she knew. She also decided to take in paying lodgers, leaving Dad to sleep downstairs sometimes on the sofa in the small front room. It was a sign of how accommodating he was that he put up with it without a great deal of protest. Ira, who was nearly twenty, protested more and kept her room. André would appear sporadically and ask for money and leave in a cloud. Of the children, Dad was already the helpful one.

With lodgers came a heightened sense of foreboding and a more intimate view of the threat from across the Channel. Heinrich "Heini" Grunwald, a mathematically inclined half-Jewish young refugee from Vienna, came to stay with them in 1936 or 1937. After the Anschluss, he was followed by a pair of sisters from Austria, and then by an older couple who managed to get out of Danzig on the eve of the war. The world was becoming more troubled and Dad was more attuned to its political complexities than other boys of his age: "I was really quite a political animal, I suppose...Most of the boys weren't interested in politics." On the wall of his room he was marking a map of Spain with the key battlegrounds: Guadalajara, Lleida, Jaén, Guernica. In the local library, he had long discussions about General Franco with the librarian, a fellow republican sympathizer, and wondered why his favorite writer, the prolific Percy Westerman, the author of such popular yarns as *A Mystery of the Broads* and *Standish of the Air Police*, had taken the nationalist side.

Because his parents could no longer afford the fees at High-gate, Dad won a scholarship that took him to a new school across the Heath in Hampstead. Down the road Oswald Mosley's Blackshirts were holding rallies and denouncing the over-running of the country by refugees. Fascism seemed to be on the rise in England, and in Hampstead, around his new school, there was plenty of anti-refugee feeling openly expressed. At UCS, as University College School was known, the Leftist tra-dition of Oakeshott Avenue now made itself felt. His parents forbade Dad from joining the cadet corps and along with some other juvenile pacifists, he spent long afternoons weeding the playing fields. When he began polling fellow pupils to gauge opinion on the Spanish Civil War, the headmaster feared he was breeding a dangerous radical and called him into his study and urged him to think less about politics and to make more friends.

The looming crisis began to prey on his nerves. He was wait-ing at Gospel Oak station one September morning on his way to school when he glanced across the tracks to a deserted platform on the other side and spied a disused line with weeds growing out of it. He started fantasizing about phantom trains speeding through, like the one in Walter Forde's popular 1931 film *The Ghost Train* that terrifies a small group of passengers stuck at night in an isolated country backwater—a potent incarnation of the nightmares of revolution that troubled the "deep, deep sleep" (in Orwell's phrase) of middle-class Britain, faced with the increasing threat of extremism from across the Channel. In the railway carriage that took him to school, heavy leather straps held down the windows and he wondered worriedly how easy it would be to cut them if there was an accident and they needed to get out. On his twelfth birthday, his parents gave him a bike. He took enthusiastically to cycling, at first over the

Heath to school and then farther and farther afield, a glimpse of freedom, a way of banishing the anxiety of being trapped.

There was always a coming and going at Oakeshott Avenue. To Max, and especially to Frouma, friends had an almost existential significance, reinforcing family as a resource in hard times; their closest ones they saw regularly over decades. These were people they trusted, often living nearby, who had shared many of the experiences of their generation and background. Most of them had taken politics seriously their entire lives, and understood the stakes for Europe.

I only became aware of how remarkable some of them were long after Dad's death. I had started to notice a familiar name — Zukerman, often abbreviated as Zuk — cropping up in Frouma's letters, and one thing I did know was that Dad had been friends with a boy called Dick Zukerman. I remembered him because he and Dad had stayed in touch over the years, and when I was growing up he would sometimes come to visit us, a warm and charismatic man in his forties. The Zukermans and the Mazowers had been good friends, close enough for Frouma to have entrusted Dad to them for summer holidays by the sea, and later, in the panicked days of September 1939, to their care for a spell in the country to get him out of London and away from German bombs.

What I had not understood until I was guided by Frouma's letters — and found myself in the middle of something much larger — was exactly how Dick and Dad had come to be playing together. Dick's father was a journalist called William Zukerman who had been born in Tsarist Russia. Like Max and Frouma, he had gotten out, and like them he was on the Left but not a communist. What he was or became, in the Bundist spirit, was a vocal Jewish opponent of Zionism, and after the creation of Israel in 1948, he was a prominent and early critic of what he called American Jewish tribalism. In 1949, settled by then with his family across the Atlantic, he wrote a prescient essay entitled "Jews as Conquerors," one of several in which he deplored the treatment of the Arabs in the new Jewish state and likened it to the way the Jews themselves had been treated before the war in Europe. Today William Zukerman's writings have been rediscovered by a new generation of American Jewish critics of Israel. But between 1920 and 1941, when Zionism was not the obsession it has become today, he was the European correspondent of a New York Yiddish daily, sending dispatches from across the Continent. In 1936 he reported on the rise of fascism in Britain and the Battle of Cable Street; in 1937, he published *The Jew in Revolt: The Modern Jew in the World Crisis*; the following year his attention turned to anti-Jewish policy in Poland and the changing political outlook there. His wife was also very much part of their circle too, not least because she had a sister in Moscow with whom she was in touch, and she and Frouma relied on each other from time to time to evade the Stalinist censorship by sending coded messages through their loved ones in Russia: you only did that with someone you trusted.

In early 2016 I found that Dick, just shy of ninety, was living in very active retirement in Vancouver. Since I wanted to track the network of my grandparents' friendships, it seemed like he might be a good starting point. I called him up and asked if he could remember any of the people his parents and the Mazowers had known together. It was some eighty years in the past and only one name came to his mind, he said, but it was quite a name: Emma Goldman, probably the most famous American anarchist of the twentieth century. Dick thought he recollected at least one occasion on which she dined with his parents when the Mazowers had also been there. Whether or not they all ever ate together—and the odds are he was right—it turns out that that they certainly knew each other. A kind of proof: On the shelves in Dad's office we found one of Zukerman's books with a handwritten inscription by the author to Goldman. Somehow it had never reached the intended recipient and ended up with us, probably because Max or Frouma had failed to deliver it.

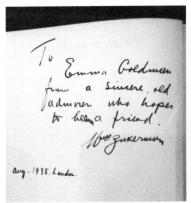

"To Emma Goldman, from a sincere old admirer who hopes to become a friend." The date is August 1938. William Zukerman and Goldman had in fact known each other in some small way a long time because back in 1910, the twenty-four-year-old Zukerman had written for Goldman's anarchist journal, *Mother Earth*. But that Dad's family had ever moved in the same circles as this world-renowned subversive was something I had certainly not expected.

Their acquaintance seems to have begun around 1937 when Goldman, who had been stirring up trouble, and hearts, on both sides of the Atlantic for forty years, arrived in London as a representative of the powerful anarchist grouping in the Spanish Civil War. She set to work as strenuously as only this passionate, egocentric professional revolutionary could, drumming up support and speechifying at Speakers' Corner in Hyde Park. But her habitual energy hid a growing inner sadness. It was not a happy time in Goldman's life and friends mattered to her more than ever. At sixty-eight, she was growing old for the life of a nomadic activist, especially as her longtime companion, Alexander Berkman, had just died in terrible circumstances in France—ill with cancer, he had tried to commit suicide and died painfully and slowly with Goldman by his side.

She had never liked London or understood the English, so families from the world of her youth provided solace and shelter. One of these yielded her London "headquarters" in those months, as she threw herself into what was to be her last great cause. The location was, to my astonishment, a tiny spare bedroom in a modest Golders Green apartment, and it was there that another forgotten name from my childhood rose up to greet me. I remembered Liza Koldofsky as a thin, elderly Russian lady who always had sweets available for small visitors and let us watch her television in her scrupulously neat dark home. We lived only a few streets away, and when we were kids, we used to call in to see her whenever we visited our doctor because she was across the road from him. It had just been her—there had been no husband when we knew her. Now it turned out that this frail ghostly figure, soon departed from our lives, had lived in Golders Green since before the Second World War and had been Emma Goldman's landlady and close friend, and the likely link between her and the Mazowers.

Goldman, the Zukermans, and now the Koldofskys—threads in the tangled skein of this vanished micro-society of the Russian Jewish emigration that I was trying to unravel. Liza's husband had been a pro-Bundist journalist in London in the Tsarist years, a union organizer in Canada, and a manager of American Jewish relief funds during the Russian Civil War. He had been targeted as a communist by the Canadian police and as an anti-communist by the Bolsheviks. He was clearly a capable, idealistic, and very brave man who like all the others in this little group had survived a period of extraordinary turbulence. The worst of it had come during the Russian Civil War, when the Jewish populations of the former Pale had been devastated by a series of pogroms, mostly carried out by the White armies, which had left thousands, if not tens of thousands, dead. In those days when international relief work was in its infancy and conditions were unbelievably dangerous, Semyon Koldofsky negotiated with Bolsheviks and anti-Bolsheviks alike in order to bring aid to the devastated shtetls of the Pale and had managed the task well. He had first met Emma Goldman in Moscow during those years, when, as she later wrote in a tribute to him, "life was cruelly hard and the struggle bitter." By the late 1920s, eking out a living as a translator and a penniless journalist, he and his wife had settled in London.

And where exactly had they chosen to live? Right there in the undistinguished suburb where my brothers and I would later be raised, in Golders Green, only a few doors down from my old kindergarten. They had found a small flat in Beechcroft Court, a cheap apartment block that backed onto the new aboveground section of the railway—the trains heading up to Brent Cross and Hendon screeched past their windows from morning to night. That then was where Emma Goldman holed up, at least until Semyon died prematurely, worn out by ill health, poverty, and overwork, at which point Liza, who earned a pittance sowing curtains for friends, moved to the modest semi on nearby Sneath Avenue, where she was still living thirty years later.

In the 1960s London may have been swinging but Golders Green felt like a place where nothing ever happened, the epitome of suburban blandness. As a boy, I knew of course that the tree-lined streets that were so familiar to me had not been there fifty or sixty years earlier. In fact I think now that is what first drove me to immerse myself in history because when I was about ten or eleven I would make visits to the public library on Golders Green Road to find out what I could about the area's vanished farms, the old field boundaries, the medieval origins of local names. Sitting quietly in the reference section, obsessively mining the riches buried in Eilert Ekwall's *Concise Oxford Dictionary of English Place-Names*, I suppose I was trying to uncover the deeper past that would root me to a spot that otherwise seemed to offer so little. What I had missed was that it was precisely Golders Green's lack of history that had been the draw for others, that it was in this ultra-new suburb — with its thousands of houses built in scarcely a decade, with no one already there to claim prior ownership — that these newcomers to England found themselves most at home, most easily able to sink into the comfortable anonymity that they valued. The Ridgeway, Woodstock Avenue, Wessex Gardens — the very names of its streets had marketed an anodyne vision of English pastoral to new entrants to the metropolitan middle class. From the start it had been a kind of survivors' paradise.

I suddenly saw Golders Green with new eyes, a place exploding into being as the result of one of those amazing speculations that had transformed huge swathes of London every bit as radically as older landgrabs had transformed the empire. In 1900, it was still a rural backwater of dairy farms and scattered villas with a population of a few hundred. But once the high-flying American businessman Charles Yerkes, a land developer, convicted larcenist, and blackmailer, managed to persuade Parliament to give him permission to extend the railway line north beyond Hampstead Heath, land values had shot up, the fields were plowed under, and hundreds of houses were built annually, before and after the First World War. No wonder Max had felt the lure of property development. By 1923 Golders Green had more than twenty thousand residents. There was a shopping parade and you could watch films at the local Ionic and variety shows at the Hippodrome, a gargantuan theatrical mélange of Roman, Greek, and Egyptian. All this was thanks to the trains that ran past the Koldofskys' window, in and out of one of the busiest underground stations in the capital.

"Give Golders Green back to the British Empire," joked a comedian at the Hippodrome in the late 1930s. The neighborhood had gotten a reputation early on for attracting Jewish families from the East End, and refugees from the Nazis settled there too. Yet neither group had much in common with the Russian political émigrés among whom Max had lived before 1914. By the 1930s, many of them had gone, and Max and Frouma kept their distance from anyone who was too credulous about the regime. Goldman — who certainly was not — was just passing through, but the Koldofskys and the Mazowers and the Zukermans were all very close and saw each other regularly. The Mazowers were in Highgate, half an hour from Golders Green by bus. The Zukermans and Koldofskys lived only three streets apart. Round the corner was another member of their circle, David Mowshowitch, who was probably one of the best-informed men in England on the nationalities situation in Eastern Europe.[2]

And there were younger friends, figures from the next generation who were equally powerful sources of political insight: Eva Broido's daughter, Vera, who had fled through Polotsk with Max, was done with Raoul Hausmann by 1934 and settled in London. During the Spanish Civil War, she often came round for tea with Dad and his parents. The man she was to marry, Norman Cohn, had just come down from Oxford and was also in digs nearby. In 1938, he spent three months living in a slum in the East End charting the rise of anti-Semitism across the United Kingdom for the pioneering social research group Mass Observation: The report he helped to author was the first serious study of racial prejudice ever undertaken in Britain.[3] Friends like these were a kind of political education in themselves, and they had an enormous influence on Dad at an impressionable age.

Thanks to Goldman—or, rather, thanks to her letters—something of this remarkable network of people swam back into view. She had left a truly voluminous correspondence at her death—even her lover Berkman had been staggered at her capacity for letter-writing—and it helped me to appreciate just how intense, and how political, these overlapping friendships had been. Through the second half of the 1930s, she would write regularly to the Koldofskys on the notepaper of Solidaridad Internacional Antifascista, the London-based body of which she was honorary secretary and which numbered George Orwell and Havelock Ellis among its sponsors. There was news from Spain and her reports on the state of politics in France, which Goldman found depressing and introverted. And in each of these letters there was a brief message for the Mazowers and often for Zukerman and Mowshowitch as well. In Paris, waiting for a visa to Spain, she asked Liza to "remember me most kindly to the Mazowers." "Affectionate greetings to the Mazowers," she wrote from Canada on September 12, 1939. "Remember me to Mr. Zuckerman. Remember me also to Mrs. Mazower and Mr. as well," in January 1940. Sending Liza some articles on Stalin's malign influence in Spain, the Red Army purges, and Soviet overtures to Hitler, she asked her to "please let the Mazovers [*sic*] read the articles and then send them to Doris Zhook, 12 Hillside Gardens Edgware Middlesex." (Zhook was an anarchist veteran—she and Goldman went back to the 1890s.)

What all this points to is the afterlife of a late-nineteenth-century Russo-Jewish socialist tradition—one that had begun with the Bund and then been overtaken and overshadowed but never entirely erased by Bolshevism. Some of these people were Bundists, others were Mensheviks or anarchists, but the labels did not matter much anymore and perhaps they had never mattered as much as historians make out. What lingered invisibly in London's Metroland, passing down through the generations, was an outlook, no longer confident of its capacity to shape the future but still engaged, highly informed, and faithful to its original values. Certainly not everyone in Dad's parents' milieu had been as political a creature as Semyon Koldofsky or William Zukerman, let alone Emma Goldman. There were businessmen, more or less successful, import-export traders in timber or coal, a doctor or two, journalists, and some research scientists; there was a tailor and a pioneering Yiddish art critic who had written early appreciations of Chagall and Modigliani. But of these a surprising number were or had been on the Left, former revolutionaries focused now on making their homes in this country where they had chosen to settle, behind the privet hedges and lawns of the very suburban streets that would end up exercising such a subliminal pull on my father that we would end up growing up there. Neither of the other two Mazower children, Ira and André, showed any interest in their parents' circle, and both in their different ways made it clear that they wanted to throw off the part of their background that these circles represented. Max and Frouma did nothing to stop them. Whether they were eating properly was always a more urgent subject for Frouma's concern and Max's approach was to allow his children to guide themselves. It was their son Billy who was most attentive to the grown-ups. I imagine them clustered around the radio for the news from Spain, the latest horrors in the Third Reich, and the unfolding tyranny in Moscow, the faint but intense buzz of conversation in Russian that reaches him while he is with Dick in the next room, playing corpses, a favorite game, lying on the living-room floor pretending to be dead while Max emerges silently in his smoking jacket, an early-evening drink in his hand. In this atmosphere, Dad's political consciousness matured rapidly, and unlike that of his half siblings, it quickly came to replicate his parents' orientation. He went through a brief communist phase but by the time he was fourteen his mother was reporting half in amusement, half seriously, that he was "through with communism and is now simply a socialist."

The first time it occurred to me to think about Dad's life more systematically, about the world of his childhood and how it had formed him, was when the Hayward Gallery hosted an exhibition about art in the era of the interwar dictatorships. The centerpiece was a re-creation of the 1937 Paris International Exposition, at which, famously, the German and the Soviet pavilions faced off as if foreshadowing architecturally the imminent war, collectively looming over the optimistic internationalism of the previous century that the Eiffel Tower had once incarnated. I went down to the South Bank with Dad to see it, and at one point, as we went around, he turned to me and said, "I was there, you know." I could hardly believe it; it was a shock to imagine him, standing there full of life in front of me, back in history, on the wall. But it was true—he was never wrong about such things: He had been there.

August 8, 1937, was a blisteringly hot summer day in Paris, and when Dad got up that morning at his aunt Niura's house, she was already fretting about letting him stay out in the sun too long, especially in his new suit and tie. It was his first visit without his parents but there was no chance of his being neglected. As he was only twelve, Heini, Max and Frouma's lodger, had accompanied him across the Channel to suburban Beauchamp, north of Paris, where Niura lived with her husband, Yasha. After breakfast in the garden, Yasha, Heini, and Dad caught the train into town. At the Gare du Nord, his uncle Vitalie was waiting for them, and the four men—Dad, Heini, Yasha, and Vitalie—went around the newly opened Palais de la Découverte, and then crossed the Seine to tour the grounds of the exposition. Heini, the refugee from Nazism, was on his way back to Vienna to try to get his family out; Yasha was a tough White Russian who had fought his way to France through not one but two civil wars; Vitalie had served in the Red Army before making his own escape from the Soviet Union. The intensity of the ideological confrontation looming over Europe needed no explaining to men like this, and it was in their company that Dad in his boyhood came to know and love France. They joked around in French—first language for none of them though Vitalie and Yasha were fluent by this time—and headed back to Beauchamp around four for tea. I have the letter that Vitalie wrote his wife later that day describing it all. Dad, whom they had got to know a little a year or so earlier when they had visited London, is *"vraiment un garçon épatant et il est beaucoup plus attaché à nous maintenant."* The boy had tired easily—it had been *very* hot—and anyway the sights themselves had been disappointing. Back at the house, the dog adores him and so does Niura. He charms them all. He tells Niura that he loves Alice, Vitalie's wife, better than his sister, Ira. He is palpably energized by the company of younger, more communicative men than his ailing father, and by the affection of the lively women who dote on him. After the strains of home, the doctors, the worries from Moscow, the lack of money, Paris must have been a shot in the arm.

When I was sent to stay for the first time in Beauchamp with Niura and Yasha, I was about the age Dad had been when he went in 1937. The line wound out of the Gare du Nord through the Paris outskirts, just as it had done in his day, and there were the same quiet hedge-lined streets once you stepped off the train. The tall iron gate that Niura always kept shut defended a rather lifeless front garden. The bell rung, Niura would emerge from the house, trimly patting her always neat bun, not a hair out of place: She had a slightly coquettish manner, attenuated by age. This was not the house they had lived in before the war—they had left the avenue Hébert place with its wild garden and old trees—but it was in the same sleepy district and is the setting in which I always think of Niura and Yasha. Inside it had the stillness of a house without children, and Yasha was retired, ailing, and seemingly charmless. Even so, the Toumarkine warmth meant one never felt unwelcome. My halting French was met with fond kisses and a stream of Russian endearments and food quickly emerged from the kitchen for the *golodnyye sobaki*—hungry dogs. Then off I would be sent to the local boulangerie for baguettes, French or no French, as Niura had once sent Dad out too.

The haven at Beauchamp had been a precarious one in those days, much more precarious than I had realized. Niura, the youngest of the Toumarkines, had left the USSR shortly after Frouma, passing through London before settling in Paris where she had gone to a party of Russians and met Yasha Stepanof, a stocky hard-drinking railway engineer. Both of them had the Nansen passports issued to refugees by the League of Nations, which meant that they were officially stateless; neither of them acquired French citizenship until after the war. There had been a rocky few years in the mid-1930s in which Yasha had lost his job, and they thought seriously for a time, despite Yasha not being Jewish, of emigrating to Palestine. Nothing came of that and luckily he found work again in the design offices of a large French rolling-stock manufacturer. He was an accomplished draftsman who had been trained in the imperial engineering college near Smolensk before World War I and he had learned his trade the hard way—on railroads in Finland and the Caucasus. In Beauchamp, stretched out on the chaise longue in the living room, he would regale his nephews with stories. Unlike Max, he was happy to talk and had a vast technical knowledge. He spoke to Dad about the Trans-Siberian Railway in the old days and the workers whose hands he had seen frozen to the rails. It was the cold, he said, that had started him drinking—he did not hide his problem with the bottle, a problem that in later years was to get so much worse that Niura would often have to go out in the early hours to get him out of the gutter and bring him home. He had fought the Reds at Sebastopol, and needed little prompting to unbutton his shirt to show the Bolshevik "gift" he had received there, a bullet wound in his shoulder. Like others in the White armies he had escaped across the Black Sea to Constantinople. He had then made his way to Bulgaria where he built roads and offered his services, as thousands of other Russian soldiers did, to the Bulgarian army in its bloody coup against the agrarian Left. This fighting was behind him by the time he settled in France late in 1923. He had briefly been married before, but his first wife, Bulgarian to judge from her name, had died shortly after their move to Paris. Once he met Niura they settled in Beauchamp and lived near the railway sidings and his workplace.

Yasha was old and cantankerous by the time I got to know him. But in pictures from the mid-1930s he seems much more at ease and more affectionate, if not with his wife—theirs was never a happy bond—then with his nephew. It was, I think, from his White Russian engineer uncle that Dad learned about planting vegetables, putting up sheds, and keeping chickens, practical lessons that were to prove useful on Oakeshott Avenue when the war started. It was in Beauchamp too that Dad found how much he loved playing with their dog, Pchelka (Bee), with the result that in the spring of 1939 their charlady in Oakeshott Avenue thrilled him, and his mother, by bringing round an eight-week-old puppy to take their minds off the international scene.

There were other lessons too in Yasha and Niura's stormy, nerve-racking relationship, something Dad had not experienced at close quarters before. Niura was lively, conscious of her appearance, a great confidante—even the secretive André seems to have confided in her—and to judge from her love of hamming it up for the camera, the extrovert in the family. But she was unhappy that she had no children, and her husband tended to flirt heavily, especially when he was drunk—and with his friends he drank a lot. They had frequent and explosive quarrels, loud enough to worry Dad when he was there, and to make him wish he wasn't: His parents wondered how bad things got when no one else was around. Perhaps as a result, Niura was often mysteriously ill during those years. At the same time, she was a devoted and loving aunt, and like Frouma, her cooking covered all of Russia's holidays and traditions: borscht, blinis and cakes, homemade curd cheese, stuffed carp. Despite the domestic turbulence, Beauchamp became a refuge for her nephews and nieces, and visiting her in Paris was a rite of passage that all the Mazower children—André included—went through in the 1930s.

Back in Highgate, the plight of Heini Grunwald brought home the lengthening shadow that was being cast by Nazism. They were certainly aware of it before, but the plight of Jews trying to get into Britain could not and did not leave them unmoved. Dad once commented to me that Ira was the least Jewish of all of them, and when I asked what in fact it meant for the Mazowers to be Jewish, given their Christmas trees and Easter feasts and unease with Jewish festivals and total horror of synagogues—the whole Bundist suspicion of more or less any form of organized religion—he said that what it evoked for him was chiefly that sense of solidarity that he and his parents had felt with the refugees trying to escape Germany and Austria after the Nazis came to power.

Six or seven months after Heini and Dad had gone to Beauchamp, the Wehrmacht marched into Vienna and the refugee crisis came to Oakeshott Avenue. Heini's uncle and father (his mother had died when he was young) had fled Austria on the day of the German takeover, made their way through France to the Channel, and were expected in London any minute when the telephone rang: It was them. They had been refused entry at Folkestone and sent back to France, so Heini went to Paris the same day to try to sort things out. Not only did he fail but he came close to being refused entry back into England too. A fragment of one of Frouma's letters to her brother in Paris conveys her state of mind, plunged suddenly back into the uncertainty and terror of flight:

> [On Friday Heini] immediately left by a night steamship.
> In the middle of the day on Saturday, [he] shows up all of a

sudden, in a terrible condition, unshaven, thin and pale, and he tells us that his father and uncle have returned to Vienna and that he was detained on his way back here in Newhaven, and they didn't want to let him through. After four hours in detention, they let him in, but marked his passport that he is only permitted to stay in England for one month, because he revealed that he has twenty pounds in the bank and they said that is enough for one month…

I tried to calm him down as best I could; I told him we will go to Stevenson and ask them to take steps, and we will petition his college director, in a word not allow him to leave. Now I will have to charge him much less of course since I cannot turn him away in such circumstances. I sent him to take a bath and he went to sleep, since as it turned out he had not slept for two nights. He slept from 2 p.m. on Saturday until 11 a.m. on Sunday, and woke in better shape.

Today he went straight to the bank manager and then, based on the results of this conversation, we'll decide what to do. The French are acting so much nobler than my compatriots. We have only a single dream now—that you get naturalized. Recent events in Russia have alienated both the socialists and the conservatives here. It is not clear where Stalin's policy can lead and an alliance with Hitler is not out of the question. I am so afraid for our folks there…

In the end Heini managed to stay, and his father joined him in England and they moved out of Oakeshott Avenue. But the struggle was coming closer, and I can't help noticing how when Frouma writes about Heini and the problems he faces it immediately arouses her fears for her own family. "The massacres in Moscow and Spain have alarmed us a lot," Frouma wrote to her brother in September 1938, "and we are immersed in these concerns at the moment." And a week or so later: "My kids are quite calm while Maxi and I are, obviously more worried." Max did not show it directly—perhaps his chronic ill health reflected his anxiety—but Frouma did. As 1939 began, she feared waking up to the sound of German bombs, and found the Londoners' sangfroid made her more conscious of her own unease: "[It] does not look as if a war can break out any minute. People paint houses, plant flowers and trees and think about vacations and soccer and now about the king's trip to America." "For now the sun is shining and airplanes are flying, but they are ours—I would like to think that this nightmare will somehow get resolved without war."

Both Frouma and Max fretted about their relatives and urged the Toumarkines in Paris to obtain French citizenship. "We are very worried about you and Yasha," Frouma wrote to her sister. "My God, when will your French realize that their quarrels just play into the hands of the fascists?" Despite her fears she let Dad go to Paris that August. He took his camera and this time he caught the ferry to Dieppe alone; the images in his album are of the last prewar summer: picnicking with Niura in the long grass of the Oise, fishing from the riverbank, playing with the dog. Beauchamp had become an extension of home, a place with its own rituals: the morning coffee on the table in the back garden, or shaving his uncle on the porch outside, something it is hard to imagine his father, who was rarely out of a suit and tie, ever letting him do. He wrote to his mother and reassured her he was having fun: "I haven't yet made the acquaintance of the boys next door but I caught sight of the smaller one looking at me through a window in their house so I tried to look *British* which was a rather complicated procedure because I was on hands and knees playing with the kitten." A few days after, less than a week before the outbreak of the war, he pushed his way onto a crowded boat and made his way back across the Channel, annoyed that Hitler had disturbed his stay and prevented him from getting through either the mystery novels in the living room or the seven bottles of lemonade that his aunt had ordered.

CHAPTER SEVENTEEN

The War

We were once on holiday by the sea in Cornwall, a fairly large clan by now, and Mum and Dad were already grandparents several times over. Dad and I were walking down a dune to the beach behind the others, and I asked him how people had felt when the war ended. Exhausted, he replied, not needing very long to think it over, "We were all exhausted."

An exhausting experience, and an inexhaustible subject, the war dragged on one way or another for him for more than ten years, and in that time he went from being a schoolboy to being a trained soldier with multiple technical skills who had been through bombing and air raids and knew about weapons and had seen the devastation they caused. In 1937 he was still reading *The Modern Boy*. By the time he had finished his national service, it was the spring of 1948 and these things were long behind him. The war made him more conscious of his relatives abroad, of his origins, of the differences between him and the more insular men serving with him. But the war also made him more English because he was fighting for his country and sharing in the experiences that bound an entire generation together. Or maybe it would be easier and less misleading to say simply that the war saw him become capable of and primed for certain decisions about the shape of his life to come, decisions that fate was on the whole kind enough to allow to come true.

Thirteen at the time of the Munich crisis, and already as tall as his mother, Dad initially took a boyish view of things, regarding the whole business as a bit of a relief after the unreal peace, and a lot more exciting. War's imminence meant putting together sheds and chicken coops and measuring vegetable beds and fitting blackout curtains. His practical bent was evident, and his weekly sixpence was disappearing on carpenter's wrenches and other tools from Woolworths. When it was announced that Anderson corrugated-iron shelters were to be distributed, he took charge of the digging. Max was too old and ill for such exertions, and André was rarely at home, so Dad became the man of the house. Yet he still thought air-raid precautions a great game and became obsessed enough for the same headmaster who had been worried about his political leanings to call him in and suggest he should spend less time digging shelters and more time making friends. It does not seem to have done much good, and as he entered adolescence, he gives the impression of having become more emotionally dependent on his family than before.

For a while it was perhaps understandable if war seemed like a game. Through 1939 Britain remained untouched and so did France. Only in the spring of 1940 did events escalate, as one country after another collapsed in the face of the German advance. But even France's defeat in June did not dissipate the energy of the times for him. Two days after Dunkirk, Dad wrote to Niura and Yasha—they had already fled Paris—and his letter conveys his excitement: Life is going on "normally" at school, but he and the other boys have formed a firefighting team in case there are air raids. To his delight, his parents had bought him a hand pump for his birthday. And he was happy that someone had moved in next door who put up with his endless discussion of gas masks and bombs. ("The family won't let me talk!") The day after Petain announced France's surrender, this new neighbor came round—he wrote captions for the *Daily Sketch*—and he and a photographer got Dad to dig a large hole in the back garden and pose for a picture burying his bike under a pile of leaves. With the studied matter-of-factness of an era less easily flustered than ours, the journalist then wrote his piece, "What to Do if This Country Is Invaded," reminding readers that it was just as important to hide bicycles as cars and passing on other useful bits of official advice: Stay where you are, hide your food, and avoid spreading rumors. Everyone was doing their bit. It was, Dad remembered, *"great fun,"* almost as though the closer the prospect of a Nazi takeover came, the less serious it seemed, or rather, perhaps, as though the more serious something was, the less one should show it.

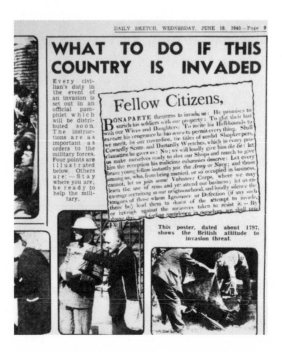

It was only in August, when his form master took Dad and some boys from school to Kent to help bring in the harvest, that he came face-to-face for the first time with the reality of death. The weather was hot and they had ended up at a farm near Biggin Hill, which happened to be the site of a major RAF base that guarded the southeast of England and the approaches to London. After several days of making sheaves of corn and sleeping at night on the bare floor of a laborer's cottage, they were given Sunday off. It was the start of the Battle of Britain and there was a dogfight overhead, a distant display of bravado high above them, but as they watched it ended abruptly with the German plane plummeting with a "great howling noise," machine guns firing, the pilot dead. Bullets hit the roadway, the boys dived into the ditches on either side. There was an immense explosion and falling debris, and then a cap fluttered down—a moment he never forgot.

From the slopes of Highgate, he saw the skyline of the city sprout the paraphernalia of air defense—gun emplacements, fire-watch posts, and the barrage balloons that flew overhead from moorings on the Heath, like a scene out of his beloved H. G. Wells. Night after night, the residents of 20 Oakeshott Avenue tracked the German squadrons flying in, the red glow of the flames and the smoke as bombs fell across the Thames valley and large swathes of the city were destroyed. The northern suburbs were not immune and several bombs fell close to the house. When the alarm went off, they were supposed to make their way in the dark to the Anderson shelter in the garden. But it was damp and claustrophobic, the two pairs of steel bunk beds took up all the space, and after a mouse made an appearance, Frouma refused to go back, so they set up camp chairs in the tiny downstairs cloakroom, trying to ignore the blasts that made the entire house shake. Small incendiary devices lit up the night and one burned a hole in the garden fence. Another came through the roof of their house in the course of a particularly fierce raid, and it was after that that his parents decided that London had become too dangerous for him. Because the headmaster refused to evacuate University College School—his reaction to the warning sirens was to herd the boys down to the cellars—Dad was sent to the west of England to continue his schooling.

To the end of his life, Dad had a capacity for solitude. He did not mind his own company, and while he was by no means a solitary person, he was often happiest when others were nearby but not on top of him—gardening, perhaps, offered the ideal relationship to the world, or reading in an armchair or in the bath, or, of an evening, holing up in his shed from which he would generally return to the house with a slight air of reluctance. Even in hospital, in the last few months, one would come into the ward and find him reading. He did not usually need people around him for distraction, could seem slightly abstracted in company, and was known to fall asleep in the presence of guests at his own dinner table. When he awoke—or was woken—he was always quietly but spectacularly unregretful. He avoided parties and was not one to hold forth, or to put a high premium on being entertaining.

Growing up in Oakeshott Avenue with older parents had provided lessons in the pleasures of his own company, since André had left the house and Ira was nearly ten years older. As a dutiful son much of his social life was spent accompanying his mother to see her friends, a world of sweets and conversations in Russian with Mrs. Koldofsky and those other ladies whose faces were increasingly lined by hardship and widowhood.

Now, evacuated from London at the age of fifteen, he was to encounter a more intense kind of isolation. He had transferred to the Regent Street Polytechnic School, which had left its peacetime premises in central London and relocated to Minehead in Somerset, a normally sleepy coastal town now crowded with evacuees and soldiers. The school prided itself on its technical orientation but what it did best was to mold boys from middle-class backgrounds to fill the middle-management positions of the British Empire. By the time he got there, they were already disappearing into the armed forces, and the first deaths—two Old Boys, pilots in the RAF—were posted in the school newspaper.

In the winter of 1940, Dad arrived on the train from London, accompanied by both parents. With their help, he found lodgings with a family of bridge-playing fanatics called the Newmans, who lived in a gloomy late-Victorian place on one of the roads leading west out of the town. It was cold and the snow on the hills was deeper than he had ever seen. Dad, who knew from his own experience what it was to have boarders disrupt the domestic routine, was now a boarder himself. One sure sign of his sense of being on his own is that when his parents left, he began to keep a diary, something that was to become a lifetime habit. His 1941 Schoolboy Diary, filled with useful information about logarithms and cricket and the British Empire, had been given to him by his mother, and it became a kind of surrogate companion, an effort to exert some measure of control over his new life in its unfamiliar setting.

Although on the surface he was quick to settle in, or doing his best to make it seem so, underneath he must have been finding it hard. One evening he was making his way home in the blackout through the backstreets of the town when he stopped for a moment to look up at the stars, which seemed very bright, and as he set off again, he suddenly realized that his usually infallible sense of direction had deserted him and he had no idea which way to go. He experienced a feeling of complete disorientation for the first and possibly only time in his life, and a panic took hold of him which he still remembered many years later as like "being in a forest and not knowing which way to go." Perhaps it is not coincidental that a man who was given to taking holidays in the places he had first visited as a child, never showed, to my knowledge, the slightest interest in returning to Minehead. Along with Yorkshire and his time in Germany doing national service, Minehead was a setting that defined much of his experience of the 1940s, and none of the three were places he wanted to share with us.

The school was his third in five years and it did not help that he was a year younger than most of the boys in his class because

he had taken his exams early. There was a new form to be
assigned to, and a new set of customs and habits, those invisible
intimidating codes that English schools seem designed to impose:
Elgar on the gramophone before assembly; watching the other
boys head off to chapel on Sundays; house games. Dad's house
was Kerridge-Swan, a name emblematic in its obscurity; he rose
to become subprefect. There were occasional stately visits from
the eighty-four-year-old chairman of governors, the fabulously
named Sir Kynaston Studd, a former lord mayor of London, a
devout Christian, and once a world-class cricketer whom some
still remembered for the time back in 1882 that he and his two
brothers, the so-called "set of Studds," had helped Cambridge
University to a famous victory over the all-conquering Aus-
tralians. Cricket was big at the school as a result; so was Freemasonry. Studd was a leading Freemason; many of the masters
belonged and quite a few boys later joined too. I find it hard to
think of anything Dad would have found more alienating.

He now had to get on with a different set of boys, most of
whom had come up together through the school over the past
few years. For anyone as immersed in his home and family as he
was, it cannot have been easy. At one Sunday service in March
1941, already "saddened by memories of France," he noted in
his diary that he felt from the others "a curious feeling towards
me." He wrote no more about this and never mentioned it
again so it is hard to say what he was alluding to—being Jewish, having foreign parents, or something else entirely? What
did bring him together with the others was walking, cycling,
and above all politics. The immediate future for his generation could not have been more uncertain but beyond it, and
maybe as some kind of substitute for thinking too much about
their own personal destinies, was the future of their country. A

debating society of earnest sixth formers met in the Methodist Hall and Dad became a stalwart. He chaired one or two meetings and spoke about his vision of the ideal state; a boy named Coleman gave "an impassioned denunciation" of German fascism, and there was an argument over whether Britain and Russia were democracies.

In his new wool suit, polished shoes, and dark striped school tie, a heavy greatcoat protecting him against the harsh Somerset winter—he looks serious, no longer exactly a boy. He joined the Air Cadets and acquired a uniform and got his first basic training in Morse code. There was shooting practice in the local quarry. A future airman was the part he imagined for himself, and he visited the local RAF base and carefully noted in his diary the Beauforts, Mosquitoes, and Lancasters flying over the Bristol Channel. The Luftwaffe came across the estuary from time to time and hit the towns of south Wales—the antiaircraft guns could easily be heard—but no bombs dropped on Minehead. Butlins, a harbinger of a new future had they but known it, was quiet and guarded by concrete bunkers and pillboxes. Only the Rex and the Regal provided Hollywood glamour at the gray English seaside.

Beyond the hills that guarded the town, the moors beckoned. Across England, the war was unleashing an extraordinary
process of national rediscovery and self-romanticization, a col-
lective effort of imagination and cultural creativity that was visible everywhere from T. S. Eliot's *Four Quartets* to the paintings
of Eric Ravilious. In Minehead these London boys discovered
the "country scene," and the school magazine filled up with
essays on hawking and timber-felling, bluebells and the beauties of the West Country. It was at this time that Dad's own
deep but rarely articulated sensitivity to the English landscape
blossomed, his liking for its fields, hedges, hills, and villages
humanized by history and settlement and cultivation. For the
first and perhaps the only time in his life, he expressed himself
in verse. "Carrier Pigeons," a poem by "W. MAZOWER, L6.
Arts," sees birds as the war's true heroes, *English* heroes from
the dales of the heartland, calm intermediaries, succoring and
homing, with the courage not of those who fight but of those
who carry words and save the day, in a long line of the generations that have fought for the nation's liberty.

It was perhaps a compensation, this meditation on the outward view, for some inner turmoil. When I asked him once near
the end of his life if he had been unhappy in Minehead, he had
said not. And when I persisted, asking him whether he had been
happy, his response was that he had enjoyed the countryside,
that he was a keen cyclist. The landscape suffuses the pages of his
diary, and the quiet of Selworthy Beacon and the natural world
move through these months in counterpoint with the war's
advance into the Far East. He walked and biked along the coastal
road, often with classmates, sharing the cake that Frouma sent
regularly from home. It is a spectacular setting, along the edge
of Exmoor, with the yellow gorse flowering into the spring and

the hills cut by some surprisingly steep wooded valleys, but it can also be bleak and chilled by the winds coming in off the Bristol Channel. Two years later, when he was already up at Balliol College but thinking back to Minehead, he copied out an extract from John Keble's classic of nineteenth-century devotional verse, *The Christian Year*. What spoke to him in Keble's lines was certainly not their religious dimension but the connection they drew between the experience of wandering, the promise of England, and a certain modesty of ambition—not grand vistas but homely scenes and simple views, the ground underfoot.

> Needs no show of mountain hoary
> Winding shore or deepening glen
> Where the landscape in its glory
> Teaches truth to wandering men.
> Give true hearts but earth and sky,
> And some flowers to bloom and die
> Homely scenes and simple views
> Lowly thoughts may best infuse
>
> (Selworthy
> Somerset   1941)

And then one day in June 1941 he came in from making haystacks in the fields on what was an unseasonably cold and cloudy summer's afternoon and heard the radio announce the news that he, at the age of sixteen, instantly understood changed everything: *"Sunday, June 22: Germany attacks*

Russia!!!!!!!!!!!!!!!!!!!!!!" The entry in his diary is marked with a force
even greater than that he used three years later in a very different spirit, when news came in of the liberation of Paris. For now
events were unremitting in their grimness, and while he worked
for his exams, he monitored the front as it overran places that
for him were much more than just names on a map—"Grodno
in danger," and then, revising his Virgil, on June 30: "Jolly hot!
Germans attacking Minsk." On July 17: "Picked whortleberries
in morning. 1 and ½ lbs. Got 6d cash from Mrs. N. No letter
at post office from parents. Got most of my marks. Smolensk
threatened."

If, like a lot of the boys, he was homesick, his desire to see his
family must have been intensified by the dismaying news from
the east, and his relief when he gets home leaps off the page.
April 10, 1941: "Caught 9.30 train. Changed at Taunton. London
at 2. Home 3.30," as though recording the train schedule itself
assured a kind of normality, and indeed he always remembered
the trains and how well they were running through the war.
He goes straight into the garden to mow the lawn, happily
active amid the daily alerts, the sirens, the sound of anti-aircraft
battery, and evenings spent behind the blackout curtains. The
bombs had stopped raining down on the city so furiously. He
planted onions, carrots, and tomatoes and built a hutch for
rabbits and chickens behind the house on Oakeshott Avenue.
When he was not in London, he worried about his parents, neither of whom could easily have coped physically with a serious
emergency, and as often as not, news from home left him feeling down. His mother wrote on his birthday in June encouraging him to share the sweets she had sent with his classmates and
reporting on their new life: the rationing, the friends moving
away to safer suburbs farther out, André passing through in his

new officer's uniform, and the detailed bulletins from the garden that she knew would bring him some comfort: "Potatoes on the upper bed, lovely, no sign of them below, no beans, carrots very poorly coming up. Peas are splendid. Tomato plants were caught by frost and turned yellowish." It was not just the garden that he missed. It was trips to the Forum in Kentish Town to see films with his parents, their walks around Kenwood, the Vienna Café in New Oxford Street. In new lodgings across from the Newmans in 1942, he tried to re-create something of his home life, helping his landlady, Mrs. James, by tending her back garden, but for once it did not work. That spring he was beset by real anxiety, and for the first and only time in half a century's worth of diaries, he jotted down a dream.

8 May 1942
Lecture on India. The first dull day for a long time. Had a curious dream last night. I was being sent on a bus to some hospital with Oppé and crowds of other boys. I wanted to get away but was forced to shake hands with a reception committee. Then I escaped and hid in a gun'n fish shop. Air pistols 11 and 4 shillings. Then I woke up.

With the Third Reich extending its control over the Soviet Union, this was a sinister vision in difficult times. He must have been in some kind of nervous state because his mother phoned him from London a few days later, a rare enough occurrence. Then, even more unusually, she came up to visit him and to see the headmaster, and the next day he decided to go back with her to London where he spent nearly a week before returning for his exams.

Maybe it was just homesickness, but he was also probably feeling under pressure because he had decided to apply to university. Max had come round to the idea—at first he had muttered Dad should train as a builder's apprentice, prompting an explosive reaction from Frouma—and after his parents encouraged him to think about history, sensing his liking for the subject, he did well enough in his examinations to make this a possibility. That summer Max sent him an affectionate letter, hoping to get him home to coincide with his own leave in August, and giving him encouragement. "Dear Billy," he wrote. "Come home as soon as you can...You will find the house overrun by chickens and Russians. I am afraid you will run back to Minehead!" And then, enigmatically: "I am glad you took a decision, and doubts do not trouble your mind anymore." What doubts were these? They may have been the usual ones raised by leaving school and deciding where and what to do next. But they must have been unusually intense for Max to have commented. He had signed off: "Cheerio! Spirits up and 'cares' down! With love, Dad." The stoical life-hardened Bundist had acquired a British stiff upper lip and for just once we catch a glimpse of that resolute approach to putting difficult things behind one that was perhaps Max's most emphatic message to his son.

That Dad's anxieties were prompted solely by loneliness, or by the challenge of getting into Oxford, I doubt. He was worried, and with good reason, about the fate of his relatives in France and Eastern Europe. In Poland and Russia, we now know, the fate of his uncles and their families was to be grim beyond any imagining. But Beauchamp was just across the Channel and the Germans were there too, and no word had come from his uncle and aunt for more than a year.

On Oakeshott Avenue, where Frouma was sick with worry, all they knew was that Niura and Yasha had returned to Beauchamp in the summer of 1940 once the Germans had taken over, but Vitalie had remained with his wife and little girl in Lyon, in what became the unoccupied zone. From there some intermittent correspondence with those abroad was still possible. In March 1941 Dad wrote to his uncle from Minehead and on May 9, a month and a half before the invasion of the USSR, a telegram arrived at Oakeshott Avenue with the news that they were all well. Two days later, a postcard arrived for him with more details: "After the war," Vitalie wrote—evidently he assumed the Germans had won and were destined to rule Europe for many years—he had regained his job as an electrical engineer. He added, without going into details, that Niura was living in difficult circumstances (*"dans une ambiance loin d'être agréable"*). His wife, Alice, added a few equally enigmatic words: They were far from their Paris friends, living in a tiny apartment with nothing to recommend it, but they were nevertheless grateful to be where they were.

About a year later, on July 18, 1942, another telegram got through. This time the resourceful Vitalie reported that Niura and Yasha were in good health: He was working, and she was with him—an innocuous few words to allay an unspoken fear.

The war was more than twenty years in the past when I first got to know my great-aunt Niura in Beauchamp and I am struck now that it never occurred to me to raise the subject of how she had survived the occupation. I don't remember feeling it was taboo. But much later, after her death, Dad told me she had not liked to talk about that time, so perhaps I had felt some subliminal deterrence or the subject had been avoided without my noticing it. One thing Dad had gleaned after the war was that Yasha had expected Niura to go out and do the shopping early on even after she had pinned the yellow star on her overcoat. And there were certainly some bitter and unpleasant local memories because when Patrick, her nephew, stayed with her after the war, she used to point out the collaborators to make sure that he did not play with their children on the swings in the park. Between early 1941 and the summer of 1942 there had been a barrage of legislation against Jews, and they were obliged to wear a yellow star and to register at their local police station. Stateless Jews such as Niura were especially vulnerable to blackmail and worse. In the Beauchamp region an increase in anti-Semitism was reported by the local prefect from the very beginning of the occupation, and "adventurers" and "gangsters of the press" were said to be stepping up their activities. In the spring of 1942, the first transports for Auschwitz left from the Paris suburbs carrying large numbers of Russian and

Polish Jews. There was one on March 27, four in June, and then a stream of transports starting on July 17. Vitalie's telegram had arrived from Lyon at the moment of maximal danger; perhaps it was a coincidence, perhaps not.

After the war the family in London learned what had happened and how our relatives in France had survived. For one thing, Yasha was not Jewish and so Niura's married name—Stepanof—helped hide her background. With his drinking and womanizing, they had not had an easy relationship before the war, and Niura had often been depressed and ill, but it turned out to have been helpful to be with him. Not only had he an attested pedigree as a long-standing anticommunist who had fought for the Whites against the Bolsheviks; he was also a highly prized draftsman working for one of France's main builders of railway rolling stock, a protected industry vital to the German war effort. Niura had begun wearing the star when the first decree was promulgated. But when Vitalie heard, he telephoned her and insisted that she take it off and not report to the police. Niura listened to her older brother—Yasha does not seem to have intervened either way—and the result was that she remained in their home through the war undisturbed.

Vitalie—seated on the left with his unit in an anti-aircraft battery on the eve of the German invasion—was more vulnerable both because he was male and because he had to travel widely for his work, including into the occupied zone. But although his Jewish background put him in acute danger, his too was a marriage that provided some protection. Alice came from a Catholic milieu, which had not prevented her being warmly enfolded into the embrace of the Toumarkines: At their wedding there had been telegrams of welcome and congratulations from Moscow and London and there were frequent invitations to visit both cities. Alice's mother was a conventional bourgeoise in her views and somewhat anti-Semitic, but her father was a very different spirit: an architect and a painter, an open-minded and artistic man, who liked his son-in-law. He had been wounded in the First World War, and had gone on to design the family home, a cubist villa that stood out in their leafy bourgeois Paris suburb. Even before the war they had agreed—and Frouma too had given the idea her blessing—to bring their little girl up as a Catholic, partly in order to please Alice's mother, and baby Monique was baptized in 1940.[1] Once the Germans took over, a friendly priest supplied them with fake baptismal papers. They kept up the pretense for years and their son, Patrick, who was born in 1944, was baptized and confirmed in Notre-Dame des Champs in Montparnasse, and seems only to have realized that his father was Jewish when he was sixteen.

Vitalie was once caught on the street in a roundup by Lithuanian militiamen working for the Germans in Lyon. Fortunately they failed to identify him as Jewish and he was released after two days. That was his closest brush with deportation. Protected by his employer, he continued working for his engineering firm, and since one of his jobs was to maintain refrigerated units for markets and shops, he had access to a ready supply of vegetables and kept his wife's parents, hungry in their Vesinet villa, supplied with potatoes. After the Germans took over the whole of the country, he moved Alice and Monique down to what they imagined would be the safety of the Vercors plateau, only to find that in the final months they were caught in the midst of bitter fighting between German troops and the Resistance. Many Jews were being hidden in the mountains by farmers, and when Vitalie went back after the war to thank the cowherd who had lodged them, he decided to reveal that he was Jewish. "But of course," she told him. "We all knew that." Frouma's brother and sister had passed through the war unscathed, principally because others around them had either looked after them or had, at the least, not informed on them. They had been very lucky.

CHAPTER EIGHTEEN

Oxford and What Came Between

Immigrants cluster together and in this way they shape each other's lives. The Koldofskys and the Zukermans, the Kidels, the Broidos, the Japolskys: These were some of the names the social life of 20 Oakeshott Avenue revolved around, newcomers on the North London heights, doling out biscuits and sweets and Russian endearments in their curtained living rooms. Among them was the Riga-born businessman Solomon Bielinky, a figure of means, a successful coal trader in whom Max confided, and a fiver from Bielinky arrived in an envelope for Dad on his birthday every year until he was about twenty. Bielinky's son, a few years older than Dad and intimidatingly self-assured, had gone up to Balliol in 1940 from University College School, Dad's old school. An equally self-confident nephew had trod the same path the year before him. In both cases, it was obvious that their studies would be truncated since eighteen was the call-up age, but Bielinky's advice for them and for Max, when he came asking about his son, was to get your foot in the door at Oxford as soon as possible.

In this way not only Oxford but Balliol in particular became the aspiration, the college of H. H. Asquith's men of "effortless superiority," the powerhouse of the British political elite in the mid-twentieth century, and, not least as a result of the deliberate policy then pursued by the college's socialistic master,

A. R. Lindsay, a funnel for the bright upwardly mobile sons of the middle classes. Balliol was their portal to an English life that Lindsay hoped they would modernize and invigorate. The son, Louis Bielinky, would be awarded the Military Cross in the invasion of Italy with the Royal Irish Fusiliers in 1944 and became a high-flying Treasury official before dying tragically young in 1953. The nephew, David Ginsburg, became a long-serving Labour MP. Where they trod, Dad followed.

On a chilly damp night in the autumn of 1942 he saw Oxford for the first time. He was young and it did not seem welcoming. In the blackout, Balliol's impassive Gothic façade must have loomed even more cheerlessly as he came up Broad Street from the station than it would thirty-odd years later when I went up and entered the college gate to take the entrance exam in my turn. But the rain pattering down on the old flagstones would have sounded the same, and the impossibly narrow twisting staircases leading to unheated rooms probably induced a similar sense of anomie. A question from this charged occasion stuck in his memory: Dad was asked which era he would most like to have been born into. The second half of the eighteenth century, he told them. At the interview, he was questioned about this answer, which he always remembered and which testified to his rationalism, the value he attached to calm and civility, a capacity to find humor in life, and perhaps too his suspicion of unregulated passion. Dinner was served at a long candlelit table lined with young men eyeing each other suspiciously over the dishes, the college servants hovering, and a disorienting sense of competitiveness.

He stood at the threshold of a different England from any he knew. Oxford was a laboratory of the mandarinate, sharp minds half hidden behind cultivated manners, a little aloof but with urgency in the questioning, in the hands of a generation of men who had already known more than their share of war's pain and could measure the seriousness of the times and the temper of the young men knocking at their oak doors. Maurice Roy Ridley, the college chaplain, was a Keats scholar. In 1913, the young, handsome Ridley had won the Newdigate Prize for his poem "Oxford." As he read it aloud at the Encaenia ceremony, he had made such an impression on the young Dorothy L. Sayers that she later turned him into the hero of the detective stories that made her famous and immortalized him as Lord Peter Wimsey. This man Ridley was one of the two Balliol fellows who interviewed Dad.

The other was a powerhouse. Benedict Humphrey Sumner taught Russian history, indeed he was one of the pioneers of that subject in England, despite having visited the country only once. And he was, though largely forgotten today, a historian of genius. He was tall, wiry, pipe in mouth, a physically imposing man of reserve but great charm and energy who would die still relatively young as the warden of All Souls in 1951, worn out by overwork. He had fought on the western front before being invalided out; subsequent intelligence work led to the Paris Peace Conference and several years with the International Labour Organization. With interests that extended across Europe, from the Ottoman Empire to the latest trends in Soviet scholarship, Sumner was anything but parochial. At the time Dad encountered him, he was not merely tutoring in history but working for the government as well, analyzing conditions in Nazi-occupied Europe at a Foreign Office think tank that had been parked in Balliol for the duration of the war. As if that was not enough, he was also writing the brief survey on Russian history that he published the following year, a book far ahead of its time in arguing for the existence of fundamental continuities between the Soviet regime and its predecessors. Dad, who was to develop affection and deep respect for Sumner and his book-lined rooms, must have made a good impression on these two remarkable men because they told him he had a place and could begin in the New Year.

Only seventeen, he was at Oxford. He had finished school a year early, and so he began his undergraduate career at the start of 1943, choosing history and Russian, probably the only Russianist of his year, certainly the only one at Balliol.

It was wartime, a time of rationing and improvisation. There were still the watchful porters, the gates locked at night to keep women out and the men in. But there were relatively few students and some of the college buildings had been put to other uses: In the Garden Quad, Arnold Toynbee, along with Sumner and others, was helping to lay the foundations of the postwar Anglo-American alliance, though a stripling like Dad would not

have known it. Air raids were the pressing fear, and the possibility of a conflagration that would consume the library, and
there were hair-raising drills across the rooftops. Students came
and went, as they were called up, entering an army that had not
recovered from the shock of Dunkirk. Most of those who were
there were a year or two older than Dad, and many had already
started the previous autumn when he was still finishing up at
Minehead. With the call-up on everyone's mind, the times did
not conduce to lasting friendships and Dad did not make any.
Ernest Gellner, later one of the country's leading sociologists,
entered the college that year. Yet despite both of them living on
the Holly Lodge Estate — the Gellners' house was scarcely one
hundred yards from the Mazowers' and the families knew each
other slightly — he and Dad did not mix. Another Jewish refugee was John Hajnal, a quiet man, shy, politely spoken, and brilliant, who had also gone to UCS and came up to Balliol when
he was even younger than Dad; he became an eminent demog-
rapher, one of those remarkable scholars who achieves lasting
renown with one classic article, and was the only member of
the college intake of that year whom Dad kept up with in later
life, perhaps because by coincidence he settled at the end of our
road to raise his family. In general those men Dad was drawn to
tended not to be intellectuals nor to achieve fame afterwards.

Like Dad, most of them were waiting for the call. Unlike
him, most of them would find frontline action within a year or
two anywhere from the European theater to the Bay of Ben-
gal. Afterwards, if not ensconced in Whitehall or the City, there
beckoned years on the North-West Frontier, in Burma, or on
the Gold Coast, entering into colonial administration or a Cal-
cutta trading house. The prospects were still imperial, almost
Victorian, although many at Balliol were on the Left and would

have welcomed the sudden postwar collapse of the empire had anyone seen it coming. Something else they cannot have anticipated was that despite plenty of close shaves, only one or two of the sixty or so among them would be killed during the war. Dad's classmates did not experience anything resembling the bloodletting that Sumner's generation had known, although they probably expected to. For all the risks involved in the invasion of Europe, the sheer murderousness of the trenches was not repeated.

For Dad the entire atmosphere was a revelation. A slow start in the first cold days of January suddenly gave way to animation, and his embrace of this new world completely changed his personality. After several years of feeling isolated and perhaps slightly depressed, he now flourished and a more sociable side to his personality emerged. When he went home that Easter vacation, he once told me, his mother was completely amazed. He had been a very silent child while he was at school, she had said, but when he came home he didn't stop talking. It was a new experience for everyone.

"I was suddenly liberated." Those were his words. Liberated from what, I now wonder. From the brooding impassivity of his aging father, from the solicitude of his infinitely anxious mother? Above all, from the weight of being the good son? He would never entirely shake these things off, nor even really seek to, but a time began that was an experiment in independence. A smart sports jacket and tie now replaced the more formal school suit. He started to speak like an Oxford man. Photographs show him at ease in deep armchairs. He has a room of his own. The chubbiness of the schoolboy has been replaced by a more confident glance. He was not ambitious. But he has gotten into Oxford; he has made it.

Highgate, Somerset, and Oxford: At each step in Dad's life, England took on new depth and meanings. This was the golden age of the country ramble, the Youth Hostels Association, and the group hike, a way for the young and the Left to lay claim to a new kind of civic consciousness and a new kind of comradeship, leaving their footprints on soil that the great interwar aristocratic sell-off had liberated for the nation to enjoy, the age of the democratization of landscape. The author and rambling campaigner Tom Stephenson published *The Countryside Companion* in 1939, with its praise of "rugged peaks" and affirmation of the social virtues of the outdoors. *How to See the Countryside* came out the following year, reminding readers to dubbin their walking boots and take care of their maps. It was now that Dad began the hiking holidays that became an essential psychic safety valve in his life for the next decade, and it was no coincidence that it was happening as his own political commitment intensified. Barely a week goes by without him recording a serious walk in his diary, a good ten or fifteen miles is common, sometimes extended over a weekend, often longer, with an ever-changing cast of companions. At Easter 1943—in the vacation that followed his first term at Balliol—he kitted up much as Stephenson recommended, packed his rucksack, and headed for the Lake District around Derwentwater and Coniston Water with a group of fellow students as if to pay homage to the hills and mountains of his native land.

He was also exploring his connection with Russia in a more rigorous way. The middle of the war was the apogee of the Anglo-Russian alliance, a time when the United Kingdom and Russia briefly came closer than ever before or since. In the 1941 Hampstead by-election there was even an "Official All-Out Aid for Russia Candidate." He did poorly, but that was partly because the Communist Party of Great Britain had thrown its weight behind the Conservative candidate for the sake of national unity, and admiration for the courage of the Red Army was widespread across the political spectrum. Oxford did not celebrate the USSR with the zeal it showed towards the United States and the Dominions, but the hammer and sickle did flutter alongside the Union Jack over Carfax in the town center during Help for Russia week. Dad now immersed himself for the first time systematically in the country and language of his parents.

The growing world importance of Soviet power had not yet really impinged on the university's sluggish consciousness and would not for some time. (Two years later, Isaiah Berlin would write in tones of despair about the obstacles to building up Russian studies in Oxford and in England more generally.) Hardly anyone at Oxford read Russian in those pre–Cold War days, and the university's tutor in the subject was lucky if he had a finalist a year. It was a quiet life for Sergey Aleksandrovich Konovalov, who had arrived in England at the end of the Great War, the son of a minister in the 1917 Russian Provisional Government. Imposing, elegantly dressed, reserved, he wrote about the minutiae of seventeenth-century economic history and his lectures were notoriously dull; against the odds he would later brilliantly engineer the expansion of Russian and Slavic studies at the university. But in 1943 his was still a one-man show. His deep voice lingered in Dad's memory, as did his devotion to the Romanovs and his Orthodoxy, a different Russia from the one Dad had grown up with. Like many dons, Konovalov was not much of a teacher; like many Oxford students, Dad did not need one. A typical immigrant's child, he had learned his parents' language by ear; datives and genitives kept getting confused. All someone with his cast of mind needed to sort this out was time and now he had it. In 1944 he kept his diary in Russian for practice, and he did this for an entire year.

Russian brought together Oxford and his life at home. In early 1943 the British and Americans were still contemplating a landing in North Africa, as they viewed the epic struggle unfolding on the borders of the USSR. The launching of a second front was the question of the day and it split the university Labour Club down the middle: Communists and fellow travelers were backing Stalin's call for immediate Anglo-American landings while Dad's cousin David Ginsburg was running a breakaway Democratic Socialist group that represented those not so inclined to go along with the line from Moscow. Dad was not yet eighteen, but despite cheering on the Red Army, as almost the entire country was doing, he kept his distance from the Stalinists.

He had not forgotten the Hitler-Stalin Pact of only four years earlier. He knew too that his uncle Lev had disappeared in the Terror. And it was while he was at Oxford that the news broke that Bundist leaders Henryk Erlich and Victor Alter had died in Soviet detention. Maxim Litvinov, now the Soviet ambassador in Washington, D.C., announced to the world that the two men had been convicted of spying—ridiculous charges to anyone who knew them as the Mazowers did.

There was even one occasion when the long arm of the NKVD reached inside the house on Oakeshott Avenue. Needing money, and with the war having temporarily stifled the influx of refugees, Dad's parents had begun taking in lodgers from the Soviet trade delegation, which had been set up across the road from them in Highgate. Their first guest, a captain in the merchant navy, was a handsome, sociable man who rolled up his jacket sleeves when he met them to show off the collection of wristwatches that he was going to sell back home. They got on well, kept off politics, and said nothing about their family in Moscow. He stayed some months, and when he left, they decided he had been sent to test the waters and to see whether Oakeshott Avenue was a subversive environment. Others followed, so apparently it had been deemed safe. Frouma provided Sunday lunch, cooked dishes from her childhood, and made a fuss at Easter and on weekends. When he was down from college, Dad would be deputed to escort the visitors in groups around the sights of London; on a visit to Hampton Court he took a picture of them posing politely in front of this relic of British feudalism. Normally tightly chaperoned—most weekends they were bused to a house in the countryside to avoid forming close friendships with their hosts—his guests enjoyed themselves and taught the young Oxford undergraduate Russian obscenities that were unknown to his college mentors. Politics remained untouched: "We were very aware that they were walking on eggshells and one didn't want to embarrass them."

So no one in the family forgot the occasion when one of their lodgers, who had been living with them for some time,

knocked ashen-faced at the front door in the middle of the day.
Flanked by two unsmiling heavies, he went upstairs, packed his
things, and left, never to be heard from again. "Are you leaving?" Frouma had asked him from the landing. And he, looking
like death, said, "Yes, I'm going back to Russia." They never
found out what he had done, but it is not surprising that the
more pro-Soviet members of the Oxford Labour Club struck
Dad as naïve: He was immersed in Stalinist realities to a degree
that not even his tutors could match.

One more thing came out of Oxford, the most important.
Before 1943 the pages of Dad's photo album take us past childhood scenes of life in Highgate into Minehead in winter, the
loneliness of a schoolboy far from home staring out of his

bedroom window across the fields. There are the wartime back-streets of the once bustling seaside town where nothing seems open. There are boys, of course, in groups or alone, and some men, teachers too old to fight, others in uniform or hiking in a line across muddy fields.

And then we turn the page and there is a dark-haired girl, or really she is a young woman, unnamed, curled up in a chair and holding a cat in the garden at Oakeshott Avenue; and then there is a cluster of fellow students from one of the women's colleges sunning themselves on the steps at the end of the spring term. And then a whole gaggle of college friends, male and female, are boating on the Norfolk Broads, and there is that Easter hiking tour in the Lake District, eight of them in shorts and walking boots high above Coniston Water. Next summer, we glimpse outings and picnics in Hitchin and Cockfosters. Dad is usually behind the camera, but one senses the change in mood and possibilities. A few faces would remain, but mostly they come and go—laughing as they pick grapes after the war in the south of France, browned by hard walking in the Dolomites, later on framed by quiet Oxford rooms or the Devon coast. Some pose carefully; others smile politely or laugh or grin because they are friends and like him and the sun is shining. One or two are saying something else, something more.

Who these girls were and what they meant to Dad were not matters that could easily be discussed between him and me. Perhaps this was out of a kind of mutual discretion or shyness, and there was maybe also some feeling that broaching the subject meant being disloyal to Mum, even though she did not come into his life until many years later. At school I had been taught always to avoid the first person singular—we were told that one of the virtues of Latin was its impersonality. If I was not the right person to probe my father about his early encounters with the opposite sex, he was not a man to volunteer such things. Yet once we started our conversations about his early time in Oxford, the subject came up, as it was bound to. In fact, it was initiated by him, amid pauses for thought and recollection:

Dad: "Now social life was quite good. We had play readings with women from women's colleges. Society functioned more or less. The Labour Club functioned."

Me: "To what extent was social life an extension of what you were used to at school? To what extent were you entering new worlds?"

Dad: "Oh, it was a completely new world."

Me: "In what kind of way?"

Dad: "Well, in school I hardly knew any girls at all."

It was in Minehead, he said, that he had first kissed a girl. But Oxford was where it all began really. At a play reading, he met Patty Nichol, whom he remained friendly with for the next few years. A fellow student tried to warn him off; she was Bert Parnaby's girl. Dad thought that was a matter for her—she could make her own mind up. His world was not one in which men spoke for women; he was drawn to women who spoke for themselves.

He had grown to just over six feet tall and by the early 1940s was losing his slight boyish chubbiness and was in good shape. Dark-haired, with the sensitive Toumarkine mouth, he was a handsome young man, sure of himself without being overly assertive. Slightly reserved, perhaps, outside the family, but a man of obvious affections and kindness, not underhanded. And unlike many Englishmen, especially the tongue-tied public schoolboys whom an American undergraduate at Balliol of those years remembered being hopelessly ill at ease around the opposite sex, Dad had grown up in the company of women.

First and foremost, there was his mother to whom he was tied so close. She missed him when he was in Minehead as much as he missed her, and she was aware of the strength of her feeling for him. "I'm still in love with my son, though I know he is far from perfect. He is very morally clean, serious and always diligent about his work," Frouma would write to her brother in 1945. "My son is not bad at all, and he turned twenty; I could really say I am grateful to my fate for these twenty years of joy." In Paris there was his aunt Niura and Alice, Vitalie's wife, to whom he was also very attached. There had been few girls his own age at home, apart from one or two of the Oakeshott Avenue lodgers. But after he arrived at Oxford, his circle of women friends began to expand and college beauties gaze fondly into the lens for the seventeen-year-old freshman.

Cleo, Patty, Magda, Lalage, Barbara: names on the pages of his diary. None of them meant anything to me. I was curious to find out more about that phase of his life in which nothing was determined or decided, in which all outcomes seemed possible, especially since in every case he had allowed these ties to wither and had not shown any interest in returning to them. What had happened between them was not something it seemed likely could ever be reconstructed, nor did it seem the most important thing to try. In connecting them to other unguessed and later buried dimensions of my father in those years—the new energy manifested in his sudden talkativeness, interest in poetry, dabbles in acting, and other aspects of his youth that melted imperceptibly into what became a more retiring personality with age—what I was after was something else: a provisional sketch of the road map of the emotional landscape of England in wartime that he had known and traveled, the intersections that had brought him and these shadowy figures together for a while, and then their separations, the circles their own lives turned out often to have traced back to their points of origin in ways that seemed not unlike his own.

Cleo, it transpired, was a young woman called Cleome Birkinshaw, a spirited undergraduate a little older than Dad, who was reading English. They were both part of the group of students that went walking in the Lake District over the Easter break. He was smitten and later he remembered her very high forehead and long black hair—that and the fact that her father was in the colonial administration in Malaya had given her an aura of exoticism. Her mother and sisters lived on the south coast, and after Coniston and Derwentwater the two of them hitchhiked back to London and because there were no trains for her to catch by the time they got there she spent the night at Oakeshott Avenue before heading down to Bournemouth. Frouma, he remembered, had not entirely approved—she thought the girl had been allowed to run wild—but he had not cared and letters passed between them until after 1945 when they lost touch. Dad's memory was good: Her father, who had trained at Kew Gardens before the First World War, was indeed in the Malay service—a botanist, he had named all three of his daughters after plants—and he was then starving in a Japanese internment camp and barely survived the experience. Years after Cleo and Dad had gone their separate ways, tragedy blighted her life. I discovered that she had married an army man, a British intelligence officer who served in Malaya as her father had, and shortly after they went out there together, he was killed, blown up by a roadside bomb during what was generally referred to at that time as the Emergency. She never spoke about it and never remarried, and curiously spent her last years in a nursing home in North London, barely half a mile from Highgate. So far as I know Dad never saw her again and I doubt he had given her another thought until he and I began talking and her name came back.

Then there was a group of young women, mostly four or five years older than him, who went down to London after Oxford and roomed together. One of them was Mary Stapledon—"intellectual, kindhearted, feminine," as another friend recalled her. Her father was the philosopher Olaf Stapledon, then perhaps at the height of fame as the author of *Last and First Men*, the first novel of his Future History / Last Man series, and his astonishing 1937 novel *Starmaker*, a story spanning two billion years which Jorge Luis Borges later acclaimed and which inspired generations of science-fiction writers. Never I think more than a friend with whom Dad shared teas and walks and concerts, Mary later married a young Indian medical student and became a doctor, and after Dad died and I found her name in his old diaries I traced her to an address in Belsize Park, only to find she too had died a few months previously.

What made Mary Stapledon typical of the women he befriended in those years is that she was on the Left and intellectually inclined, and in these and most other ways the very opposite of his sister, Ira. His mother watched, and occasionally commented, with curious amusement at this new element in their lives. "Billy has many girl acquaintances and invites all the girls over to our house," Frouma wrote to Vitalie. "They are all students, very serious girls, usually without heavy makeup and in low-heeled shoes, but so far he was never seriously involved with anyone. He told me once, in all seriousness, that he would not marry until the end of the war, having no desire to leave a widow." The seriousness that Frouma highlighted was spot-on: Dad's friendships in these years, both male and female, tended to be joined under the banner of a higher purpose. At university it was Labour Club politics, exciting and intense, on the ascendant against conservatives and communists alike, and this continued once he was back in London, where he joined the Labour Party in 1945 and that September was elected to the central committee for his ward in St. Pancras North. Like his father, Dad was a natural organizer with a calm, authoritative presence. By some mysterious alchemy he had transposed his father's youthful commitment into a mid-century English key. The fight for socialism and the rights of labor went on, only now it was not part of an underground revolutionary struggle against Tsarist autocracy but an open electoral battle for control of the parliamentary democracy that presided over the world's largest empire. Where his father had once mobilized the workers in the backstreets of Vilna, Dad now stood on voters' doorsteps in Highgate and Kentish Town.

What remained of the Bund cheered on the party's rise. They regarded Labour theoretician Harold Laski almost as one of them: An obituary of him a few years later noted proudly that his role in infusing the British Labour movement with the spirit of socialism could be attributed to the stories he had heard as a child of the Bund's struggles in Russia. A Bundist journal expressed confidence that Labour would succeed in the all-important task of "peacefully reconstructing the oldest capitalist country into a social democratic one," thus showing "all mankind the way to its socialist salvation."

As his father had done half a century earlier, Dad found political engagement invigorating his personality: Socialism brought sociability and many if not most of his friends, male and female, came out of this milieu. There were evenings spent in now-forgotten Leftist youth organizations such as the 18 Plus Group and the League of Youth, earnest discussions and debates at the Fabian Society. There were the hikes, of course, and films and concerts, but this was the political core, exhilarating as they worried away at the shape of a better and more just future and felt the burden of responsibility on their generation's shoulders. It is hard now, I think, to recapture what it must have felt like to have been twenty years old and to have gone—the sheer euphoria of it—in only a matter of months from the last terrifying German rocket attacks on the capital to news of total victory in Europe and then on to Labour's triumph in the general election, a time like no other before or after.

One of Mary's housemates was an ardent socialist named

Lalage Sharp. Nearly four years older than Dad and active in
Labour Party work, she was a comrade. On the afternoon of VE
Day, May 8, 1945, the two of them and another Labour friend
from Oxford, Marna Buckatzsch, walked together into Tra-
falgar Square through the flag-strewn streets and went on to
Buckingham Palace to hear King George VI proclaim the end of
the war. At Mansion House, Winston Churchill made a speech
and the three of them were out in the celebrating crowds all
night. Dad got back to Highgate only in the early hours of the
morning, having walked the entire way home. The very next
day they met up once more and caught the train to Seaford and
went hiking along the cliffs before returning to the women's
lodgings on Ormond Street for dinner. One almost senses the
energy coursing through them. A month later, he and Lalage
were canvassing for the party ahead of the general election in
the streets below Oakeshott Avenue, and after more tramping
across Sussex Downs that first summer of peace, he was back
in time to learn the great news that Labour had won. "Terrific
excitement," he noted in his diary. Their lives continued to
intersect for the next six years, by which time both Lalage and
Marna had become councillors on Holborn Borough Council—the firebrand Lalage pushing through the construction
of new public housing. In the summer of 1949, she and Marna
headed off to Tito's Yugoslavia to build railways in the mountains of Bosnia, a project for idealistic young British socialists
that for them and many others sharpened the contrast between
the spirit and energies they found there and the disillusionment
they had come to feel with the Labour government at home.
Their generation was already feeling let down by the older figures running the show under the sober Clement Attlee. Like
them, Dad continued his Labour Party work for five or six years.

But in 1945 that sense of deflated expectations, which I think he came to share, lay in the future, and the Ormond Street house that Lalage and Mary lived in brought him in touch with a cluster of highly educated, internationalist women who embodied the possibility of change. They knew foreign languages, valued the arts and self-improvement, and took the politics of the public good seriously. Later Marna Buckatzsch was involved in the founding of Amnesty International. Magda Skoupilova had gone through the war in Prague before landing in Ormond Street as well; she married a British journalist and ended up writing about Europe for many years for the *Financial Times*. Lalage went on to join the staff of Political and Economic Planning, perhaps the most important British social-policy think tank of the mid-century, before marriage and children took her out of Ormond Street and Dad's life.

All of them were, in one way or another, the sort of women you would have expected a young man of Dad's background to have been drawn to. Yet his longest-lived friendship of all was with someone who, although she was certainly on the Left, had not studied at Oxford and was neither a Londoner nor middle class. She was a Yorkshire woman from the collieries called Megan Bentcliffe, and they had met in 1944 at a student conference when she was in her early twenties. For the next few years, they were in close touch, and as they were more often than not living in different places, letters went between them, a correspondence that lasted into his time in the army and beyond. He used to see her when he was doing his officer training in Yorkshire as she was teaching by then in Doncaster. But she often came down to London too and was at Oakeshott Avenue when Dad and Ira gave a New Year's Eve party at the end of 1947. Their closeness seems to have ended only in 1951.

The distance between Oakeshott Avenue and the working-class northern streets where Megan had grown up was more than just a matter of miles; her world and his could scarcely have been more different. The mining villages of the Dearne Valley were closed South Yorkshire communities, isolated and rural, which had unexpectedly found themselves at the heart of the mid-nineteenth-century industrial revolution. Several generations of their men had labored in the rich coal seams. Her father had fought on the western front with the Yorks and Lancs, and then, a colliery clerk, he had brought his daughter up in one of the two-up two-downs that fringed the nearby pits. Her mother, a miner's daughter, had died before Megan was ten, and so had a younger brother; she grew up with a step-mother and a much younger sister. This was a world with a strong sense of class and intense local pride, clogs for shoes, and a dialect on the streets so impenetrable it kept away foreigners — a category that to the villagers of Brampton, Wombwell, and Wath-on-Dearne meant chiefly the men from Scotland or Newcastle or Staffordshire who were coming down in the 1920s looking for work. The Asian corner shops would not arrive for another half century, and the few Jewish peddlers and pawn-brokers in nearby Barnsley were mistrusted.

That Megan's path had ever crossed with Dad's was owing to two things. One was the grammar school down the road from her home. Like its partner school in Mexborough that produced the poet Ted Hughes only a few years later, the school at Wath-on-Dearne had been set up after the First World War for miners' kids, boys and girls together, grouped into houses called Athens, Sparta, Carthage, Rome, and Troy. The West Riding Education Authority was a renowned pioneer, admirably reluctant to accept the low expectations inbred into the English class system and their schools showed the result: Against the odds, a handful of Wath's smartest boys were sent on to university each year. But a girl was a real rarity and Megan must have had drive and intelligence and independence of spirit to kick so hard against expectations. Prefect and house captain, she matriculated at sixteen, got a scholarship earmarked for the children of miners, and left Yorkshire to travel south to study at Bedford College.

The second thing that brought her and Dad together was the war. By the time she and Dad met, she had already spent several years in the southeast of England, had a degree in English, and spoke more than passable French. In 1945 she returned to Yorkshire to train as a teacher, and when Dad was posted to Germany for his national service, she bought him a German grammar, a teacher's gift. I have no idea how close they were because no letters have survived, but his diaries record that plenty were going in both directions. She and Dad remained in touch until 1952. After they went their own ways, she married an engineer and spent the next half century with him. To the best of my knowledge, she and Dad never saw each other again. She became a teacher, as she had planned, and in retirement lived in a neat brick semi, hydrangeas in the front garden, in the village outside Rotherham where her father had lived before her. A stone's throw away were the pits at Cortonwood where the epic struggle between the miners and Mrs. Thatcher began in 1984; the tussle must have erupted more or less out-side her house. Today an ASDA supermarket sits atop the old shaft, King Coal looks like a parenthesis of a century and a half in a much longer rural South Yorkshire story, and kingfishers have returned to the Dearne. Somewhere in the back of my mind is that signpost at the top of Highgate West Hill with its arrow pointing to "The North." One of the roads not taken was where Megan had returned to her roots. In the late 1940s, Dad had sometimes visited her at Brampton and Wath, enduring the bumpy drive over the moors by bus from Doncaster, but he never talked about the impression those mining villages, still not far removed from how life had been half a century earlier, had made on him, a North Londoner, Oxford educated, the son of foreigners.

When I came across Megan Bentcliffe's name in his diaries, I hoped to find her and talk with her. I wanted to take the whole thing out of the realm of feeling, to gauge the impact of the times, the countervailing pull of place, the Brownian motion of human beings. In the summer of 2015 I found her address and wrote but there was no reply. When I tried the phone, a voice message warded off incoming calls. Then this stopped and there was a busy signal instead and after this continued for more than a day I got to thinking about all the reasons why a ninety-two-year-old woman's phone would be left off the hook for so long, and eventually I found the number of her local police station. The duty sergeant on the other end heard me out politely. It felt absurd to be ringing from New York about someone I had never met who might have known my father seventy years ago. It turned out that having your phone off the hook was insufficient reason for the police to act. The following day, the busy signal was still there. Only some weeks later did I discover that she had moved a couple of years earlier into a nursing home — I had been telephoning an empty house — and a little after that, the carer at the home felt able to tell me that she had died at about the time I had written to her. That was coincidence but what struck me as more than this was that like Dad she had passed away less than a mile from where she was born.

I can't now remember whether it was at the bottom of our garden or in the garden next door — in those days it was all a bit overgrown back there — but in the early 1960s when I was very small there was a massive wartime concrete bunker we used to sometimes play in. The walls were rough and thick, and I remember the total blackness inside, the low ceiling just above your head that seemed to press down, the smell of musty decay, like something once monstrous, out of time. I was four or five, I suppose, and I never dared to go very far in. The war was less than twenty years in the past and remains of this kind could easily be glimpsed amid overgrown nettles through broken fences in the North London backstreets. Today they are mostly gone. The bunker certainly is; it had served its purpose and was not worth keeping. Oddly, I don't remember its demolition.

Dad's experience of military service also served its purpose. There was, in the end, not a great deal of glory in it, and much being moved about thanks to a series of training stints and exercises that equipped him with a formidable array of practical knowledge but dragged on so long that his real period of soldiering did not begin until the fighting in Europe was over. The endlessly deferred horizon of expectation, the frustration and uncertainty, and not least his protracted contact with the officer class—crusty, small-minded, inhabiting a xenophobic country all its own—contributed to a gnawing sense of wasted time as the decade progressed. It was not as though the army took him to the battlefield or to any kind of ultimate test: The reality was much more prosaic. First stop was a technical college in Wandsworth where he also served out the final year of the war in the Home Guard; then, in March 1946, after his selection for officer cadet training it was on to Bodmin on the Cornish moors for the basics; and then to the huge prisonlike Marne Barracks at Catterick in Yorkshire, where after a brief stay at Sandhurst, he was commissioned into the Royal Corps of Signals before being posted to Hamburg as a second lieutenant in the spring of 1947.

It was his fretful, resourceful mother who had been responsible. In Minehead he had dreamed of joining the air force. Frouma had not, however, gone through war and revolution and exile, brought up her son in England, and seen him admitted to Oxford, only to face losing him to the RAF. Knowing his mathematical mind, she persuaded him to apply for a War Office engineering cadetship and thus diverted him away from the front. It meant more studying, but at Wandsworth Technical College, not Oxford. His parents were relieved. Not only was he back living with them but the path before him seemed to be heading in a familiar direction. They gave him an Engineer's Diary for 1944 to help him along. There were after all plenty of engineers in the Mazower family—among them Frouma's brother Vitalie, her brother-in-law Yasha, and half the Toumarkines in Moscow. There was also Vera Broido's older brother,

Daniel, a remarkable man who among other things invented the first bar-code system and was prominent in the prehistory of analog computing. So it is not surprising if writing to Vitalie in February 1945 Frouma told him with evident relief that "engineering definitely captivates [Bill] and if God willing, he survives the war, it will be his future profession." It was her hope, clearly, although this was not how it would turn out, even if in later life Dad retained the engineer's love of precision and rationality and utility.

Enrolled at his college on the other side of the war-damaged capital, he left home before the trolleybus began running, to reach Wandsworth for classes that started at six. In 1944 and early 1945 German rockets were raining down on London, but he never spoke about them. As formative in its way as Oxford, the college gave him the rudiments of a proper scientific education—serious chemistry and physics, which he had not studied at school, combined with the practical business of using lathes in an engineering workshop. I realize now that his extraordinary skill with all things electrical, not to mention woodworking and construction, was the product not only of talent and inclination but of targeted wartime training as well.

Back at home, and not, I think, unhappily, he dismantled the bomb shelter, took down the blackout curtains, and resumed his life as a vegetable gardener. He noted the milestones, the political landmarks interspersed with the weather and holiday plans: "April 17: Heatwave still continues. Buchenwald unearthed." "May 24 (Empire Day): Wrote to Devon. Alfriston fixed. *Himmler se suicide.*" He was waiting for the interviews that would determine whether he would get an officer's commission or something less prestigious, and whether he would be sent to India or closer to home. In November he received a letter from

the War Office asking him if he intended to remain an Englishman, as both his parents were foreigners when he was born, or
if he intended to take a second citizenship. He replied that he
had no such plans, and shortly after that he finished his exams
and was quickly approved for officer training. But one detects
an undercurrent of restlessness that no amount of Labour Party
work assuaged. He was walking long distances whenever and
wherever he could. He also now became obsessed with radios,
as if they were a vital lifeline to a world cut off by the war. "My
personal life consists of two things," he wrote his uncle Vitalie,
whom he was missing, "radios and politics." He would build
increasingly complex valve radios and take them apart again, as
if to focus on things that could be mended, not those that could
not. At one stage there were no fewer than six homemade sets
lying around the house, testimony to an underlying dissatisfac-
tion. Rio de Janeiro, Delhi, New York, Madrid, Warsaw, Danzig: On November 19, 1945, he noted he had managed to listen
in to them all that day. Meanwhile he awaited the army, and
travel abroad was all but impossible.

At the beginning of 1946, his fate passed into the hands of
the War Office and the round began of provincial camps and
parade grounds, checkpoints, barrack duties, and weekends
off. He was not learning about lathes now but about grenades
and Bren guns. I remember my surprise after his death when
I opened his bedroom cupboard and there behind his jackets
I found a baseball bat, a last-ditch defense against intruders
who had never materialized. Weapons and aggression of any
kind had seemed so foreign to him. But a son's imagination is
limited and I now see that thanks to the army he knew how
to box, ride a horse, shoot deer, and drive a lorry along with
the other things that are easier for me to visualize: more radio

sets for his Signals training, forced marches through the Yorkshire snow followed by snowball fights or—when the weather
improved—a tug-of-war. Although he formed few friendships
with the other men, he was not a loner, and he often hitched
into the nearest town with one or two of them to watch films
or to while away a weekend afternoon on the beach at Whitby.
But apart from brief leaves that he spent at home, or in France,
he was stuck in Catterick through the terrible winter of 1946, a
time of peeling potatoes, of monotonous futility.

In April 1947 he finally learned he had been assigned to the
British Army on the Rhine, and after a visit to Paris with his
seventy-three-year-old father—Max was in poor health, which
he would never really escape from this point on—he returned
to his regiment at Thirsk and sailed across the North Sea to
Germany, or what was left of it. They landed at Cuxhaven, the
main port for the British Zone.

Hamburg might have been a city in ruins but in the officers'
mess the conditions were far better than back home, and on
their first evening Dad and the other new arrivals were greeted
with champagne, apricot brandy, and ice cream. The extrav-
agance of it bothered him. That sweltering summer of 1947,
after work they would take their armchairs and sit out on the
grass under the birch trees. In one of his photos from those
afternoons, a couple of members of his unit have stripped to
the waist and are making themselves at home with their legs
outstretched. Dad is with them but he is not lounging: wearing shirtsleeves, braces, and sunshades, he sits a little apart.
He looks thoughtful. Some weekends were spent with friends
boating on the lake at Plön, others on the beach. He shot deer,
visited the small Baltic fishing ports around Lübeck, and went
riding on the country roads outside Bielefeld. But it was not a
happy time. The work—monitoring telephone conversations

across the city's exchanges—was uninteresting, the office dull. He wrote letters, dreamed of trips to France and London, and buried himself in the German grammar that Megan had given him. Books piled up on his mattress.

It was not only that he felt slightly alienated from many of his English messmates, abroad for the first time, ignorant of the language, and now enjoying the kind of access to girls and foods and comforts they had never known before. There were also the locals, burying a recent past that seemed all too close. In later life, I don't remember him singling out the Germans for particular hostility. But feelings were running higher after the war, even his: On landing at the docks, he once told my brother, the immediate impulse of this least violent of men had been to take a machine gun and shoot the first Germans he saw. After less than a month, he wrote to his uncle: "Life here does not agree with me: it is too luxurious on our side and sets a bad example to the Germans. I don't feel comfortable when I am surrounded by them. I can never chat with one of them without feeling a tinge of suspicion that I am talking to a former SS man and the certainty that at some point or another they applauded Hitler. They entirely lack the ability to laugh and always look so down that I have a great desire to see the French again with their air of vivacity...Work is boring. Unfortunately most of the officers here are not pleasant and life could certainly be more amusing. Write me in French or Russian, it is all the same. If you've read *Les Grandes Vacances* or the book by Rémy or something similar please send me them because I am desperate for something to read." Worst of all, he was cooped up indoors. "It is the first time in my life that I have to sit down in an office all day and I really don't like it," he wrote, little knowing that was how he would spend much of the next forty years. He would go

on hikes when he could, a walk of a few miles of an evening was
the least of it. Even out under the pines he noticed the marks of
the war. Walking alone in the Teutoburg Forest one hot evening in May, with the thickly wooded slopes below him, the
very slopes where just two years earlier there had been fierce
fighting in one of the last battles before the German surrender,
he lay down in the grass at the top of a hill and slept.

"March 27, 1948: Went with Tripp, Bill, Adams, Evans to
Russian border at Besenhausen by lift in Dutch lorry. Talked
to guards. Then walked & hitched to Witzenhausen in US
Zone. Train back to Gottingen from Eichenberg." The border
with the Soviet Zone was a tourist attraction for many British
servicemen in those years, but for him it had much more than
merely the allure of the forbidden. Drawing him on more than
one visit, it was the closest he had ever gotten to Russia, the
country of his parents' birth, the country he had never entered
and would not for many years.

This stretch of time, full of unease, loneliness, and boredom, brought one encounter he never forgot. There was a

German family in Bielefeld—the Roeperts—whom Frouma had told him to visit. They were relatives. Ida Berlinraut, Frouma's cousin, had left Russia to marry a German called Edouard Roepert before the First World War and had been living in Germany since then. She was Jewish; he was not: They had a son. To their good fortune, the Gestapo had somehow overlooked her background and so despite everything she had spent the war a housewife inside the Third Reich, avoiding the bombers and listening to Joseph Goebbels denouncing Judeo-Bolshevism on the radio. What was more, her son had been called up and had served on the eastern front. Once the war was over, she had written to Frouma, so Dad hitched a ride to Bielefeld to see them and spent several days in their company. He told me later that his cousin had seemed traumatized by his experiences. To Dad the meeting must have brought home the element of sheer chance and good fortune that had led him to end up as a Sandhurst-trained second lieutenant in the British Army. He might have been feeling bored but his cousins, Max's nephews, had suffered much worse fates—Zachar's daughter had died in the Vilna ghetto; Semyon's son, Ilya, had frozen and starved to death in the siege of Leningrad. Now, it turned out, Ida's son had endured the war in the east in the ranks of the Wehrmacht. Did he need any further demonstration of the debt he owed his parents? Within the ambit of his family alone, the entire spectrum of the war's European destinies was contained.

For the remainder of his time there, he kept to himself, writing letters and counting the days. The Princess Royal, the future Queen Elizabeth, recently married, paid a visit to Hamburg and he was among the men presented to her, but the event counted for nothing in his recollection. It is as though afterwards he wanted to put the whole period out of his mind. He was happy to forget the drinking, the machismo, the boredom, and the fräuleins who did not interest him. In the photos of time off with men in his unit, he stands apart, as if he is waiting for life to begin again. In his album, Germany looks pretty enough away from the wartime devastation, but there was nothing for him there and never would be. In late May 1948 he took the ferry from the Hook of Holland and went straight to the barracks at York to be demobbed and came home to London the same night. He carefully packed away his army boots with hobnails so thick they are today almost unwearable. His suit went to the tailor to be altered, and he ordered a tweed jacket and corduroy trousers. He was ready to get on with things.

"You realize, Mark, this was all fifty years ago." It was more, actually, but that scarcely mattered. I had rung Mike Walker out of the blue, and although he had never met me, we were on first-name terms from the start. "I remember Bill of course, a singularly nice chap, he really was."

WALKER, Michael Herbert— b. May 15, 1928; o.s. of R. H. Walker, cotton merchant, Littleborough Lancs. Educ. Giggleswick [praep., capt. cricket]. Served in the Army Sept.

1946–Feb. 1949; R.A. Educ.; Egypt Nov 1947–Feb. 1949. Balliol 1949–(E.T.W., P.P.S.); 3rd Phil., Pol., Econ. 1952.

I had come across his name in Dad's diary and then in the Balliol College Register, and I thought he might remember Dad because another Balliol man had sent me a photo of the two of them kitted out for squash. They are standing outside Holywell Manor, where Mike had rooms: Dad has cycled over and with his socks rolled down, his collar open, and the racket under his arm, he looks at ease, the clouds lifted.

Mike couldn't remember much beyond that they had been good friends, and that Dad was an "exceedingly nice guy." Other Balliol men—he singled out William Rees-Mogg, the future editor of *The Times*, as an example—were a "loud noise in the JCR." He and Dad were not like that: "A lot of us were very ordinary chaps." But squash turned out to have been more important than I had thought. There was a college team and Balliol had an annual fixture with one of the women's colleges, which was how Mike had met his wife, at a college tea party. She was with him in the room when I called. And he did remember Dad as a squash player: "a very fit guy, extremely competitive."

Competitive. That was not what I had been expecting and it got me thinking—about my father's body, about his physicality and his mental outlook, and more generally about all those ways in which a child forms a picture of their parent and in doing so misses so much. Recovering Dad's world has meant tracing back deep into the past things I already knew about him, finding in the child the elements of him that were familiar to me. But it has also revealed parts of him to me that were forgotten, erased, and often just plain surprising. We always knew, for instance, that he had a sweet tooth. Frouma lovingly but accurately described him as "morally serious" and it was true; sweets were probably the closest he came to allowing himself to give in to impulse. This was why he could always be tempted by ice cream, and why when we grew up it was a kind of family joke that he would keep the chocolate hidden away in a locked cupboard, only to be brought out occasionally after a particularly delicious meal. The very first time he remembered his mother shouting at him—he had been about three—was when they were on Hampstead Heath and he had put a sheep's dropping in his mouth, thinking it was a sweet. Then there was the boy who delighted in being useful about the house, in making and mending; he too was instantly recognizable in the man. And so was the streak of stubbornness in those things, the few, he had really set his heart on, that balanced his capacity to accommodate and help. But I was discovering other sides of him, aspects that I simply could not have guessed had once been there. There was the intense sociability of his early twenties, hosting lunches and dinners and parties. There were the movies and unbelievably frequent trips to the newly built Forum, its great gaudy art deco columns gracing busy Kentish Town, where he went so often with his mother and father. There was Pchelka, his aunt and uncle's dog in Beauchamp: I started to notice how many photos he had taken of it in the late 1930s, the more striking to me because we had not grown up in a household with animals.

Now from what Mike told me, there was something more. Evidently there had been a time when, however briefly and if only on the squash court, he had wanted to win. Not that it was difficult to imagine that he had been very fit in those days (military training would have seen to that, along with his naturally muscular physique and the mountain hikes), but in later life it was hard to have envisaged anyone less competitive, and he always seemed to have conquered as successfully as anyone else I knew the impulse to show off or to get ahead of others. Working as a middle manager in one sector of a vast multinational company, he had shown no interest at all in climbing the greasy pole to executive glory. Competitiveness is often the fuel of ambition, and Dad was, or so he seemed to me, the least ambitious of men. So this was a conundrum. But it was a welcome one because it made what I can only call his tranquillity of mind, at least as we saw it in the larger things of life, the product of an inward struggle or deliberation rather than merely a gift. This energy had not dissipated later on—he was never lacking in energy—but it had been diffused into other things, and lost its competitive dimension, though how this had happened was a mystery.

I was grateful to Mike Walker for our conversation because it reminded me of much that I valued in Dad. Was it perhaps something inherent in their generation, that surface diffidence and modesty and courtesy that masked, in the right circumstances, a real underlying warmth and slight melancholy and the desire to help and be useful? At least in Dad's case, being useful was almost the leitmotif of his existence. His diaries noted meticulously not only the few days he marked out as "lazy" but the far more numerous occasions when he repaired a lamp, or put up shelves in a landlady's bedroom, or fixed the wiring, or mended the radio. If the diary was any judge, these were the things worth recording, more important than dreams or love affairs.

His first experience of Oxford had come as a seventeen-year-old in 1943. His second was six years later with the army behind him. The first time round, he had sailed in, wanting to enjoy everything. By the late 1940s, the Cold War was in full swing and the passage to adulthood and independence seemed less certain than he had imagined. A lot less certain. As the clock wound down on his time in Germany, he got a nasty shock when he learned that he did not have an automatic right to return to Oxford. In the spring and summer of 1948, he tried to get back into Balliol and applied to several London colleges too, but the universities were inundated with returning ex-servicemen and he was rebuffed each time. It started to seem he might not go back at all. He earned some money as a research engineer in an electrical factory, a long commute each day out to unglamorous Enfield, but these were unhappy months for him, perhaps the unhappiest of his life. Already frustrated by the time he had wasted in the army, he was back in London and at home, living on his nerves in a kind of limbo. His health suffered.

For the first time, I think, he was in some measure defying his parents' wishes. Max was now ailing and unable to work—and his parents wanted him to go back and finish training as an engineer so as to get into regular employment as soon as possible. He resisted, not wanting to give up the thought of further studies. Only in the summer of 1949 did he learn, to his enormous relief, that Balliol would take him. But the sense of uncertainty did not immediately dissipate. Perhaps in deference to his parents' wishes he went up to read mathematics, but a day into the course he realized it was not what he wanted at all, and he did something very uncharacteristic: He changed his mind and, with Ira's encouragement, announced that he was going to study politics, philosophy, and economics instead. The dons gave no resistance. His parents wondered what had gotten into him and hoped it would all be of some use in the end.

Balliol in 1949 was a very different place from six years earlier. It was no less democratic—one of his friends was Tommy Ward, a man in his thirties, a carpenter's son out of a Liverpool council school and married, a species of undergraduate all but unknown in most Oxford colleges in those days. But the college was now full of older men who were coming out of the army and in a hurry to be done. I had asked Mike Walker what they had thought about the war after they went up: "Most of us wanted to raze it from our minds." Getting on with it—their outlook was practical, experienced, with an eye already turned finally to making a life of one's own. There were decisions to be made and one looked forward not back; the untoward was an irritation to be surmounted not a trauma to be scrutinized.

Introspection could easily be written off as feeling sorry for yourself, which was not a habit of mind the war had fostered. Having had enough of being ordered around in the ranks, and in many cases seen active service and been decorated for it, these were not men to take easily to being treated as if they were fresh out of school. There was another striking difference with 1943: Americans had arrived at the college in force. There was a sizable cohort of them, mostly older men, the spearhead of the new Cold War alliance. Dad's year included at least one future CIA operative, a future Librarian of Congress, and a distinguished philosopher of history alongside the inevitable diplomats, lawyers, and journalists. Greece to the new Rome, England's place in the universe was changing.

The switch to politics, philosophy, and economics was—in retrospect—a kind of last sign of his political commitment, at least in the intense form it had taken on since the Spanish Civil War, an effort, subconscious I think, to resist the pull of the vocational and the practical. Yet it was, in its own way, a very practical choice. The Mazowers were not, on the whole, a speculative family, and if it is not clear why Dad chose to study philosophy, it is also true that the subject as it was taught in postwar Oxford was proudly down-to-earth.

There were exceptions, mostly imported. "March 7, 1950: Heard Brock on 'Existentialism'—incomprehensible!" he wrote during his second term. The somewhat forlorn figure of Werner Brock, a former assistant to Martin Heidegger in Freiburg, had fled to England in 1934 and became a leading popularizer of the great man's ideas there. Brock had been battling against the current for more than a decade to spread a vision that was completely at odds with the increasingly powerful British analytic tradition. Its proponents valued clarity and precision whereas Brock and Heidegger sought to use language to probe its own limits. In self-assured Oxford—anti-metaphysical and intellectually complacent—this was not likely to prosper: People didn't want obscurity, however profound. The year before Dad heard him, Brock had published the first translation in English of Heidegger's thought under the title *Existence and Being*, a book now eagerly studied by historians of the spread of philosophical ideas. It was a brave venture at a time when Heidegger's reputation was at its nadir because of his flirtation with Nazism. Dad's main philosophy tutor at Balliol, Patrick Corbett, could not have been more different: He was a brilliant teacher who basically combined the commonsense approach that was sweeping the philosophy of language in Oxford with a liberalism that valued reason above all things. Common-sense philosophy was, in a way, a kind of reasoning for the age of Labour, anti-elitist and problem-solving rather than problem-creating, premised on getting things done through what could be understood in common. As philosophy it now seems antiquated next to Brock and Heidegger, but as a train-ing for linguistic precision, a kind of supercharged version of the values of clarity and saying what you mean of the kind that had been dear to Max, it had no peer. Some found the Oxonian manner—the inevitable pipe, the crisp articulation inflected only by the equally inevitable slight fake stammer—intimidat-ing; Dad didn't. It came naturally to him to respect words as tools. What could not be said straightforwardly could be left unsaid or figured out later. His Oxford training helped reinforce this attitude.

He was less at ease with the flash and dazzle of his economics tutor, Thomas Balogh, one of the most important and certainly the most colorful of the economists active in twentieth-century

Britain. Having started out in Budapest in the 1920s as a youthful supporter of Admiral Miklós Horthy, Balogh had come to England and moved steadily to the Left. A. R. Lindsay had appointed him to teach economics and he helped turn wartime Oxford into one of the principal centers of what would later become known as Keynesian thought (although in fact Balogh and several of his colleagues were as significantly involved in the challenge to laissez-faire as Keynes himself). Balogh's behavior as a college tutor was unconventional: He was notorious for lying down or wandering off to the bathroom while students were reading their essays aloud; he liked students to call him by his first name and addressed them as "little poppet" and "darling." Dad did not warm to him—unflamboyant himself, Balogh's flamboyance did not put him at ease—and recorded with relief on December 1, 1950, his "last essay for Balogh."

Twenty-five years old, Dad now straddled two worlds. He remained attached to his childhood home on Oakeshott Avenue, and it was still his base outside term time; but his childhood was over and the house was growing quieter. André had departed for Spain, reappearing for a week or two each year; Ira was hard at work in the West End and about to begin married life with her new husband. Max was growing visibly older, fretting about his medications, his enforced idleness, and the lack of money. Looking after him was exhausting Frouma. In a photo Dad took at this time from inside the living room through the French doors into the garden, his parents are together at the bottom of the garden, two small elderly figures, survivors in a way, enjoying a North London summer day.

As his father's life wound down, Dad was becoming aware of what his could be. That summer, he headed back across the Channel for a holiday picking grapes in Provence. In shorts and a short-sleeved shirt he trekked up mountain slopes, chopping wood in a chalet on the flanks of the Alps; later there were the sands at Bandol, the bay at Sanary-sur-Mer, surrounded by the smiles and handshakes and embraces of men and women his own age, looking forward to what the world has to offer now that the war is in the past. In these months, he walked and walked, great hikes with friends across the Dolomites and into Austria and Switzerland, as though he were testing and hardening himself, taking to the heights to see the way ahead.

Friends were getting married, and I wonder if it is a sign that his thoughts, as his mother's had been on his behalf, were turning towards matrimony that he formed a couple of friendships, so far as I can tell for the first time, with girls who were, in one way or another, Jewish. One of these was a shy beautiful eighteen-year-old refugee, Barbara S., who had just arrived in England and knew almost no one when mutual friends encouraged them to meet. Lodging in Oxford, she visited him in his rooms and they took pictures of each other, pictures that had struck me when we looked at the photo album. I went through several other Barbaras, some living, some not, before I found the right one, married to a distinguished biochemist and living in very active semiretirement in Switzerland. We chatted, and she was enchanting, friendly, and happy to cast her mind back sixty-five years. It had not been an easy time for her, alone in a new country and unsure of her future, and although she and Dad did not see much of each other after that, what had stayed with her was his kindness, a big man but gentle. It was something she appreciated; for her war had been an exceptionally traumatic time, spent mostly underground in German-occupied Amsterdam before she was reunited with her father. In fact, she stayed only a few months in England in 1950 attending art school in Oxford before going back to Amsterdam, and by the time she returned, Dad had finished his studies.

There was also Ruth Spielman and her brother, Roger. Their background was quite different. The Spielmanns, as they had originally spelled it, were paid-up members of the Anglo-Jewish elite — the "cousins," as the historian Chaim Bermant once dubbed them. Claude Spielman, their father, had won the Military Cross in the First World War before joining one of England's oldest engineering firms, based in Darlington, which he ended up running. Ruth and Roger had grown up in the family residence, Hurworth Grange, a Victorian pile on fourteen acres on the banks of the Tees, in the company of a dozen or so servants, two chauffeurs, and several gardeners.

After Oxford Dad had headed north again. He had accepted a position as a trainee manager with Lever Brothers and was sent to Selby in Yorkshire, and there were factory foremen and sales managers to fill his waking hours, the mysteries of the Engineering Department and Administration, Marketing, Transport, and Wages to be interpreted as he rested after work in his lodgings. But early on the morning of Friday, May 2, only a few months into his training, Dad learned that his father had died suddenly of angina. He caught the train straight down to London and was in Oakeshott Avenue by lunchtime. The following day, at St. Pancras town hall, he registered the death: "Mordchel Mazower, aged 79, birth date approximately 1873." The funeral was held at Golders Green crematorium, and Edvard Grieg's "Morning" was played while Max's body was turned into ashes. That same evening Dad returned to Selby and shortly after that he was moved again, to Sheffield and a new set of digs. His father's death seems to have brought a kind of decision. The security of employment inside a large corporation appealed to him, and he stuck with Lever Brothers for thirty years. But he hated the grime of Sheffield, and with nothing to keep him in the north, he decided to return to London. It is as though one sees crystallizing in his mind the resolution to root himself close to his birthplace, driven by the sense of responsibility he felt to his mother, now widowed in a country he belonged to and knew far better than she did.

Sometimes he would get away to spend weekends with the Spielmans at Hurworth, where there were long walks and lunches with local colonels and their wives. It was not a friendship he ever mentioned to us, but it is suggestive of the way the social landscape of England had opened itself up to him, that he moved easily in these years, sometimes in the same day, from the wealth of Hurworth Grange to the poverty of the Doncaster mining villages, from Anglo-Jewish aristocracy to West Riding workers. Afterwards, his range of acquaintances would narrow, for many reasons I think, some of them willed and some of the times, as the energy of the war decade, which drove so many to mobilize and socialize around politics and the army, gave way to a life of family and domesticity that was focused on North London. But I like to think of him in those last few months of his father's life, a young trainee manager, with the army and Oxford behind him, jumping out of Roger's car in the drive at Hurworth in the winter of 1951, and walking with the Spielmans across their snowbound estate down to the Tees.

The Shed

There are many ways to tell a life. There is the unfolding of genius, beloved by the Romantics. There is the debunking of genius, beloved by those who followed them. There is the Odyssean quest, the pursuit of psychic stability, facing down ghosts and exorcising demons, the story of pain overcome, and the revelation of hidden secrets and of the effort required in keeping them buried. This is what biography often does in an age magnetized by the omnipotence of trauma: It reassures us that traumas can be identified and surmounted, the sinful dead and the perpetrators identified, the victims consoled. But these genres and tropes betray the limitations and perhaps the poverty of our literary expectations and psychological assumptions. What would it be to tell the story of a life that illustrated the unfolding of a different, much older theme: the pursuit of contentment and well-being? Of life lived across generations as a story not so much about suffering and the isolation and loneliness of an authentic individuality as about resilience and tenacity and the virtues of silence and pragmatism and taking pleasure in small things?

Dad's capacity for this kind of pleasure was connected to a strong sense of purpose and seriousness. "Billy is the same helpful boy he always was," his mother wrote to her sister and brother in France as the war ended. He was the good son, which meant to be of use to those around you, and the value of this was deeply inculcated into him by both of his parents. Growing up in an era of falling bombs and tight money, he was the one who kept the house in order, and landladies as well as his parents benefitted from his love of making things work. As a mischievous twelve-year-old, he once sabotaged the wiring in Oakeshott Avenue for the sheer pleasure of impressing the family by bringing the lights back on. As a grown man, he could not walk home past a rubbish skip without plundering the contents for anything that might be added to the woodpile in the garden or stored in the loft, deposited against life's mishaps, malfunctions, and eventualities. He had the craftsman's knowledge that accidents and breakdowns are a part of life. When they happened, they were to be fixed without fuss. If they were not soluble, there was no point talking about them.

This approach meant saving words for when they could affect things and make them better. It was not that he mistrusted words, not at all—the faded red covers of that mid-century classic of teach-yourself philology, Frederick Bodmer's *The Loom of Language*, protected a book he prized, and there was always a dictionary to hand at dinner to check on meanings and derivations—but he did like them to be exact, and exactitude was harder when it came to the category, a large one, of those things it was not generally worth talking about. Among these were metaphysical speculations, disappointments, and pain. His parents had, I think, taught him this lesson, each in their way, and the result was that it did not come at all easily to him to talk about personal difficulties. As a teenager, in the first pages of his diary, even when he did note openly—as he soon ceased to do—those days of being "depressed," his language was allusive. We never heard about the ill health he had suffered as a boy, nor the period of lassitude and frustration that came over him after he finished the army and could not get into university. This softer version of his father's stiff upper lip was the obverse of his pragmatism, and it was characteristic of many in his generation. I soon realized that when he skated over things, it was where he needed to be gently pressed about something that had happened and that he had not wanted to think about for one reason or another—things to do with his half sister and half brother, for instance. When I did probe, I never encountered protest, and sometimes found a willingness and even enthusiasm to contemplate things he had not thought about for decades. But I did not probe very deeply because I suppose I have more admiration and respect than I perhaps should for the ethos that underpinned his reticence, a reticence that was never more admirable than at the very end of his life when his stoicism impressed itself upon all of us afresh and upon his doctors as well.

The turbulence and upheavals of the twentieth century had a direct impact on Dad and shaped him particularly through their effects on his parents and siblings. They affected him too insofar as he understood his relationship to the place of his birth in a very specific and deeply felt way and because he knew what good fortune was whenever he looked at his family tree. In tracing his life, I have tried to show this, to convey how these family experiences and the social possibilities in the country of his birth came together in his childhood to foster a certain outlook that prepared him for the life he was to follow. Max's political ideals provided the basic orientation—socialist but not communist (and yet not ardently anticommunist either)—that Dad learned in the light of English conditions as he came to political consciousness during the Spanish Civil War. It is striking that it was his half brother's support of Franco into the 1960s that convinced Dad they had nothing in common. But then, fairly or not, he had already found André wanting because of his attitude towards his parents. Frouma's belief in family, her commitment to nurturing those ties through visits and letters with her siblings in Russia and France, left an even greater mark on him than his father's politics—and turned out to be more enduring—because he was so close to her and because she expected so much from him. The responsibility he felt as the son of immigrants never left him. He could not emulate her letter-writing, though at times he tried, but he remained devoted to his uncle and aunt, and above all to her, and made sure his children followed in his steps.

A psychic balance all his own helped him blend the world of his parents, a very specific Russian Jewish atmosphere preserved in Highgate living rooms, with many of the middle-class values of interwar England into which he was raised. It was not that he never felt embarrassment—the complementary mortifications he once mentioned to me were, first, whenever people mistook him for a White Russian, and, second and conversely, the times he went with his mother to some more observant Jewish family friends and felt out of place. But neither kind of embarrassment was insurmountable. At the same time, a series of networks so natural that they seemed to have always been there smoothed his path and gave social confidence: circles of friends of his parents, Mensheviks and Bundists born before the century had begun; the Fabian Society; and the Labour Party. Oxford and the army were equally powerful as entry points into ways of speaking and thinking about oneself that became part of the essence of the man.

There were role models, negative and positive, in a half

brother and half sister from whom semi-detachment was key. Both André and Ira responded to the family's revolutionary past in romantic ways that he could not share—in André's case through a kind of exaggerated conservatism, the Catholic Church, and conspiracy theories; in Ira's by glamorizing the Tsarist era and creating a series of aristocratic literary fantasies. Suspicious of excesses of the imagination, Dad's response was practical: to make sure the money was there for a family life. But this never led him to making money for its own sake. His father, impressive in many things, some of them hidden, had acquired the savings to support them in a few fortunate years around 1912, but afterwards, when money got much tighter, Max's business acumen was found wanting. Among the familial maps that one could draw across North London is one of the properties that at various times Max toyed with buying and that would have made his fortune had he done so. Success in making money was not a trait of the Mazowers and too much attachment to it was undesirable, which is why the Jaguar parked outside our door when Ira and Jeff came to call was always grounds for suspicion. Neither was worldly ambition or seeking the limelight; getting things done was more important. Max's entire early life was an illustration of the virtues of political commitment behind the scenes.

To a surprising degree, this was a life Dad chose, pushed I think in particular by his father's death in 1952, and once the uncertainties of the late 1940s were behind him, there seems to have been little wavering. He chose a job that would give him stability and allow him to raise a family. He chose to be more present in his sons' lives than his father had been in his. He chose to marry and was fortunate as well as thoughtful enough to know instantly when he had found the woman he wanted to make a home with. By the time he began working at Lever Brothers, his mother was already on the lookout for a prospective daughter-in-law. There was a couple called the Kidels, who had lodged with them in Oakeshott Avenue before the war and later moved down the road. On Saturday, March 14, 1954, they invited Frouma and Dad, now twenty-nine years old, to meet some friends who had a daughter they thought he might like. That was the evening he and Mum met—through old-fashioned matchmaking in the Eastern European style. Mum's father, Reg Shaffer, was a self-made businessman who owned a small textile manufacturer in Manchester. His wife, Ruth, who looked after their home in London during Reg's frequent trips north, was the daughter of a well-known Jewish novelist, a serendipitous connection because Max had published this writer, Sholem Asch—a giant in Yiddish literature—back in another world and another time, in a Bundist journal he had edited before the First World War in Vilna. Mum was nineteen, an only child, home from a not terribly happy stint in Paris and training to become a physiotherapist. Little more than a year after that dinner they married. They both wanted a family and children followed, four of us, all boys, all close. They moved into the house that became our home in 1959: They would occupy it into the next century. Frouma was only a couple of miles away. Set amid the Golders Green streets that Dad knew from his visits to the Zukermans and the Koldofskys when he was a boy, the house is not unlike the one in Oakeshott Avenue, a little older but in a very similar style, semidetached, with French doors at the rear that gave onto a long garden that ended in trees.

Dad's shed first went up just below the house, and my brother Dave and I, then aged two and three, are caught on film washing its wooden sides with water—we're trying to be helpful. By the late 1960s, by which time our brothers, Ben and Jony, had arrived too, it had been moved to its present location farther down the garden and along the wall on the other side. As we grew up, this was Dad's domain. It was small and functional and there was room only for one person to work, with perhaps a small boy alongside. Standing at the workbench, you looked out across the garden to the large cherry tree we used to climb; behind were shelves of screws, nails, and other items, all neatly housed in an assortment of small containers and carefully labeled.

He had fastened the tool cabinet to the wall at the end and this was where his chisels, hammers, saws, and mallets were housed. I don't remember him ever buying tools, which may be because these were things he had begun collecting as a school-boy at the Woolworths in Kentish Town and then supple-mented during the war. None was for show and none looked new, and there was always a smell of sawdust and usefulness; an apron was worn lest there be hard words when he came dirty into the house. Once the shed acquired a light, he could spend hours there in all seasons.

The shed became not so much a refuge as a kind of home within the home, the place where he could be himself, freed of the responsibilities that he shouldered so readily. It embodied his very practical and precise intelligence, his patience and care with objects. But its charms lay too in its surroundings—part of a garden, surrounded by greenery in the city that had wel-comed his parents and whose northern suburbs were his as much as they were anybody's. It embodied a commitment to the domestic that brought him lasting happiness. Not for Dad the allure of fame (he was too much his father's son for that) nor the happiness of creative solitude (he was too much his mother's). He valued money for the stability it provided but he was neither avaricious nor acquisitive, and when he died there were no more than two suits in his wardrobe and a jacket or two. He valued constancy and honesty and loyalty to those close to him. And durability: What he built, he built to last. The shed is empty now and the tools have found new homes, which is what he would have wanted. But it still stands in the old place, and the trees and hedges are starting to grow up around it and honeysuckle is beginning to unpick the lock.

One afternoon in August 1997, eighteen minutes and thirty-seven seconds into the last tape of our conversations, we were called down for tea.

Dad: "Okay. Let's stop…"

Me: "Shall we stop there?"

Dad: "Yes, let's stop there."

Acknowledgments

The primary sources used in this book are chiefly family documents—letters, diaries, photographs—in the possession of my mother. I transcribed a long interview with my father, conducted some years before his death, and also drew upon the many letters to and from his mother, Frouma, which my cousin Patrick Toumarkine was kind enough to make available to me.

The main archival sources include the State Archives of the Russian Federation (GARF) in Moscow, notably files 102 and 124 (on Max's and Sofia Krylenko's revolutionary activities), 539 (Semyon and his family), 1742 (Lev Toumarkine), and 10035 (Sofia Krylenko's rehabilitation file). The Archives générales du Royaume in Brussels, Belgium, include files 996537 (Sofia Krylenko), 1002985 (Olga Krylenko), 791610 (Vladimir Krylenko), and 912047 (Constantin de Meyer). I should also mention the Eastman archives at Indiana University; the Emma Goldman Papers at the University of California, Berkeley; the International Institute for Social History in Amsterdam, Netherlands; the Liège municipal archives; and YIVO in New York.

Two books were invaluable: *My East Is Gorgeous* by Ira J. Morris and *Daughter of the Revolution* by Vera Broido, both of which contain accounts that I have drawn upon or cited directly. Other sources include Elissa Bemporad, *Becoming*

Soviet Jews: The Bolshevik Experiment; Walter Benjamin, Moscow Diary; Gill Bennett, Churchill's Man of Mystery: Desmond Morton and the World of Intelligence; Oleg Budnitskii, Russian Jews Between the Reds and the Whites, 1917–1920; Andrew Cook, Ace of Spies: The True Story of Sidney Reilly; Corpus: Within Living Memory, edited by M. E. Bury and E. J. Winter, for André's recollections of Corpus Christi College in the 1920s; Documents Concerning the Destruction of the Jews of Grodno, 1941–44, volume 1, edited by Beate and Serge Klarsfeld; Max Eastman, Love and Revolution: My Journey through an Epoch; T. S. Eliot, The Letters of T .S. Eliot, Vol. 4: 1928–1929, edited by Valerie Eliot; Victor Erlich, Child of a Turbulent Century; Naum Jasny, Soviet Economists of the Twenties: Names to Be Remembered; Miklós Kun, Stalin: An Unknown Portrait; Lars Lih, Bread and Authority in Russia, 1914–1921; Ivan Maisky, Journey into the Past; David Matless, Landscape and Englishness; Vladimir Medem, The Life and Soul of a Legendary Jewish Socialist: The Memoirs of Vladimir Medem, edited by Samuel Portnoy; Monnika Minninger et al., Antisemitisch Verfolgte registriert in Bielefeld, 1933–45, which mentions Ida Roepert; Benjamin Nadel, "Bundism in England," Jewish Socialist, 6–7; Leo Pasvolsky, The Economics of Communism; Arthur Peacock, Yours Fraternally; Polin 6: Jews in Łódź, 1820–1939, edited by Anthony Polonsky; Kevin Quinlan, The Secret War Between the Wars: MI5 in the 1920s and 1930s; Helen Rappoport, Conspirator: Lenin in Exile; Rudolf Rocker, The London Years; Gabriella Safran, Wandering Soul: The Dybbuk's Creator, S. An-sky; Karl Schlögel, Moscow, 1937; Andrew Thorpe, The British Communist Party and Moscow, 1920–1943; Henry Tobias, The Jewish Bund in Russia from Its Origins to 1905; Nick Toczek, Haters, Baiters and Would-Be Dictators: Anti-Semitism and the UK Far Right; Scott

Ury, *Barricades and Banners: The Revolution of 1905 and the Transformation of Warsaw Jewry*; David Vital, *A People Apart: A Political History of the Jews in Europe, 1789–1939*, which has a good discussion of the Gomel pogrom on pages 530–31; Claudia Weill, *Les Cosmopolites: Socialisme et judéité en Russie, 1897–1917*; Nathan Weinstock, *Couleur espérance: la memoire ouvriere juive autour de 1900*; and *The Worlds of S. An-sky: A Russian Jewish Intellectual at the Turn of the Century*, edited by Gabrielle Safran and Steven J. Zipperstein.

I am grateful to the following for their assistance: Nile Arena, Lilly Library, Indiana University; Nick Baldwin, Great Ormond Street Hospital archives; Christophe Bechet; Jennifer Bell; Gill Bennett, Lillah de Bie, University College School; James Billington; Adam Bosiacki; Lalage Bown; Anthony Camp; Anna Carlen; Tanya Chebotarev; Michel Closquet, Archives of the Ville de Liège; Deborah Cohen; Robert Crossley; Phil Dykes; Candace Falk, Emma Goldman Papers, Berkeley; Jean-Francois Fayet; Katie Giles, Kingston University Archives; Tatiana Glezer; J. H. Goldthorpe; Barbara Gray, King Edward VI School archives, Chelmsford; Ernest Hecht; Henley Henley-Smith, Highgate School; Peter Holquist; Sonia Hood, Friends School, Saffron Walden; Philip M. Hudson; Lucy Hughes, Corpus Christi College, Cambridge; Anthony Ismailoff; George Jones; Rosie Kennedy; Oleg Khlevniuk; Mark Kidel; Peteris Kimelis; Anna Kisselgoff; Tim Knebel, Sheffield Archives; Steve Kotkin; Tamara Lansky; Natalia Malihina, Memorial Society, Moscow; Richard Meunier, St. Bartholomew's Hospital; Alan Montefiore; Mark Nowogrodzki; Julie Parry, People's History Museum; Bert Patenaude; James Peters, Manchester University Archives; Silvio Pons; Richard Ramage, St. Antony's College,

Oxford; Melvin Richter; Anna Sander, Balliol College, Oxford; Nicholas Shakespeare; Peter Slezkine; Daniel Snowman; Belinda Spinaze, Fryer Library, University of Melbourne; John Stewart; Filip Strubbe, Algemeen Rijksarchief, Brussels; Sacha Toumarkine; Susan Trackman, the archives of Highgate Scientific and Literary Institution; Jane Tucker; Alexei Tumarkin; Annabel Valentine, Royal Holloway Archives; Godfrind Vinciane; Tony Watson; Nadine Werner, Walter Benjamin Archive; Joshua Zimmerman; and George Zukerman.

A very special thanks to Riccardo Mario Cucciolla, Victor Petrov, Gil Rubin, and Carolina de Stefano for helping me in the YIVO Institute for Jewish Research and the Moscow archives, since without them much of this would have remained unknown; to my cousin Boris Kobrinsky for sharing so much of his knowledge about the family in Moscow; and to Jane Gorjevsky and Tarik Amar for translations from the Russian. Rina Turner provided translations from Yiddish. My brother David helped with his great expertise in all matters Yiddish. I am indebted to Mike Allen, Elizabeth Donaldson, Barbara and Jack Dunitz, Richard Jefferies, Andrei M., Anthony Platt, Patrick Toumarkine (both for conversation and for sharing the letters from Frouma to her brother and sister, his father and aunt), and Mike Walker for their great kindness in fielding questions from a (to most of them) complete stranger about events that happened more than sixty years ago. I owe a great debt to Peter and Gilly Wesley for opening up 20 Oakeshott Avenue with such charm and helpfulness. My thanks to Marwa Elshakry, Constantine Giannaris, Kostas Kostis, Peter Mandler, John Palatella, Rachel Phipps, Alexander Star, Inigo Thomas, and Simon Winder, and to my colleagues in the Heyman Center

Fellows seminar for reading earlier drafts of this manuscript and suggesting improvements. Judith Gurewich has been a publisher *sans pareil*, who brought the acutest of editorial eyes to my words. It has been a privilege working with her and the whole Other Press team. I end by thanking Mum, Dave, Ben, and Jony for their immense and unquestioning support without which this book would not have been written.

FAMILY TREES

MAZOWER FAMILY

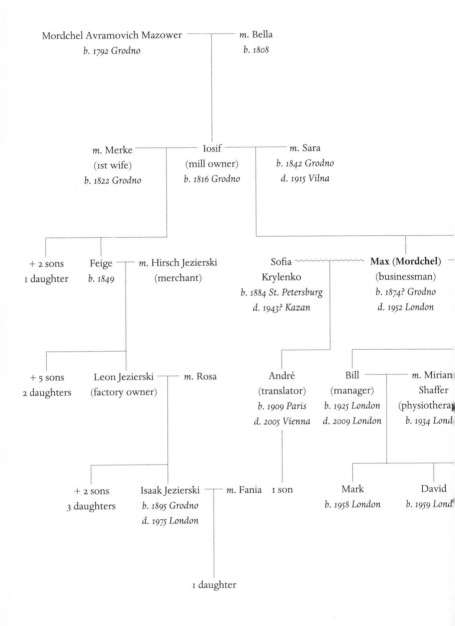

Mordchel Avramovich Mazower —— m. Bella
b. 1792 Grodno   b. 1808

m. Merke —— Iosif —— m. Sara
(1st wife)   (mill owner)   b. 1842 Grodno
b. 1822 Grodno   b. 1816 Grodno   d. 1915 Vilna

+ 2 sons   Feige —— m. Hirsch Jezierski   Sofia   **Max (Mordchel)**
1 daughter   b. 1849   (merchant)   Krylenko   (businessman)
   b. 1884 St. Petersburg   b. 1874? Grodno
   d. 1943? Kazan   d. 1952 London

+ 5 sons   Leon Jezierski —— m. Rosa   André   Bill —— m. Mirian
2 daughters   (factory owner)   (translator)   (manager)   Shaffer
   b. 1909 Paris   b. 1925 London   (physiothera
   d. 2005 Vienna   d. 2009 London   b. 1934 Lond

+ 2 sons   Isaak Jezierski —— m. Fania   1 son   Mark   David
3 daughters   b. 1895 Grodno   b. 1958 London   b. 1959 Lond
   d. 1975 London

1 daughter

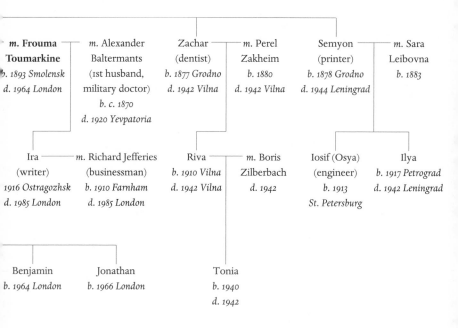

m. **Frouma** **Toumarkine**	*m.* Alexander Baltermants	Zachar (dentist)	*m.* Perel Zakheim	Semyon (printer)	*m.* Sara Leibovna
b. 1893 Smolensk *d. 1964 London*	(1st husband, military doctor) *b. c. 1870* *d. 1920 Yevpatoria*	*b. 1877 Grodno* *d. 1942 Vilna*	*b. 1880* *d. 1942 Vilna*	*b. 1878 Grodno* *d. 1944 Leningrad*	*b. 1883*

Ira (writer)	*m.* Richard Jefferies (businessman)	Riva	*m.* Boris Zilberbach	Iosif (Osya) (engineer)	Ilya
1916 Ostragozhsk *d. 1985 London*	*b. 1910 Farnham* *d. 1985 London*	*b. 1910 Vilna* *d. 1942 Vilna*	*d. 1942*	*b. 1913* *St. Petersburg*	*b. 1917 Petrograd* *d. 1942 Leningrad*

Benjamin	Jonathan	Tonia
b. 1964 London	*b. 1966 London*	*b. 1940* *d. 1942*

TOUMARKINE FAMILY

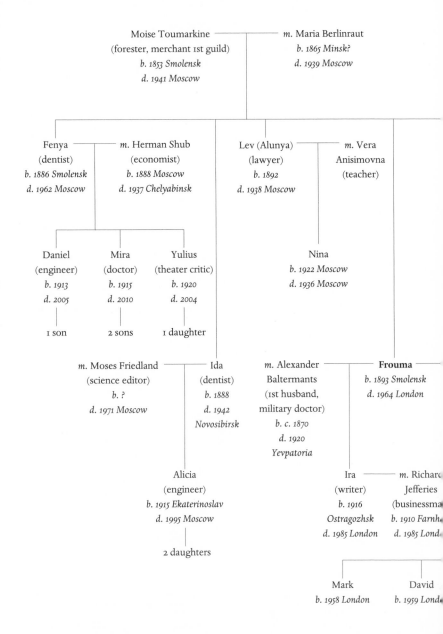

Moise Toumarkine
(forester, merchant 1st guild)
b. 1853 Smolensk
d. 1941 Moscow

m. Maria Berlinraut
b. 1865 Minsk?
d. 1939 Moscow

Fenya
(dentist)
b. 1886 Smolensk
d. 1962 Moscow

m. Herman Shub
(economist)
b. 1888 Moscow
d. 1937 Chelyabinsk

Lev (Alunya)
(lawyer)
b. 1892
d. 1938 Moscow

m. Vera
Anisimovna
(teacher)

Daniel
(engineer)
b. 1913
d. 2005

1 son

Mira
(doctor)
b. 1915
d. 2010

2 sons

Yulius
(theater critic)
b. 1920
d. 2004

1 daughter

Nina
b. 1922 Moscow
d. 1936 Moscow

m. Moses Friedland
(science editor)
b. ?
d. 1971 Moscow

Ida
(dentist)
b. 1888
d. 1942
Novosibirsk

m. Alexander
Baltermants
(1st husband,
military doctor)
b. c. 1870
d. 1920
Yevpatoria

Frouma
b. 1893 Smolensk
d. 1964 London

Alicia
(engineer)
b. 1915 Ekaterinoslav
d. 1995 Moscow

2 daughters

Ira
(writer)
b. 1916
Ostragozhsk
d. 1985 London

m. Richard
Jefferies
(businessman)
b. 1910 Farnh..
d. 1985 Lond..

Mark
b. 1958 London

David
b. 1959 Lond..

N.B. *All the Toumarkine children were born in Smolensk.*

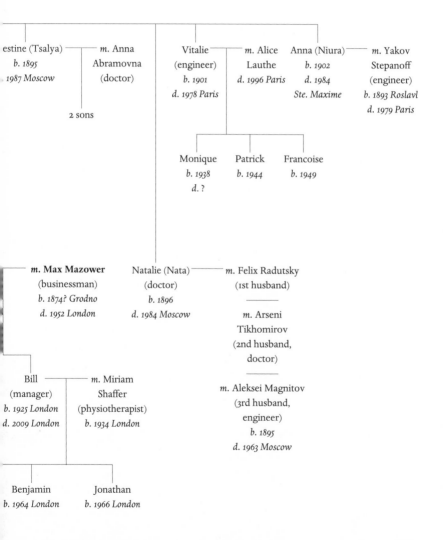

estine (Tsalya) ⎯⎯ *m.* Anna
b. 1895 — Abramovna
1987 Moscow — (doctor)

2 sons

Vitalie ⎯⎯ *m.* Alice — Anna (Niura) ⎯⎯ *m.* Yakov
(engineer) — Lauthe — *b. 1902* — Stepanoff
b. 1901 — *d. 1996 Paris* — *d. 1984* — (engineer)
d. 1978 Paris — *Ste. Maxime* — *b. 1893 Roslavl*
— *d. 1979 Paris*

Monique — Patrick — Francoise
b. 1938 — *b. 1944* — *b. 1949*
d. ?

m. **Max Mazower** — Natalie (Nata) ⎯⎯ *m.* Felix Radutsky
(businessman) — (doctor) — (1st husband)
b. 1874? Grodno — *b. 1896* — ⎯⎯⎯
d. 1952 London — *d. 1984 Moscow* — *m.* Arseni
— Tikhomirov
— (2nd husband,
— doctor)
— ⎯⎯⎯
Bill ⎯⎯ *m.* Miriam — *m.* Aleksei Magnitov
(manager) — Shaffer — (3rd husband,
b. 1925 London — (physiotherapist) — engineer)
d. 2009 London — *b. 1934 London* — *b. 1895*
— *d. 1963 Moscow*

Benjamin — Jonathan
b. 1964 London — *b. 1966 London*

Notes

INTRODUCTION: ON WEST HILL

1. Aves was an associate of Charles Booth, the Victorian antipoverty campaigner. Aves's notebook, "Walk with District Inspector Mountfield of the Highgate and Upper Holloway sub-division of the Y division of the Met[ropolitan] Police, District 19 [Kentish Town], 13 December 1898," pages 159–61, is held in the Charles Booth archive at the London School of Economics.

CHAPTER ONE: THE BUNDIST

1. From "The Salt Sea" ("In Zaltsikn Yam," 1901) by S. An-sky, written in praise of the "Great Jewish Workers' Bund," translated by Daniel Kahn, available at yiddishkayt.org/the-salt-sea. The Bund's anthem was also by An-sky. On the personality of the Bund, see Vladimir Medem, *The Life and Soul of a Legendary Jewish Socialist: The Memoirs of Vladimir Medem*, translated and edited by Samuel Portnoy (New York: Ktav, 1979), 236.

2. Max's surname as given in the Russian police archives should probably be rendered Mazover. I have changed this in accordance with the family's later spelling.

3. See Gur Alroey, "Demographers in the Service of the Nation: Liebmann Hirsch, Jacob Lestchinsky, and the Early Study of Jewish Migration," *Jewish History* 20, nos. 3–4 (2006), 265–82.

4. Sholem Levine, *Untererdishe kemfer* (New York: Solom levin

bukh-komitet, 1946), 164–66. Many thanks to Gil Rubin for the research and for the translation from the Yiddish.

5. The Okhrana was the secret police under the Russian Empire. Founded in 1881, it was active after until 1917, when it was dismantled by the Provisional Government.

6. See the excellent Scott Ury, *Barricades and Banners: The Revolution of 1905 and the Transformation of Warsaw Jewry* (Stanford, CA: Stanford University Press, 2012).

7. The following year, there was a police raid on the Nadezhda office in Warsaw, which turned up a cache of Bundist and other revolutionary materials. Whether this was a relic of Max's stay or an indication that the company itself was being used by others in the revolutionary movement is impossible to say. Ibid., 98.

8. He had probably translated the book into Yiddish from a Russian translation, not from the English original.

9. The Soviet secret police went by several names over the years: Cheka, 1917–1922; OGPU, 1922–1934; NKVD, 1934–1943; KGB, 1943–1991. Even this is a simplification. All these names are used at various points in this book.

10. In the same issue we read of another breakout from the main prison in Kiev. Among the escapees was Max's contemporary, a Russian Jew from Białystok named Meyer Wallach, better known to the world by his revolutionary name Maxim Litvinov, the long-serving Soviet foreign minister.

11. Medem, *The Life and Soul*, 227–28.

12. S. An-sky, *In Shtrom*, cited by Jonathan Frankel, "'Youth in Revolt': An-sky's *In Shtrom* and the Instant Fictionalization of 1905," in Gabriella Safran and Steven J. Zipperstein, eds., *The Worlds of S. An-sky: A Russian Jewish Intellectual at the Turn of the Century* (Stanford, CA: Stanford University Press, 2006), 147.

CHAPTER TWO: 1905

1. This document is held in the International Institute of Social History in Amsterdam. The Institute was established in 1935 to preserve the papers of the European labor movement in the face of the rising threat of the Nazis; today it is known as an important repository that holds the papers of figures such as Leon Trotsky and of other Leftist groups that were caught between Bolshevism and fascism. But the first collection of documents it purchased was a large part of the archive of the Bund. This it obtained from a comrade and close friend of Max's, Franz Kursky, who took the files from Vilna to safety in Germany in 1920, and then, when Hitler came to power, sought a new home for them. The files had not yet been catalogued when the Germans reached Amsterdam; the Institute was plundered by the Nazis during the war and stripped of its collections. We do not know how much was lost but what remained was returned to Amsterdam after 1945. Fortunately, plenty survived and the Institute's online catalogue lists nearly four hundred and fifty Bund files, as yet largely untapped by historians. ARCH00195/37/33, contains leaflets from Łódź during the 1905 revolution.

2. My thanks to Gil Rubin for tracking down this and the Gomel proclamation, and to Rina Turner for translating them.

3. Y.S. Hertz, *Di geshikhte fun Bund in Łódź* (New York: Farlag Unzer Tsayt, 1958), 135–37, 150. Thanks to Gil Rubin for his wonderful help discovering this and other sources, and for his translation from the Yiddish. Also *Chicago Tribune*, June 24, 1905.

CHAPTER THREE: THE YOST TYPEWRITER COMPANY

1. Elissa Bemporad, *Becoming Soviet Jews: The Bolshevik Experiment in Minsk* (Bloomington and Indianapolis, IN: Indiana University Press, 2013), 54.

CHAPTER FIVE: BRITS AND BOLSHEVIKS

1. Ivy Low [Litvinoff] papers, "Materials for Autobiography," 32, 37, St. Antony's College, Oxford.

2. Intriguingly, the Okhrana reported a Bundist agent called "Daniel" active in Warsaw in 1910 and 1912. It is unclear if this refers to Max, or someone else. He is described as a member of the Bund Central Committee.

CHAPTER SEVEN: THE AFTERLIFE

1. Miklós Kun, *Stalin: An Unknown Portrait* (Budapest and New York: Central European University Press, 2003), 285.

2. *Henryk Erlich and Victor Alter: Two Heroes and Martyrs for Jewish Socialism* (Jersey City, NY: KTAV, 1990); "NKVD Documents Shed New Light on Fate of Erlich and Alter," *East European Jewish Affairs*, 22:2 (1992), 65–85.

3. Benjamin Nadel, "Bundism in England," *Jewish Socialist* Nos. 6–7 (Summer–Autumn, 1986).

CHAPTER TEN: ANDRÉ

1. By coincidence, *Warrant for Genocide*, the definitive history of the *Protocols of the Elders of Zion*, was written by Vera Broido's husband, Norman Cohn. On Cohn and the origins of his interest in the study of anti-Semitism, see chapter 16. The Omni publishing house is included among twelve "anti-Semitic radical traditionalist Catholic groups" by the Southern Poverty Law Center in its *Intelligence Report* of Winter 2006.

2. For a vivid account of the college when André was there, see Joseph C. Harsch, *At the Hinge of History: A Reporter's Story* (Athens, GA: University of Georgia Press, 1993), 2–4.

CHAPTER ELEVEN: THE KRYLENKO CONNECTION

1. Walter Benjamin, *Moscow Diary*, edited by Gary Smith, translated by Richard Sieburth (Cambridge, MA: Harvard University Press, 1986), 26–27.

2. The date of birth that the British police had on file for him in the Central Register of Aliens, and that he had presumably gotten from whoever had brought him over to England, was off by a day— March 2—as was the birthday present the Hudsons had given him in 1917. I deduce from this that probably neither André nor Max had possessed a copy of his birth certificate before he decided to apply for French citizenship. Indeed, in 1932, when he applied to be naturalized in London, he said he still did not have a copy. See HO (Home Office) 144/18052 (U.K. National Archives).

3. See A. Bosniacki, *Utopia-wladza-prawo: Doktryna I koncepcje prawne "bolszewickiej" Rosji, 1917–1921* (Warsaw, 1999), 182. Hence when Max was arrested by the Cheka in 1919, his acquaintances in the revolutionary administration likely included not only senior Chekists but also Sofia herself in a senior position within the judicial apparatus.

4. See Paul Avrich, "Bolshevik Opposition to Lenin: G. T. Miasnikov and the Workers' Group," *Russian Review* No. 43 (1984), 1–29; also "Lignes directrices de la K.A.I. [1922]," in *La gauche allemande: textes du KAPD, de l'AAUD, de l'AAUE et de la KAI (1920–1922)*, edited by Denis Authier (Naples: La Vecchia Talpa, 1973), 124–26.

5. Max Eastman, *Love and Revolution* (New York: Random House, 1964), 432–34.

6. In the meantime, Max, who had his own family as well as Frouma's in Russia to worry about, kept utterly silent about his Krylenko connection, and I doubt he had any contact at all with Sofia after the early or mid-1920s at the very latest. When André was young, Max would have been a natural intermediary for their correspondence, but with time it is likely that André and his mother communicated independently of him.

7. An entry in the Liège population register sows further confusion: it records that DE MEYER, Constantin and KRYLENKO, Sophie left the city for Russia on September 24, 1918, and that they had two children, entered as:

DE MEYER André (né à Paris, le 03/03/1904)
DE MEYER Nathalie (née à Liège, le 11/06/1912)

It is extremely unlikely that Sofia and Constantin were in Belgium throughout the war, or still in Liège in September 1918, since we have the record of their wedding in Petrograd in November 1914, after which time return to Belgium would have been next to impossible.

It is certainly striking that André is registered under Constantin's family name, but if he ever officially recognized him as his son, Sofia never informed her son of the fact.

There is also at least one clear error on the register—André's year of birth was 1909, not 1904, and this provides additional reason to doubt the accuracy of the entry as a whole. In all, it is a useful reminder that archival sources raise as many questions as they answer.

CHAPTER TWELVE: FROUMA

1. Dmitri Baltermants was the stepson of Alexander's brother, Nicolai Baltermants, who gave the boy his name.

2. Or was the intermediary, as Dad believed, Frouma's brother Lev, a lawyer and prewar activist in the RSDLP? For his fate, see pp. 205–6.

3. On Kogan, see Joseph Fraenkel, "Lucien Wolf and Theodor Herzl," *Transactions of the Jewish Historical Society of England* No. 20 (1959–1961), 161–88. See also "Outpost on Pampas Where Jews Once Found Refuge, Wilts as They Leave," *New York Times*, June 9, 2013; and George Fortenberry et al., eds., *The Correspondence of Harold Frederic* (Fort Worth, TX: Texas Christian University Press, 1977), 317.

CHAPTER FOURTEEN: THE SHELTERING WORD

1. My thanks to my cousin Boris Kobrinsky on whose writings about his grandparents I have relied.

2. Zalman Shazar, "My First Convention," in *Minsk Anthology, Volume 1*, translated from the Yiddish by Jerrold Landau (Tel Aviv: Tarbut Vechinuch, 1971), 438–48.

3. Wilhelm Adam, *Der schwere Entschluss* (Berlin, 1965), 457, for the reference to Nata. My thanks to my cousin Anna Carlen for sharing these stories and the reference.

CHAPTER SIXTEEN: CHILDHOOD

1. David Vital, "Our Road to Zion: A Memoir," *Commentary*, May 1, 1989.

2. Born in Minsk, Mowshowitch had been the secretary of the great Jewish historian Simon Dubnow before coming to London in 1915 and advising the Anglo Jewish elite on foreign policy. In 1919 he had left his mark on history, playing a vital backstage role at the Paris Peace Conference in getting minority rights on the diplomats' agenda. In the 1930s, he remained quiet, learned, and formidably well connected.

3. This was the Mass Observation: Anti-Semitism Survey, completed in December 1938. See the paper by Tony Kushner, "Observing the 'Other': Mass-Observation and 'Race,'" available online at www .massobs.org.uk/images/occasional_papers/no2_Kushner.pdf.

CHAPTER SEVENTEEN: THE WAR

1. Alice's father was Jean-Antoine Lauthe (1884–1963), born Guingamp, the son of an infantry officer; he attended the École des Beaux-Arts and was an architect and painter. A Chevalier of the Légion d'honneur, he was wounded in 1916 and received the Croix de Guerre.

Glossary

Arcos The All-Russian Cooperative Society, the official buying and selling agency of the Soviet Union, opened its offices in London in 1920. The Anglo-Soviet Trade Agreement was signed the following year, and formal diplomatic recognition of the USSR followed in 1924.

Bermuda Conference An international conference held in April 1943 to discuss the plight of Jewish refugees from Nazi-occupied Europe.

Blackshirts Members of the British Union of Fascists, formed by Oswald Mosley in 1932.

Bolsheviks The so-called majority faction of the Russian Social Democratic Workers' Party, which split from the Mensheviks in 1903 under Lenin's leadership.

Bund The General Jewish Workers' Union in Lithuania, Poland and Russia, founded in Vilna in 1897, and organizer of the founding congress of the Russian Social Democratic Workers' Party in Minsk the following year.

Cheka (see also GPU, NKVD) The All-Russian Emergency Commission for Combatting Counter-Revolution and Sabotage was established in December 1917 under the leadership of Felix Dzerzhinsky.

Comintern The Communist International, founded in 1919 and dissolved in 1943.

Dzerzhinsky, Felix [1877–1926] A Polish socialist from a gentry family, educated at the Vilna gymnasium, who helped found the SDKPiL (Social Democracy of the Kingdom of Poland and Lithuania) before joining the Bolsheviks. He was the first head of the Cheka.

Einsatzgruppen SS death squads tasked by Heinrich Himmler with carrying out mass killings of civilians in occupied Poland and Russia.

Fabian Society A Left-liberal think tank that exercised a major influence on interwar and wartime British social policy.

Gosplan The chief central economic planning agency in the USSR, founded in 1921.

GPU Successor to the Cheka as the chief state security organization in the USSR, also headed by Dzerzhinsky, 1922–1923. Known as OGPU from 1923–1934.

Jabotinsky, Ze'ev [b. Vladimir Yevgenyevich Jabotinsky, 1880–1940] A journalist and political activist who was leader of the Revisionist Zionist movement.

Jewish Colonization Association Founded by Baron Hirsch in 1891 to support Jewish emigration from Russia and eastern Europe to agricultural colonies on lands purchased by the association.

KAPD (Kommunistische Arbeiter-Partei Deutschlands, the Communist Workers' Party of Germany) Founded in April 1920 in a split from the KPD.

Kenwood House Formerly the house and grounds of the Mansfields, adjacent to Hampstead Heath in North London, it was opened to the public in 1928.

KPD (*Kommunistische Partei Deutschlands*, Communist Party of Germany) Formed in December 1918 out of the Spartacus League, becoming in the 1920s the largest communist party in Europe.

Kronstadt Rebellion An uprising by sailors of the Baltic fleet against the Bolshevik regime, calling for freedom of speech, new elections to the soviets, and the release of political prisoners. It was suppressed by the Red Army in March 1921 at the cost of hundreds of lives.

Kustodiev, Boris [1878–1927] Russian painter.

Litvinov, Maxim [1876–1951] Born Meir Hennoch Wallach-Finkelstein into a wealthy Jewish family in Bialystok, he joined the Bolsheviks in 1903. Lived in London 1910–1918 and married Ivy Low, was 1921–1930 Deputy Commissar of Foreign Affairs, 1930–1939 People's Commissar for Foreign Affairs, and 1941–1943 Soviet Ambassador to the USA.

Lubyanka Headquarters of the Soviet secret police and prison.

Mass-Observation Pioneering social research organization founded in the UK in 1937 by anthropologist Tom Harrisson, poet Charles Madge, and filmmaker Humphrey Jennings.

Medem, Vladimir [1879–1923] A leading political theorist of the Bund.

Mensheviks The so-called minority faction of the Russian Social Democratic Workers' Party, which split with the Bolsheviks in 1903. Banned in the Soviet Union after 1921.

MI5 The British Security Service, established in 1909 under Vernon Kell.

MI6 The British Secret Intelligence Service, established in 1909 under Mansfield Cumming.

Myasnikov, Gavril Ilyich [1889–1945] A Russian metalworker and Bolshevik who was expelled from the party in 1922 and became a leading critic through his opposition Workers' Group.

Nansen passport Travel documents issued by League of Nations High Commissioner for Refugees, Fridtjof Nansen. Initially issued to refugees from the Russian civil war from 1922 onwards.

New Economic Policy (NEP) Lenin's shift away from war communism towards what he described as state capitalism with a mixed economy that recognized the importance of private ownership and foreign investment.

NKVD (People's Commissariat for Internal Affairs) Successor to the Cheka and GPU, 1934–1946.

Okhrana Tsarist secret police that monitored political opposition within and outside Russia.

Pale of Settlement The zone of western Russia outside which Jews were deterred and often prohibited from settling.

Poale Zion A party based on a fusion of Marxism and Zionism that spread internationally before 1914. In the USSR it remained legal until 1928.

Revisionist Zionism See Jabotinsky.

Rothstein, Fyodor [1871–1953] Born in Kovno, settled in London in 1890 as a journalist and joined the Bolsheviks. A friend of Lenin's, he helped found the Communist Party of Great Britain. He returned to Russia in 1920 and became Soviet ambassador to Persia.

Russian Social Democratic Workers' Party Also known as the Russian Social Democratic Labor Party (RSDLP). Founded in Minsk in 1898, with the help of the Bund, it became the leading Marxist socialist movement in Russia.

Social Democracy of the Kingdom of Poland and Lithuania Founded in 1893 by Polish workers protesting the nationalism of the Polish Socialist Party. After 1917 its members played a leading role on the Left in Germany, Poland, and the USSR.

Soviet Trade Delegation Founded in London in 1920, before the inauguration of formal diplomatic relations between the UK and the USSR. Its home for many years was on Highgate West Hill.

Swallows and Amazons 1930 children's story by the British writer and journalist Arthur Ransome.

MARK MAZOWER is a historian and writer specializing in modern Greece, twentieth-century Europe, and international history. His books include *Salonica, City of Ghosts: Christians, Muslims and Jews, 1430–1950*, winner of the Duff Cooper Prize; *Hitler's Empire: Nazi Rule in Occupied Europe*, winner of the 2008 Los Angeles Times Book Prize for History; and *Governing the World: The History of an Idea*. He is currently the Ira D. Wallach Professor of History at Columbia University, and his articles and reviews on history and current affairs appear regularly in *The Guardian, Financial Times, London Review of Books, The Nation*, and *New Republic*.

OTHER PRESS

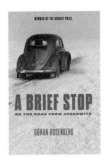

A BRIEF STOP ON THE ROAD FROM AUSCHWITZ by Göran Rosenberg

WINNER OF THE AUGUST PRIZE

A shattering memoir about a father's attempt to survive the aftermath of Auschwitz

"This exquisitely wrought book is, among other things, a meditation on the workings of memory and history in one man's life." —*Los Angeles Review of Books*

THE IMPOSSIBLE EXILE: STEFAN ZWEIG AT THE END OF THE WORLD by George Prochnik

An original study of exile, told through the biography of Austrian writer Stefan Zweig

"Richly rewardingy... a major work of historical and cultural criticism of Europe's darkest times... Zweig's haunted talent has never been better explored than in this exemplary study." —*The Times*

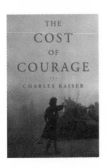

THE COST OF COURAGE by Charles Kaiser

The true story of the three youngest children of a bourgeois Catholic family who worked together in the French Resistance

"Kaiser reveals the moral ambiguity of resistance when one's enemy is as ruthless as Nazi Germany... [He] makes the most of the inherent drama in the story he tells, but his touchstone is his relentless search for truth amid the fog of war... brilliant." —*Washington Post*

"A mix of history, biography, and memoir that reads like a nerve-racking thriller." —*The Guardian* (US)

Also recommended:

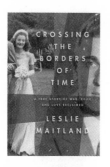

CROSSING THE BORDERS OF TIME
by Leslie Maitland

A dramatic true story of World War II, exile, and love lost—then reclaimed

"A mesmerizing memoir of one family's shattering experience during World War II. It's a tale at once heartbreaking and uplifting." —Linda Fairstein, *New York Times* best-selling author

THE BROTHERS ASHKENAZI by I. J. Singer

First published in 1936, this classic of Yiddish literature quickly became a best seller as a sprawling family saga.

"The book has the grand sweep of Tolstoy...pitch-perfect artistry and pace." —*Wall Street Journal*

"*The Brothers Ashkenazi* rates a place on any shelf devoted to modern works of art." —*Newsweek*

NOT I: MEMOIRS OF A GERMAN CHILDHOOD
by Joachim Fest

A searing portrait of an intellectually rigorous German household opposed to the Nazis and how its members suffered for their political stance

"Quietly compelling, elegantly expressed...*Not I* shrinks the Wagnerian scale of German history in the 1930s and 1940s to chamber music dimensions. It is intensely personal, clear-eyed, and absolutely riveting." —*New York Times*

▐▌ OTHER PRESS   *www.otherpress.com*